# North American
# Tree Squirrels

# North American Tree Squirrels

Michael A. Steele and
John L. Koprowski

Smithsonian Institution Press
Washington and London

© 2001 Smithsonian Institution
All rights reserved

Production Editor: Ruth G. Thomson
Copy Editor: Anne R. Gibbons
Designer: Jody Billert

Library of Congress Cataloging-in-Publication Data
Steele, Michael A.
    North American tree squirrels / Michael A. Steele and John L. Koprowski
      p.    cm.
    Includes bibliographic references (p. ).
    ISBN 1-56098-986-6 (alk. paper)
      1. Squirrels—North America.    I. Koprowski, John L.    II. Title.
    QL737.R68 S73   2001
    599.36.097—dc21                                                    2001020920

British Library Cataloging-in-Publication Data available

Manufactured in the United States of America
08  07  06  05  04  03  02  01    5  4  3  2  1

⊗ The paper used in this publication meets the minimum requirements of the American National Standard for Information Sciences—Permanence of Paper for Printed Library Materials ANSI A39.48-1984.

For permission to reproduce illustrations appearing in this book, please correspond directly with the owners of the works as listed in the individual captions. The Smithsonian Institution Press does not retain reproduction rights for these illustrations individually or maintain a file of addresses for photo sources.

*To Peter D. Weigl and Kenneth B. Armitage,*

*first our mentors,*

*then our colleagues,*

*always our friends,*

*. . . for never letting us forget that our science is*

*only as good as the questions we ask.*

# Contents

# Preface

Whether one opens this book as a seasoned biologist, an amateur naturalist, or just a casual reader hoping to learn a bit more about squirrels, we believe she or he will discover far more than a simple collection of facts about the tree squirrels. There is a story within—one that not only shares our process of discovery but also may forever change the reader's view of the tree squirrels and many other wild animals as well.

A little time with this book, and the reader should never view a squirrel in quite the same way. A walk in the park will never again be quite so casual. The notion of a bushy tail scurrying about, burying and uncovering nuts in some random, entertaining manner, will be transformed into a view of a creature that is finely tuned, from generations of natural selection, to a harsh environment—one in which every move, every behavioral choice, every moment is absolutely critical for survival. Although some may argue for the less-informed view, we concur with the physicist Richard Feynman, who wrote, "It does no harm to the mystery to know a little about it." With a little knowledge about tree squirrels, the walk in the park will be transformed into a series of compelling questions that follow naturally from each observation of the animal's behavior. This book will certainly answer some of these questions, but when the reader begins to ask questions for which we have no answers, only then have we really succeeded in our mission.

This book represents an overview of the tree squirrels—an account of their ecology, behavior, and evolution—and the story of our research. For the general reader, we seek to share not only our knowledge of the tree squirrels but also the sheer delight that comes with studying them.

For every fascinating question that we address in this book, three more will remain unanswered long after its publication. To our colleagues, we hope to convince you that tree squirrels are, as we argue throughout these pages, model organisms for testing many unanswered questions in behavior and ecology.

Much of what is discussed within these pages fails to capture the kinds of support, assistance, and guidance that goes into the more than 40 years of research represented here. An attempt to recognize everyone would surely fail; so we extend our deepest thanks to all and mention the most important players.

A few colleagues who share our love of squirrels have been especially influential in our own careers. They include our graduate advisers, Peter Weigl and Kenneth Armitage, to whom this book is dedicated, and colleagues Vagn Flyger, John Gurnell, Karl Larsen, Peter Smallwood, Chris Smith, and Luc Wauters who have especially influenced and guided our thinking over the years. We thank them all.

Throughout our graduate and postgraduate years we have been blessed with a steady flow of research funds on which our research is so dependent. For their generous support we recognize the American Museum of Natural History's Theodore Roosevelt Memorial Fund, the American Society of Mammalogists, Benemerita Universidad de Puebla, Chiricahua National Monument, the Fulbright Foundation, Highlands Biological Station, James Cook University, the Murdock Charitable Trust, the National Geographic Society, the National Park Service, the National Science Foundation, North Carolina State University, the North Carolina Wildlife Federation, the Pennsylvania Wild Resource Conservation Fund, Powdermill Biological Station of the Carnegie Museum of Natural History, the Scientific Research Society of Sigma Xi, Southwest Parks and Monuments Association, Southern Illinois University, University of Arizona, University of Kansas, U.S. Fish and Wildlife Service, Wake Forest University, Willamette University, and Wilkes University. Several other institutions allowed us access to their museum collections or other key resources. They include the National Museum of Natural History at the Smithsonian Institution, American Museum of Natural History, University of Kansas Natural History Museum, Field Museum of Natural History, Museum of Comparative Zoology at Harvard University, Louisiana Museum of Natural History at Louisiana State University, Museum of Vertebrate Zoology at the University of California–Berkeley, and Universidad Autonóma de Mexico.

There is no better work than fieldwork. But intensive field studies are not conducted alone. Through the years, we have enjoyed the company of many students, assistants, and colleagues who have made our excursions and studies pleasant and rewarding. We recognize the fine efforts of S. Agosta, W. Bachman, A. Baty, M. Beam, M. Bowen, E. Bromen, J. Butler, G. Ceballos, T. Cervenak, W. Chase, T. Contreras, M. Corse, F. De los Santos, A. Enna, L. Fairbanks, A. Faust, D. Flynn, J. Foil, J. Franchuk, R. Gardner, K. Gavel, T. Genna, L. Gizza, T. Goater, R. Gray, J. Ha, L. Hadj-Chikh, S. Hayden, J. Hazeltine, M. Heald, J. Holmgren, S. Howe, B. Hudson, P. Jaderholm, E. Jones, C. Kelley, G. Kirkland, M. Kneeland, T. Knowles, A. Kolosseus, S. Komak, E. Koprowski, E. Koprowski, Z. Koprowski, P. Lavenex, D. Lepitzki, J. Lewis, J. Luft, M. McColgin, N. Michel, K. Munroe, D. Newsom, C. Ngumezi, W. Niedermeyer, G. Psarras, J. Radillo, S. Rehberg, M. Rodriguez, A. Roth, E. Roth, B. Row, J. Rubin, K. Schauer, T. Sharpe, L. Sherman, P. Sponholtz, A. Spunar, E. Steele, M. Steele, M. Steele, Jr., T. Steele, C. Tay, W. Terzaghi, A. Tsuha, G. Turner, J. Vodzak, D. Walton, D. Warburton, M. Woolsey, K. Zitta, K. Zuby, and others whom we may have failed to mention.

Scientists are often criticized for not making their work more accessible to the public. Too often, we forget how important such an endeavor can be, but we are also too often not afforded the luxury, the guidance, and the encouragement to attempt such an endeavor. The authors of this book have been especially fortunate to receive an ample dose of all three of these key ingredients. Our respective institutions—Wilkes University (for M. Steele) and Willamette University and University of Arizona (for J. Koprowski)—have been particularly generous, allowing us the time and support to see this project to completion. Without the insightful encouragement of our university peers and superiors, this project would have surely failed.

Critical guidance came from a few individuals who share responsibility for greatly influencing the final product. Throughout the project, our writing has been guided by many scientists before us—too many to recognize here—who have shared the delight of their study animals and the fascination of their discoveries. We mention just two whose work has served as a model for our own: Uldis Roze and Keith Bildstein, both authors of previous Smithsonian Institution publications. We hope our contribution comes close to matching their fine works.

Several individuals—Debra Chapman, Margaret Steele, Jennifer Vodzak, and two anonymous reviewers—read all or part of the manuscript. Barbara Sefchik produced the maps. We are also especially grateful to the Smithsonian Institution staff, especially editors Peter Cannell and Vincent Burke, who have helped shepherd us through our frequent periods of doubt, confusion, and procrastination, always remaining patient, positive, and persistent. Copy editor Anne R. Gibbons worked tirelessly and flawlessly to help transform our scratchings into a far better written presentation. We accept full responsibility for any errors in the book, but Anne is the reason for so much that is right about it.

Finally, we thank our families—our parents for instilling a sense of wonder in each of us, our wives for encouraging our indulgence in that wonder, and our children for sharing in it. We hope our efforts here will in some small way pass on that sense of wonder to the reader.

# North American
# Tree Squirrels

# 1

# Why Squirrels?

Since beginning our research on tree squirrels—more than 20 years now for each of us—we have been asked no single question more than why do we study squirrels. While our answers vary, depending on whether it's one of our students, a neighbor, or a molecular biologist who is asking, the underlying theme is always the same. Tree squirrels are model organisms for testing and exploring important questions in behavior and ecology.

On the one hand, tree squirrels are ideal subjects for exploring the behavioral decisions animals make when consuming or storing food, and for assessing the impact they have on plant reproduction and forest regeneration—either as seed predators or as agents of seed dispersal. On the other, tree squirrels are equally important subjects for investigating the evolution of mammalian social structure, reproductive strategies, and population biology. Although both of us have studied a variety of other animals, from insects to birds, we always seem to come back to the tree squirrels.

But there are other reasons to study them as well. The diurnal tree squirrels are conspicuous, relatively common mammals. As such, these squirrels, as well as their ground-dwelling counterparts—the chipmunks, ground squirrels, and prairie dogs—are readily observed. In fact, they represent one of the few groups of mammals on which intensive behavioral observations are even possible. And as arboreal mammals, the diurnal tree squirrels fill a unique niche, at least in temperate forests where few other mammals make a living in quite the same way. In the tropics, the tree-tops are home to primates, tree shrews, and many groups of rodents in addition to a tremendous diversity of tree squirrels, ranging in size from the smallest pygmy squirrels to the 8.8-pound (4-kg) giants of Southeast Asia. But in the cooler temperate forests, among the mammals, the tree squirrels alone rule the canopy.

Finally, there are the aesthetic and humanistic reasons for understanding the squirrels. Few other wild mammals share such a close association with humans. While admittedly not the motivation for our research, it has certainly fueled much of the public interest in our work. Tree squirrels are at once a source of engaging entertainment as they go about their daily activities and, quite often, a focus of considerable frustration as they steal from our bird feeders, destroy our gardens, and strip the bark from our trees.

## OUR OBJECTIVES

We hope to fill in some of the many gaps in knowledge that still exist and provide a summary of our own research from the last two decades. In the 1980s our good friend and colleague John Gurnell provided an excellent review that focused heavily on the European literature and in particular that concerning the endangered European red squirrel (*Sciurus vulgaris*; Gurnell 1987). Our discussion, instead, centers on the tree squirrels of North America and especially the two species that we know so well from our own work: the gray squirrel (*S. carolinensis*; Figure 1.1) and the fox squirrel (*S. niger*; Figure 1.2). Throughout the book, we refer to research on other tree squirrels found in the United States and Canada, and we close with a brief species account of each of these. Figures 1.3–1.5 illustrate three such species: the Abert's, or tassel-eared, squirrel *(S. aberti)*, the Arizona gray squirrel *(S. arizonensis)*, and the Mexican fox squirrel *(Sciurus nayaritensis)*, respectively. The reader will find little here on tree squirrels of Mexico simply because so little is yet known on these species.

Our target audience is broad. We intend this book for the layperson who wishes to learn about these fascinating creatures, as well as the scientist who, like us, may appreciate their importance as model study organisms. We have attempted a light style, by sharing the process of our work in addition to the outcome, but we also make frequent forays into the current scientific literature. We hope this approach helps readers share our excitement of both the research and the basic biology of the tree squirrels.

Finally, it is our hope that this book will spark additional research on tree squirrels. We have attempted to frame our work in a way that we feel demonstrates how tree squirrels can be used to address important questions in ecology and behavior. We also provide one of the most comprehensive literature reviews available on the topic and throughout the book allude to some of the important unanswered and unasked questions. Indeed, there is much yet to learn.

## THE CHARACTERISTICS, NICHE, AND EVOLUTION OF THE TREE SQUIRRELS

Squirrels belong to the order of mammals known as Rodentia. This one order accounts for more than 1,600 species, greater than a third of the 4,500 species of mammals living today. The order Rodentia is divided further into three suborders, one of which, the Sciurognathi, contains the squirrel-like rodents. The 367 or so species in this suborder (Gurnell 1987) are further divided into 7 families. One of these, the Sciuridae, includes the tree squirrels, the ground-dwelling squirrels, and the flying squirrels.

Among the characteristics that collectively define this family of rodents, their skull and teeth are most distinguishing to scientists. Like other rodents, tree squirrels lack canine teeth, evidenced by the large space (diastema) between the incisors and the cheek teeth (premolars and molars). The total dental formula (20–22) for tree squirrels includes 1 incisor, 0 canines, 1 premolar, and 3 molars on each side of the bottom mandible. A complementary set of the same number of teeth occur on each side of the top mandible, with a second premolar possible in some species, such as the gray squirrel. This is the one dental characteristic, in fact, that distinguishes the gray squirrel skull from that of the fox squirrel, which possesses only a single upper premolar. The incisors are strong prominent teeth with a chiseled edge on the inner surface that equips the animal with tremendous gnawing ability. Like that of other rodents, the incisors of the squirrels are open rooted and grow continuously through life. Constant, heavy wear keeps the incisors sharp, but when damage occurs and the upper and lower incisors become uneven, an improper alignment or malocclusion can result. As the chipped incisor continues to grow unchecked, it can eventually pierce the skull and kill the animal.

The action of the teeth is enhanced by two prominent skull muscles: the masseter and the temporalis. The first of these represents the cheek muscles, which allow the squirrel to rotate the lower jaw and grind food on the surface of the cheek teeth (Gurnell 1987). The temporalis muscle, which attaches the posterior, dorsal portion of the skull with the lower

Figure 1.1. *(A)* eastern gray squirrel *(Sciurus carolinensis)*. (Photograph courtesy of M. A. Steele)

Figure 1.1. *(B)* its native range in North America. Ranges of the subspecies are *(1) S. c. carolinensis; (2) S. c. extimus; (3) S. c. fuliginosus; (4) S. c. hypophaeus; (5) S. c. pennsylvanicus.* (Map drawn by B. Sefchik, courtesy of M. A. Steele)

Figure 1.2. *(A)* fox squirrel (*Sciurus niger;* shown is the southeastern subspecies). (Photograph courtesy of T. Shankle, courtesy of the N.C. Wildlife Resources Commission)

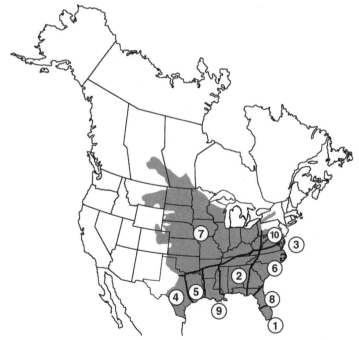

Figure 1.2. *(B)* its native range in North America. Ranges of the subspecies are *(1) S. n. avicennia; (2) S. n. bachmani; (3) S. n. cinereus; (4) S. n. limitis; (5) S. n. ludovicianus; (6) S. n. niger; (7) S. n. rufiventer; (8) S. n. shermani; (9) S. n. subauratus; (10) S. n. vulpinus.* (Map drawn by B. Sefchik, courtesy of M. A. Steele)

Figure 1.3. Abert's, or tassel-eared, squirrel *(Sciurus aberti)*. (Photograph courtesy of J. L. Koprowski)

Figure 1.4. Arizona gray squirrel *(Sciurus arizonensis)*. (Photograph courtesy of J. L. Koprowski)

**Figure 1.5. Mexican fox squirrel** *(Sciurus nayaritensis).* **(Photograph courtesy of J. L. Koprowski)**

mandible, is responsible for the powerful grinding action of the incisors. Together these two jaw muscles and the teeth help define how tree squirrels make a living eating seeds.

The tree squirrel's niche is best defined by its arboreal habits, aided by a number of anatomical adaptations (see Chapter 2). Some of the most important include powerful limbs, elongated digits, and recurved claws. In addition many tree squirrels have hind feet that can be rotated 180 degrees, allowing squirrels to scamper down trees headfirst and hang from limbs to gather food or leaves for their nests. The tail, one of the tree squirrel's most distinguishing characteristics, may also aid in balance in the treetops while at the same time serving to help regulate heat loss (Muchlinski and Shump 1979).

Keen vision is also a characteristic of the tree squirrels. Aside from the primates and a few other species, tree squirrels represent one of the few groups of mammals able to see color (G. Jacobs 1981). With eyes set wide apart on either side of the head, tree squirrels possess a magnificent field of vision. Although their depth perception may be somewhat compromised as a result, they are still able to leap through the trees at a hurried pace and catch the smallest of limbs. And although tree squirrels are exclusively diurnal, the sensory cells of the retina, called cones, function uniquely in tree squirrels to enable vision in the low light of dawn and dusk. This is particularly important for males trying to get an early start during the breeding season (see Chapter 8).

Tree squirrels belong to the ancient mammal lineage of rodents, as one of their less than flattering nicknames, "tree rat," suggests. Squirrels appear to have originated in North America and subsequently spread to Eurasia, Africa, and South America (Black 1972). Although an ill-fated introduction was attempted in Australia (Seebeck 1984), squirrels are not found on the isolated continent. The genus of tree squirrels, *Sciurus*, is represented in Europe, North America, and some parts of the tropics but the actual location of its origin is still unknown. The morphology of squirrels has remained so similar to its fossil predecessor *Protosciurus* over the past 5 million years that the foremost authorities refer to tree squirrels as living fossils (Emry and Thorington 1984). Currently, 26 species of tree squirrels in the genus *Sciurus* are recognized, with 3 species found in Eurasia and the remainder distributed across North and South America (Wilson and Reeder 1993). The evolutionary success of tree squirrels in exploiting the seed-eating arboreal niche is exemplified by the length of time the group has been a dominant component of forests and the geographic breadth that members of this group cover.

## HUMANS AND SQUIRRELS

The great familiarity of people with squirrels is suggestive of the strong relationship people have developed with squirrels. From U.S. postage stamps to city nicknames, tree squirrels are integrated into local cultures. Whether people view them as pests, as in Bill Adler's *Outwitting Squirrels* (1988), or remember them fondly from childhood, as in Beatrix Potter's classic *Tale of Squirrel Nutkin* (1903), most people have some exposure to squirrels. Squirrels do have their unseemly side and some people consider squirrels nuisances that cause power outages (J. Hamilton et al. 1989), rob bird feeders (Adler 1988), strip bark and girdle trees (Kenward and Parish 1986), compete with native species where introduced (Gurnell 1987), damage homes and other structures (J. Jackson 1983), and depredate crops of pecans, walnuts, hazelnuts, avocados, oranges, and strawberries (Flyger and Gates 1982a; Wolf and Roest 1971). But losses due to such activities are rather minimal.

The relationship between squirrels and humans is probably an ancient one. In North America, squirrels were a staple food of Native Americans and early western colonists (Barkalow and Shorten 1973; Schorger 1949). The "Kentucky squirrel rifle," or "Pennsylvania rifle," was designed to be accurate enough to hunt squirrels in tree canopies. (This rifle played a major role in the War of Independence.) In the present day, squirrels are hunted throughout their native range. In 1982 the economic impact of squirrel hunting was estimated at $12.5 million in Mississippi alone where 2.5 million squirrels were harvested annually (Flyger and Gates 1982a). Squirrels also have economic consumptive value for use in fishing lures; squirrel hair is used in the manufacture of spinner baits and trout flies.

Squirrels also have considerable value outside of consumptive uses such as hunting or trapping. As favorites of nature watchers, squirrels rank second only to songbirds as subjects of observation and photography (Shaw and Mangun 1984). A quick search for squirrels on the World Wide Web returned 358 sites, and several specialty businesses market squirrel foods, feeders, and other paraphernalia. Squirrels also provide excellent subjects for teaching ecological and biological subjects (L. Brown and Downhower 1987; Pratt 1987). Indeed, the tree squirrels are a part of our world in many important ways. It is our hope that this book will contribute to a deeper understanding and appreciation for these neighbors that grace, and sometimes plague, our everyday lives.

## SQUIRREL CONSERVATION

Although not the primary focus of our discussions, the conservation of tree squirrels is a timely and important issue, for which numerous implications follow from our efforts here. Indeed, an understanding of the basic biology of the tree squirrels is an essential ingredient for the protection and management of squirrel populations, as it is for every species. One conservation issue in particular—that of habitat loss—requires special mention.

Worldwide, the loss of habitat is a central factor in the conservation of many species, including the tree squirrels. In North America, extensive tracts of suitable forest habitat have been lost since settlement by Europeans. For example, since 1820 nearly 80 percent of forests in Illinois have been converted to agricultural cropland (Iverson 1988). And today habitat loss is the primary reason cited for legal protection provided to several subspecies of fox squirrels in the eastern United States. The southeastern fox squirrel (*Sciurus niger niger*; Weigl, Steele, et al. 1989), Sherman's fox squirrel (*Sciurus niger shermani*; Kantola and Humphrey 1990), and the Big Cypress (or mangrove) fox squirrel (*Sciurus niger avicennia;* Jodice and Humphrey 1992) are all imperiled. The Delmarva fox squirrel (*Sciurus niger cinereus;* Taylor 1974) is listed as endangered by the U.S. Fish and Wildlife Service. The loss of forested lands due to continued unplanned development can only further imperil these unique populations and subspecies.

The pattern of habitat fragmentation as a result of growing pressure from human populations is also a concern. Gray squirrels, for example, respond extraordinarily poorly to forest fragmentation in which suitable patches of habitat are surrounded by unsuitable cropland or suburban developments. In the Midwest, woodlots <102.8 acres (40 ha) in size rarely possess gray squirrels (Nixon and Hansen 1987). Fox squirrels generally fare better (Swihart and Nupp 1998; but see Weigl, Steele, et al. 1989); they are more terrestrial than gray squirrels and move more readily between isolated woodlots (C. E. Adams 1976). Yet successful dispersal often requires suitable corridors such as fencerows to link habitat patches (Sheperd and Swihart 1995). As forest fragment size decreases, the relative amount of edge to area increases, thereby decreasing true forest habitat and increasing more open woodland and woodland-edge competitors. Thus the consequences of fragmentation are far-reaching and require a deep understanding of a species' basic biology. Rob Swihart and his research team at Purdue University have wisely suggested a landscape-level approach to understanding how patterns of fragmentation influence squirrel populations (Swihart and Nupp 1998). Such approaches are essential for the continued management and protection of tree squirrels and numerous other species as well.

The isolated populations that remain in a matrix of developed land signal something about the health of any ecosystem dominated by humans. And in many of these landscapes, tree squirrels may serve as the coal miner's canary in providing us some insight and forewarning about the consequences of our land-use practices. The focus of this book is on introducing the reader to the splendid adaptations of squirrels to exploiting the forests of North America. Though squirrels are remarkably adaptable, we grow concerned when these living fossils, which have remained relatively unchanged for millions of years, are now threatened due to human action. We suggest that it is time to mind the canary. . . .

# 2

# The Squirrel Body Plan

*The winds are enough to penetrate our parkas as we stand on the snow-covered tundra-like ground. Above us, an adult female fox squirrel bobs up and down in the canopy, riding the twig upon which she sits with the skill of a world-class rodeo participant. Apparently unaffected by the chaos swirling around her, she eats catkins from the black walnut tree, her back to the howling winds, her tail held above the hunched body.*

One can only marvel at how well adapted squirrels are to exploiting a forested environment. Many of the chapters in this book emphasize a suite of behavioral or anatomical adaptations to specific problems that squirrels face with interspecific competitors, reproduction, foraging, and so on. Most squirrels have a characteristic appearance in the present day: consider the widely recognized profile of a squirrel, hunched over eating a nut, with bushy tail curled over its back. Some biologists consider tree squirrels to be living fossils because they remain virtually indistinguishable from European and North American specimens that lived more than 5 million years ago (Emry and Thorington 1984). Perhaps the dogged persistence of squirrels over time is the truest testament to their successful adaptation. In this chapter, we investigate the numerous ways in which the external and internal characteristics of tree squirrels are actually responses to the specialized arboreal lifestyle.

A number of adaptations increase the benefits of an arboreal life; however, a few significant costs act as important constraints that help shape the form and function of squirrels. Perhaps the most significant is seasonality in reproduction of tree tissues, a huge problem for tree squirrels. Periods of tree dormancy make the acquisition of energy a major challenge. Second, arboreal individuals are often more exposed to the vagaries of nature—wind, rain, even predators. Finally, a special agility is required for moving through and exploiting food resources in the third dimension, prominent activities in the everyday life of a squirrel.

## A FEW BASICS OF SQUIRREL PHYSIOLOGY

The generalized form of a tree squirrel is easily recognized. These are medium-sized mammals. Adult gray squirrels range from 10.50 to 24.85 ounces (300–710 g; Barkalow and Shorten 1973; E. Hall 1981), whereas fox squirrels are larger by as much as 50 to 80 percent, with adults weighing 17.75 to 47.64 ounces (507–1,361 g; Flyger and Gates 1982a). Males and females are indistinguishable from a distance, and there are no differences in body size. Covered by a rather thick pelage, tree squirrels are classic examples of countershading. A light-colored underside is covered by a relatively dark upper side. Advantages accrue in several ways with this type of coloration. When a squirrel forages on the ground, the darkened, grizzled dorsal pelage effectively camouflages the squirrel from predators above. When foraging in trees, a squirrel is camouflaged from below because of the pale underside set against the light-colored sky, whereas, darkened from above by the shadow of the body, the underside does not stand out to cue an aerial predator as to the squirrel's location.

Some fox squirrels in the southeastern United States are characterized by large amounts of black in their pelage. Richard Kiltie (1989, 1992; Kiltie and Edwards 1998) has examined this phenomenon thoroughly and argues convincingly that this increase in melanic forms is related to historical frequency of forest fires. Fox squirrels often forage in these open burned areas among the fire-charred trunks of trees. The black coloration may well provide value as camouflage in such environments. Entirely black individuals (melanics) are unusual but are found in areas such as

"Black Squirrel City" in Marysville, Kansas. In the northern part of the gray squirrel's range, melanics are common, especially in southern Ontario, Canada. Here the advantage seems to be related to thermoregulation. In winter temperatures of extreme cold (14°F [–10°C]), black morphs have an energetic advantage, while in summer there is no advantage or disadvantage (Ducharme, Larochelle, and Richard 1989; Innes and Lavigne 1979). Albinism is also found in gray squirrels, and many cities harbor populations that are legally protected by the populace with a great sense of civic pride: for example, Olney, Illinois; Brevard, South Carolina; and Marysville, Kansas. No advantage of albinism has been found, and given that it is a recessive trait that would easily be swamped out by alleles for normal pigmentation, it seems likely that the existence of albinistic populations may be due entirely to their protected status.

Perhaps the most easily recognized part of a tree squirrel is the bushy tail (Figure 2.1). The tail is substantial and accounts for roughly 40 percent of the squirrel's length. Nicknames such as "old bushytail" or "old shadetail" have been applied to tree squirrels. They actually derive their scientific name from their large tail. *Sciurus,* the Latin word for "squirrel," comes from the ancient Greek *skia,* meaning shadow or shade, and *oura* for tail—the combination is "shadetail." Besides its physical prominence, the tail is integral to squirrel biology and multifaceted to say the least. The tail is important in communication; both the orientation and movement of the tail are used to convey information to other squirrels and potential predators (see Chapter 9). During aggressive interactions, the tail is an important target, which can be grasped in the jaws of a rival. The tail is also used as a counterbalance when squirrels take one of their trademark leaps between trees. And it is an important structure for behavioral thermoregulation. Tails possess a bundle of blood vessels at the base that enable heat to be retained in the body core or dissipated more readily (Muchlinski and Shump 1979; Thorington 1966). When the tail is raised overhead to protect from sun or rain, the insulative value is increased by 17.8 percent—a significant increase for an endothermic animal that is attempting to maximize energy efficiency. During the heat of a summer day, a squirrel will lay spreadeagle on cool soil in the shade, flatten its tail hairs, and raise the tail to expose the vascular bundles at the base of the tail; one can actually see the blood vessels pulsing as blood is rushed to the tail to cool it.

The other prominent feature that comes to mind when one thinks of squirrels is teeth. The efficiency with which squirrels are able to process

**Figure 2.1. Adult gray squirrel in profile demonstrating generalized squirrel body form and use of the tail for insulation. Note the spot of fur dye for identification of the individual in behavioral experiments. (Photograph courtesy of C. Salonick)**

the protective structure of seeds from trees such as English and black walnut, hickory, conifer, and pecan are testament to the specialized dentition and jaw muscles that squirrels possess. The skull of a squirrel depicts this specialization (Figure 2.2). Two "groups" of teeth are obvious. The cheek teeth are composed of molariform teeth much like human molars in general appearance. Deciduous or baby premolars are replaced in juveniles by adult teeth, which are not replaced during the remainder of the life. One premolar near the front of the cheek and three molars compose the complex of cheek teeth; some tree squirrels, including gray squirrels, also have an additional peglike premolar, though this is not present in all individuals and its function is unknown. The other group of teeth are the formidable incisors at the very front of the skull. The incisors are recurved and ever growing. These are the teeth that are used for gnawing through the thick protective covers of tree seeds; their indeterminate growth is necessary to bear the wear experienced in the acquisition of food. Squirrels lack canine teeth and in their place possess a gap between the incisors and the cheek teeth known as the diastema. This arrangement is well suited to the two tasks that must be accomplished when a squirrel feeds: *gnawing* to access and fragment food items, and *grinding* to masticate items into

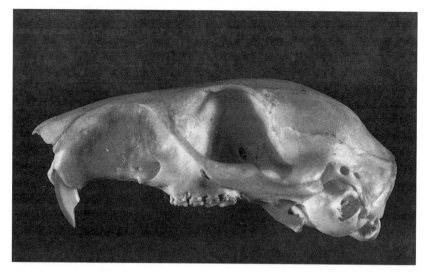

Figure 2.2. *(A)* cranium of an eastern gray squirrel. (Photograph by S. Hagan, courtesy of J. L. Koprowski)

a fine grain paste to be processed in the digestive tract. Thorough chewing of the food items significantly increases surface area of the food particles on which digestive enzymes will be able to work, and the negative consequences of chemicals such as tannins are minimized (Chung-Mac-

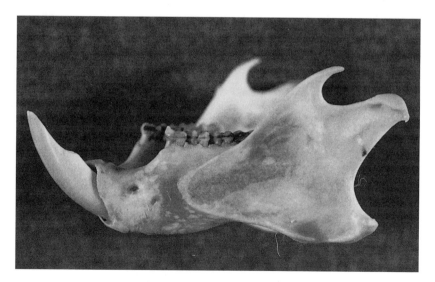

Figure 2.2. *(B)* lower mandible, including lower incisors, of an eastern gray squirrel. (Photograph by S. Hagan, courtesy of J. L. Koprowski)

Coubrey, Hagerman, and Kirkpatrick 1997). The specialized dentition of tree squirrels enables the efficient exploitation of tree seeds.

## ADAPTATIONS FOR MOVING IN AN ARBOREAL ENVIRONMENT

The acrobatic maneuvers of tree squirrels as they climb trees to escape predators, dangle between branches to collect acorns from the smallest of branches, and leap from tree to tree to find new food sources demonstrate the level to which tree squirrels are adapted to an arboreal existence. Squirrels have a plantigrade stance and thus have their entire foot in contact with the substrate. The thumb is nonfunctional on the front feet, but all five digits are functional on the hindfeet. A number of anatomical adaptations for climbing and jumping have been identified. The sharp recurved claws are exceptionally adept at grasping trees and limbs (and are capable of shredding a careless researcher's hand) and, in combination with proportionately elongated digits and foreleg musculature, enable tree squirrels to climb large-diameter trees and the smallest-diameter limbs (Peterka 1936). If one carefully watches a squirrel climb down a tree, another major adaptation becomes apparent. As a tree squirrel descends, it is able to rotate its foot 180 degrees from the normal forward orientation exhibited while walking on the ground (Figure 2.3). Although this sounds quite painful and looks a bit disturbing, the incredible flexibility of the ankle enables squirrels to quickly move up or down a tree to avoid predators, find a mate, or search for food (Jenkins and McClearn 1984).

Despite the tree squirrel's agility, accidents do occur, although fatal falls are rare. Donald Thompson (1976) reports the only known instance: he observed a juvenile fall to its death (and then be consumed by its mother!). Dick Thorington (1972) examined the skeletal remains of 65 animals and found 3 (4.6 percent) of the individuals had healed fractures of the long bones of the legs, suggesting that falls can be injurious but not lethal. During an estimated 20,000 hours of monitoring squirrels in the field, we have observed 56 major falls of >32 feet (10 m) by fox squirrels and gray squirrels; minor slips much too numerous to count can be observed on a daily basis. On one occasion, we observed a male fox squirrel fall from 85 feet (26 m) when a branch to which he was jumping broke under his weight. Within the first 16 feet (5 m) of his free fall, he had righted himself and fought to maintain this position while flattening his body over the remainder of his plunge. As he contacted the ground, he extended his legs, apparently to break his fall. He appeared dazed and

Figure 2.3. Fox squirrel descending a tree headlong. Note the high degree of rotation of the ankle joint. (Photograph courtesy of C. Salonick)

climbed the nearest tree to a height of 6 feet (2 m) where he sat visibly disoriented. Shaking his head several times and blinking his eyes repeatedly, he returned to his den about 110 yards (100 m) distant. The next morning we anxiously awaited his departure from the den cavity. Just after sunrise, he arose, apparently no worse for wear. Such is life for nature's best high-wire artist.

On a flat surface, squirrels are capable of achieving speeds of 16.7 mph (27 km/h) (Layne and Benton 1954; J. Moore 1957), and they are able to swim dog-paddle style (Applegate and McCord 1974), although sustained swimming is problematic and mass drownings have been reported during migrations from islands or across rivers (Long and Long 1986; Schorger 1949).

## SENSORY SYSTEMS

Another suite of characteristics of importance to the squirrel's ability to exploit the forest is the keenly honed sensory system. The major senses developed by squirrels include tactile, vision, and olfaction. Little is known about hearing in squirrels beyond the range of sensitivity (33–190 Hz;

Merzenich, Kaas, and Linn Roth 1976). Tactile senses are important in a couple of ways to squirrels. Clearly the ability to use touch would be important when leaping from limb to limb in the canopy. Unfortunately, little is known about the perceptive abilities of squirrels in comparison with other animals. To assist with feeling pressure (touch), mammals in general make use of specialized sensory hairs known as vibrissae, or more commonly whiskers. These elongated hairs are typically similar in structure to other hairs on the body but much thicker and sturdier. On tree squirrels, the vibrissae are always black. The base of the sensory hair is heavily innervated and possesses well-developed muscular tissue. Taxidermists often curse these small but sturdy problem areas of the body as they try to skin and prepare the mount. Essentially these sensory hairs are hot-wired to the nervous system, suggesting that they are indeed very sensitive and integral to the movement of squirrels in their environment. In comparison with those of ground-dwelling squirrels, the vibrissae of tree squirrels are much longer (Ahl 1987), likely related to the increased role in providing information in the more structurally and spatially complex arboreal environment. The nasal or facial vibrissae are well known to most people; however, vibrissae can be located virtually anywhere on the body. In tree squirrels vibrissae are also found scattered on the back of the body and a major concentration known as the carpal or ulnar vibrissae is found on the wrists. Beyond their role in gathering tactile information, the function of these sensory hairs is not known; however, we speculate that the ulnar vibrissae located on the underside of the wrist can be used to help detect tree limbs as squirrels make what sometimes appear to be blind leaps of faith between trees.

Vision is also well developed in fox squirrels and gray squirrels. At one time, squirrels were believed to only be able to function in bright light because of what appeared to be a pure cone retina, one equipped with color receptors rather than light-sensitive rods (Walls 1942). Having observed squirrels for many years, we would be surprised if this were true. Many squirrels are primarily active during the sunniest portions of the day (Gurnell 1987; Hicks 1949; Thompson 1977a). Yet the darkness of the forest can be significant, and the inability to see there would be a liability. Furthermore, on certain occasions, such as when males arise in the darkness of winter mornings to prepare for a mating bout, travel in extremely low light levels is necessary. We now know that the retinas of squirrels contain at least several different types of photoreceptor cells, which at first glance appear to be cones but nearly 40 percent of which are rodlike receptors that permit vision in low-light environments (Green and Dowling 1975; G. Jacobs 1974; West and Dowling 1975) though performance increases substantially as light levels increase (G. Jacobs, Birch, and Blakeslee 1982). Cones are known to be important in color vision and, in combination with the specialized rodlike cells, provide squirrels excellent red-green color vision that is probably important in the selection of some food items (MacDonald 1992).

The final important sense is chemoreception. Although little is known about the squirrel's sense of taste, it may be used to acquire information about potential food sources. Olfaction is clearly of importance in several ways. For years anecdotal evidence has suggested that squirrels use their powerful sense of smell to find cached food items, whereas recent studies suggest otherwise. Nevertheless, olfaction appears to be critical in deciding what items to cache (see Chapter 6). An excellent sense of smell is required in several other aspects of squirrel biology discussed later. Scent marking and gleaning information from scent marks throughout home ranges (Benson 1980; Koprowski 1993d) require a well-developed sense of smell. Many types of social encounters also involve olfaction, from the mutual sniffing of oral glands during greeting behavior by both sexes to the monitoring of female reproductive condition by males. Perhaps nowhere is a sense more directly related to reproductive success than in the location of mates. We have seen males join a mating bout after being attracted from 929.6 yards (850 m) downwind.

In relation to body size, the brain in tree squirrels is relatively large (0.25–0.35 ounces [7–10 g]; Meier 1983). Although one may be tempted to interpret the large brain as evidence of superior intelligence, the enlarged size is most likely related to the well-developed senses. Life in an arboreal environment and the increased requirements for stereoscopic vision, audition, and spatial memory all likely select for a relatively large brain size (Gould 1984; MacDonald 1997; Merzenich, Kaas, and Linn Roth 1976).

## PROBLEMS OF SEASONALITY IN FOOD RESOURCES

Because the reproduction of trees is so seasonal in most temperate species, fox squirrels and gray squirrels must cope with a huge range in available foods. From an autumn surfeit to a near absence of food in winter, tree squirrels must be prepared to deal with an over- and underabundance of food within a period of just a few months. In addition, a late spring frost can vastly change the quantity of resources by decreasing the number and quality of tree seeds available for the coming spring and summer (Nixon and McClain 1969; Koprowski 1991d). Indeed, a good year can be converted to a horrendous one in a single night of extreme cold.

Perhaps not surprisingly, tree squirrels show internal metabolic adjustments to the annual energy cycle of boom or bust. Tree squirrels, like all mammals, are endotherms. Thus they generate their own heat through metabolic processes, as opposed to ectotherms such as reptiles, amphibians, and fish. Endothermy is a high-energy strategy that requires significantly more energy per unit of body mass to subsist—often on the order of two to three times more than ectothermy. If body temperatures are to be maintained at levels different from those of the surrounding environment, then energy is required to produce or dissipate heat. The high-maintenance lifestyle and the absence of hibernation among tree squirrels combined with the need to remain active throughout the year, even under challenging conditions in northern latitudes, suggest that energetic efficiency should be a driving force in the physiological adaptations of squirrels. Body temperatures are high in squirrels, with rectal temperatures ranging from 98 to 102°F (36.4–38.7°C) for gray squirrels (Bolls and Perfect 1972; Hoff, Lassing, et al. 1976) and 105°F (40.6°C) for fox squirrels (Havera 1979). This body temperature is fueled by a heart rate of 150 to 450 beats per minute (E. Smith and Johnson 1984). The metabolic rates of gray squirrels are 1.5 to 4.0 times greater than predicted based upon their body mass (Ducharme, Larochelle, and Richard 1989; Reynolds 1985a)—the bottom line is that squirrels are geared for activity and it is energetically costly. This cost varies seasonally. Metabolic rates are lower in summer than winter (0.014–0.017 kJ/g/h vs. 0.020–0.024 kJ/g/h; Ducharme, Larochelle, and Richard 1989; Innes and Lavigne 1979). In order to sustain high internal temperatures and high rates of function, significant fuel must be provided. Thus adaptations to find food and use patches of habitat in an efficient manner are critical.

Body mass fluctuates greatly over the course of the year but in predictable fashion—mass is greatest in winter following a fall season of gluttony on tree seeds and reaches a low in summer prior to the renewal of energy-rich tree seeds (Knee 1983). Squirrels assimilate between 345 and 715 kJ/squirrel/day, and these rates typically exceed the minimum amount of energy required for maintenance, especially in autumn when squirrels eat at least 32 percent more food than is needed (Ludwick, Fontenot, and Mosby 1969). Indeed squirrels appear to prepare for the difficult weather and food scarcity that is to come in winter. But how do squirrels survive the period of winter food shortage and the potentially nasty ambient temperature and climate without hibernating like the other members of their family—such as the chipmunks, ground squirrels, marmots, and prairie dogs? Cold-exposed tree squirrels are able to mobilize energy at a rate nearly 13.5 times greater than the standard metabolic process; this performance stands as one of the best among animals (Ducharme, Larochelle, and Richard 1989). A number of characteristics are important in making life without hibernation possible. Physiological changes help meet this challenge to survive the critical winter period. Fall is a glutton's paradise in many years, with trees producing an abundance of seed. Food consumption rates are highest during this period and metabolic rates relatively low, enabling an increase in body mass of around 10 percent (Knee 1983). Metabolic heat production without shivering is also twice as effective in cold-exposed squirrels, enabling a more efficient maintenance of body temperature above ambient (Ducharme, Larochelle, and Richard 1989). Therefore, squirrels are able to accumulate fat quickly and use that fat to decrease food requirements. Squirrels reduce food intake and activity during winter, thereby minimizing exposure to the elements (Knee 1983; Thompson 1977a). The integration of behavioral modification with physiological adjustments is important in the ability of fox squirrels and gray squirrels to survive the winter. The most important behavior is to supplement the physiological storage of energy in fat with a behavioral strategy of caching food. The cache provides an energy source for the squirrel during the winter. For an animal that is literally walking an energetic tightrope without a net, squirrels are remarkably fit for such a challenge.

# 3

# The Habitat

*As always we could set our watches by the squirrel's routine. With the first light of dawn only five minutes away, we had picked up the first signs of activity. The variable signal from the radio transmitter of gray squirrel number 822 was unmistakable: the animal was active and outside the nest. The direction of the signal suggested the male was still in the nest tree. My assistant recorded the bearing, the current time, and the time of first activity and we jumped in the truck and headed to the next checkpoint. The second bearing confirmed the animal's location. We checked both radio-collared fox squirrels for signs of activity. The steady* thunk, thunk *of the signal verified what we expected: both animals were still inactive and in the nest.*

*After four years of this intensive radiotrack-*

*ing, the patterns of habitat selection, space use,*

*and activity had become quite evident. When it*

*was all over, the dozens of sleepless nights and*

*hundreds of chigger and tick bites had paid off.*

*The six-year study was our first step toward un-*

*derstanding how tree squirrels use their habitat.*

## THE SIGNIFICANCE OF THE HABITAT

Habitat use, simply defined, is the spatial and temporal use of a species' environment. It tells something about where a species lives, feeds, nests, reproduces, and escapes predators. It is the basis for understanding a species' geographic range as well as its local and regional patterns of distribution and abundance.

Although a species' distribution is in part determined by its range of abiotic tolerances, such as the severity of temperature or weather conditions, it is also dependent on how well adapted it is for living in a particular biotic environment. For many terrestrial animal species this biotic component of the habitat is defined largely as the plant community or vegetation type with which it is most often associated. Many species are dependent on this component of their habitat, exhibiting various morphological, behavioral, or physiological traits that permit them to exploit its resources. Thus a clear understanding of a species' habitat preferences is perhaps one of the first steps toward learning more about other aspects of its biology. Moreover, ecologically similar species that co-occur often show subtle differences in their patterns of resource use. Among many similar species of mammals, for example, it is argued that coexistence is possible because of differences in resource use, body size, microhabitat use, activity patterns, or a combination of one or more of these (e.g., Dueser and Shugart 1978; Glass and Slade 1980). Although such comparisons say little of the processes that allow for such coexistence, they are a fruitful way in which to learn how these similar species use their habitat in relation to one another. In this chapter we explore patterns of habitat use by fox squirrels and gray squirrels. We detail specifically a study conducted in a remote area of the southeastern coastal plain of North Carolina where both species coexist and often interact over limited resources.

Fox squirrels and gray squirrels are remarkably similar. The two are morphologically and behaviorally much alike; they show similar ecological tolerances; and they are sympatric, occurring together in the same forests, over major portions of their ranges in North America (Baker 1944; Bakken 1952; P. D. Goodrum 1972; C. Smith and Follmer 1972). Consequently, a comparison of patterns of habitat use by the two seemed like an appropriate starting point for understanding their basic biology. And that was precisely one of our goals, soon after Michael Steele began his doctoral research in 1982 under the direction of Peter Weigl of Wake Forest University. Weigl had just been awarded a Pittman-Robertson Grant from the State Division of Wildlife to study the ecology and behavior of the southeastern fox squirrels, a threatened subspecies whose decline was presumably tied to the dwindling longleaf pine forests of the southeastern coastal plain. We soon realized that a comparison of the habitat use of the fox squirrel and its ecologically similar congener, the gray squirrel, was also essential. Fortunately for us, the State Department of Wildlife agreed.

Previous studies had concluded that despite similar patterns of habitat and resource use some critical differences between the two species do exist. Based primarily on studies from the midwestern United States (Bakken 1952; Madson 1964; C. Smith and Follmer 1972), for example, it is widely held that fox squirrels prefer more open habitat, whereas gray squirrels occupy denser forests with thicker understory vegetation. It is also argued that because of their similar food preferences, these differences in habitat use are one of the only means by which the two species are able to coexist (C. Smith and Follmer 1972). Despite these claims, few studies in the Midwest have found any significant patterns of habitat partitioning between the two species (Armitage and Harris 1982; Brown and Batzli 1984). These studies, however, were conducted in homogeneous stands where coexistence was likely ephemeral and unstable, or dependent on supplemental foods from agricultural or residential areas. In contrast, in the East it has been shown quite convincingly that woodlots in which only gray squirrels reside differ significantly in habitat structure from those where fox squirrels are also found (G. Taylor 1976; Dueser, Dooley, and Taylor 1988). Thus when our initial observations in the southeastern coastal plain of North Carolina suggested similar patterns of habitat use for feeding and nesting, a more detailed study soon followed.

The southeastern coastal plain—dominated now by monocultures of loblolly pine—was once home to majestic forests of longleaf pine and oak. At the time of their discovery by European settlers, the longleaf pine forests stretched almost continuously from southern Virginia to central Florida. Today this forest type is largely gone, reduced to disjunct patches of relic forests representing little of the original cover. With the decline of these forests, many other species followed, with some, such as the red-cockaded woodpecker, eventually requiring federal endangered status. Similar concerns over the fate of the southeastern fox squirrel led Weigl to initiate one of the longest and most thorough investigations on the animal's biology. And after some initial fieldwork and some behavioral experiments with captive animals, it was soon evident that if we were to fully understand patterns of habitat use in the fox squirrel a similar comparison with gray squirrels was essential because of the similarity in the two species. What follows is an account of this comparative study of habitat use between these two species.

## THE STUDY AREAS

Our studies of habitat use were conducted in one of the few remaining tracts of longleaf pine in the North Carolina Sandhills (Moore, Richmond, Scotland, and Harnett counties) where fox squirrels are still reasonably common. The Sandhills region is located in the south-central portion of the state where the Piedmont meets the Coastal Plain. It is a region of mild relief (<328 feet [100 m]) with upland forests of longleaf pine and oak dissected by slow-moving streams and bottomland pocosins consisting of dense stands of evergreen shrubs and small trees.

Climate in the coastal plain of North Carolina consists of mild winters and extreme summers. In the Sandhills, mean minimum January temperatures remain above freezing; mean maximum July temperatures are 90 to 92°F (32–33°C), and precipitation averages about 5.07 inches (130 cm) annually with small peaks in winter and summer. Coarse sand with a heavy clay subsoil makes up most of the area's soils (Weigl, Steele, et al. 1989).

The upland forests, situated on sandy well-drained soils, are dominated by a few species of trees. Here open stands of longleaf pine are interspersed with scrubby turkey and blackjack oak; ground cover consists of wiregrass and dwarf huckleberry (Figure 3.1). Frequent low-temperature ground fires, some set deliberately for purposes of forest management, maintain an open savanna woodland with little understory. Where soils are more moist (mesic) and fires less common, denser patches of blackjack oak, post oak, southern red oak, and hickory predominate in the forest understory. In the bottomland forests, the longleaf pine is replaced by a denser canopy of pond pine, loblolly pine, tulip poplar, red

**Figure 3.1. View of longleaf pine forest in the southeastern coastal plain of North Carolina (Richmond County). Note the understory of turkey oaks and the wiregrass in the foreground. (Photograph courtesy of M. A. Steele)**

maple, sweetgum, and blackgum; a dense ground cover and understory of holly, dogwood, evergreen shrubs, greenbriar, and grapes make this nearly impenetrable habitat a haven for many wildlife species. Our specific locations for study included nine sites across the Sandhills Gameland Area, a 55,340-acre (22,000-ha) area maintained and managed for wildlife by the North Carolina Wildlife Resources Commission. One additional site was located 31 miles (50 km) to the northeast, and two others were located on the coast in Brunswick County (Weigl, Steele, et al. 1989). The habitat in these areas is similar to that of the Sandhills Gameland Area.

To determine patterns of habitat use by the two squirrel species we relied on two approaches: a survey of nest use and radiotelemetry to follow the behavior and habitat selection of individual squirrels. Both required several years of intensive fieldwork and several more years of analysis. But in the end, results of each corroborated that of the other. Although the animals showed clear differences in their habitat preferences, several unexpected results emerged.

## NEST USE

Other than food, few other resources are more important to squirrels than the nest. Leaf nests (or dreys) and natural hollows are especially critical for survival of nestlings (Barkalow and Soots 1965a; Burger 1969), protection against predators (J. Moore 1957), and shelter from adverse weather conditions (Baumgartner 1939b; Nixon, Havera, and Hansen 1984).

Early in his study of southeastern fox squirrels Weigl concluded that live trapping was too ineffective for monitoring these populations. Although other investigators working in similar forest types in the Southeast have met with some success (Edwards and Guynn 1995; Tappe and Guynn 1998; Edwards, Heckel, and Guynn 1998), capture rates in the Sandhills never exceeded 1 percent of the trapping effort. This soon led Weigl to consider an alternative for capture of the animals: the artificial nest box. Proven to be effective for the study of several squirrel species (Barkalow and Soots 1965a; Goetz, Dawson, and Mowbray 1975; McComb and Noble 1981b; Nixon, Havera, and Hansen 1984; Doby 1984) nest boxes provide not only a means for the capture of the animals but also a way to monitor the production of young, and as we discuss in this chapter, the influence of habitat on nest site selection.

By 1978 Weigl and his team of graduate students, with assistance from Terry Sharpe of the North Carolina Wildlife Resources Commission, had constructed and placed 550 nest boxes across 23 study areas. Boxes were hung in trees systematically either in transects along fire lanes approximately 574 feet (175 m) apart or in a grid pattern with a similar spacing. Each box was secured to the trunk of a tree approximately 33 feet (10 m) off the ground. Then, two to three times each year through 1986 we checked the boxes for nesting squirrels, once in the fall and again in late winter during the breeding season. On occasion we also checked the boxes in early summer to capture animals for radiotelemetry.

Box checks were labor intensive. A study of diurnal tree squirrels meant boxes had to be surveyed at dusk or after nightfall when the animals were most likely to be in the nest. And, to complicate matters, we had to carry a 30-foot (9-m) extension ladder, a holding trap, and the tagging gear through the pitch black, sometimes literally tripping over army personnel on nighttime maneuvers from nearby Fort Bragg.

But checking the boxes themselves was a blast. With one of us holding the ladder, sometimes fully extended, the other would quietly climb to the box, plug the opening with a towel, and slowly peel back the cover, peering inside with the aid of a headlamp to identify any occupants. Each box held a new surprise: sometimes screech owls, flying squirrels, opossums, raccoons, or great crested flycatchers with their nests characteristically lined with a snakeskin or a piece of discarded cellophane. On one occasion, we even found a black snake, perhaps waiting for an unsuspecting flying squirrel. But it was the gray and fox squirrels we sought. On a good night we might check 30 nest boxes and capture three or four squirrels; most often we came up empty-handed—a frustrating experience indeed.

A captured squirrel meant more work. A trap with a sliding door was placed over the opening to the nest box; the door was opened; and the nest box was shaken slightly until the animal jumped into the holding trap. On the ground the animal was then moved into a cloth cone that allowed us to restrain it until it was examined and tagged. Double zippers on the holding cone allowed us to check the animal's sex and reproductive condition, and to place numbered tags in both ears. The animal was then weighed, returned to the holding trap, and released back into the nest box.

Seven years after the first nest box checks, we summarized the patterns of nest use. By 1986, 4,040 nest box checks had yielded 218 individual fox squirrels and 105 gray squirrels—a considerable effort for such a low return. Nevertheless, a striking pattern in nest selection was evident. Among those individuals captured, fox squirrels had occupied 93 nest boxes; gray squirrels were found in only 43. Moreover, >30 percent of those boxes occupied by either species were used on more than one occasion; the remainder—417 boxes—were never used by either species. And only 3 boxes were used by both species.

We hypothesized that this strong pattern of box choice reflected a preference for a particular habitat around the nest. To test this, we randomly selected 25 boxes used exclusively by fox squirrels, 25 used only by gray squirrels, and another 25 random boxes that were never used by either species. We then conducted a detailed vegetation and habitat analysis around each nest site that included more than 36 variables. Among our measurements we recorded the species, height, and diameter of the nest tree; we also measured several aspects of the tree's architecture, including the number of branches below the box and the number of branches connecting with other canopy or understory trees. Such factors, we thought, might affect relative predation risks and the opportunity for escape if confronted by predators. We also measured the species richness, density, and spatial arrangement of the canopy, understory, shrub, and herbaceous vegetation within 65.6 feet (20 m) of each box. We also determined the boxes' proximity to certain landscape features (e.g., forest types, water). Statistical comparisons of each measure revealed only a few significant differences between the three box types. In fact there were no differences between the random boxes and those used by fox squirrels. By contrast, there were several important differences between the boxes used by the two squirrel species, and between random boxes and those used by gray squirrels. Most notably, species richness and density of understory and canopy trees were far greater at the boxes inhabited by gray squirrels. Whereas three tree species (longleaf pine, turkey oak, and blackjack oak) accounted for >76 percent of the trees identified at fox squirrel nests, seven tree species comprised 80 percent of the trees found at the nests of gray squirrels. Gray squirrels also selected boxes in trees with a greater diameter and those closer to standing or running water. Finally, we conducted a multivariate statistical analysis, which allowed us to examine the collective influence of all these variables on the patterns of nest use. The result was three measurements (factors) that in essence combined the most important variables in our data. Together, these three factors accounted for 88 percent of the variability in the data: one that described the diversity and density of the understory vegetation, a second that described similar measures of the overstory vegetation, and a third that was based on the proximity of the nest to water.

## RADIOTELEMETRY

Patterns of nest use alone provide only a limited picture of habitat use. Squirrels often nest in one habitat or vegetation type and rely heavily on others for other activities. Moreover, as some of our colleagues have noted, occupancy of nest boxes may be a misleading indicator of habitat preferences. They may encourage, for example, nest use in habitats that otherwise would not be occupied. It was, therefore, necessary to rely on another method, radiotelemetry, for a more fine-grain analysis of habitat use.

At first glance, the procedure seems rather simple: the animal is captured, fitted with a radio collar, and then tracked by the observer with an antenna and radio receiver that detects and transduces radio pulses from the animal's receiver. In practice, the procedure is far more involved, usually requiring a few years of preliminary work before serious data acquisition is possible. Our study was no exception. Beginning in 1980 James Ha, a student completing his master's degree with Peter Weigl, began the initial telemetry procedures. Ha worked out the bugs that are often typical of the beginning stages of any telemetry study. He experimented with different equipment, perfected the collaring procedure, and even wrote a

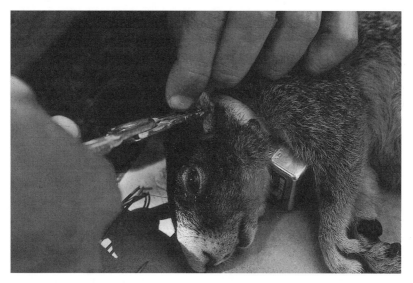

**Figure 3.2. An anesthetized southeastern fox squirrel with newly fitted radio transmitter. (Photograph courtesy of M. A. Steele)**

computer program that allowed us to analyze the data. Over the next five years, following Jim Ha's initial work, we were able to radio collar and track 17 fox squirrels and 10 gray squirrels.

A squirrel intended for radiotracking was fitted with a radio collar at the time of its capture from the nest box. While restrained in the cloth cone, the squirrel was first anesthetized with methoxyflurane, an anesthesia typically used in wildlife research. With the squirrel's nose protruding slightly from the tapered end of the cone, a jar containing cotton and several drops of inhalant was placed over the squirrel's head. The animal's breathing rate was then carefully monitored until it reached about 45 breaths per minute, indicating the desired stage of anesthesia. The cone was then unzipped and the animal quickly processed.

After tagging, weighing, and examining the animal, we slipped the radio collar around the animal's neck, adjusting it so that it was neither too tight nor too loose (Figure 3.2). We trimmed the excess collar, double-checked that the transmitter was still functioning, and slipped the now-recovering animal back in the holding cage. Barring complications, the entire procedure took less than five minutes. Once the animal recovered from the anesthesia, it was returned to the nest and left undisturbed for a week or more before it was first tracked so that the information we collected was not influenced by the handling procedures.

We used a different transmitter package for each of the two squirrel species. Both transmitters, as well as the receiving equipment (a receiver and two-element yagi antenna), were made by Telonics (Mesa, Arizona), one of several companies that specialize in wildlife radiotracking equipment. Fox squirrel radio collars consisted of a leather collar, a small rectangular box in which the transmitter and battery were hermetically sealed, and a whip antenna designed to trail down the back of the animal. With a life expectancy of more than 90 days and a detectable range of up to 2 miles (3.24 km), these transmitters provided ample information on each individual's behavior. In marked contrast, the smaller gray squirrels (up to 21 ounces [600 g] versus to 42 ounces [900–1,200 g] for fox squirrels) required a more compact transmitter. To reduce weight, the transmitter and battery were sealed in an epoxy to which a hardener was added to prevent the squirrels from gnawing the covering. The final result was a smaller package (0.63 ounces [18g]), and as might be expected, a reduction in life span and range by approximately 50 percent. The final weights of each transmitter were kept at <4 percent of the squirrels' body weights. Transmitter weights below 5 percent are widely considered to have minimal effects on behavior.

Equally important was the specific tracking protocol. Many wildlife studies that involve radiotracking focus primarily on calculations of an animal's home range, the area typically traversed by the animal in a single day or season. Although we hoped to determine home range estimates, we also sought to learn something about activity and of space use. Such calculations required several important considerations, such as how often and when to determine the animal's location. Continuous tracking, while sometimes possible with the aid of a computer and permanent monitoring station, is usually not cost-effective. In our study, as in most, monitoring had to be done manually. This meant traveling to the study area and periodically recording the animal's position. More locations meant more detailed information, but there was a limit to how often a single animal could be tracked, especially when several animals were monitored simultaneously. On the other hand, if locations were not taken throughout the day, estimates of home range and space use would be skewed. Another consideration, first brought to light by Swihart and Slade (1985a, 1985b), is the time between successive locations necessary to maintain statistical independence. Put simply, this is the time necessary for the animal to traverse its entire home range. Successive locations that are temporally too close together are not statistically independent and therefore bias home range and space-use estimates. Of course the critical minimum time between locations varies with the animal studied. For animals the size of our squirrels, we estimated this time to be 90 to 150 minutes based on comparisons made by Swihart and Slade (1985b). Although we recognized our estimate to be on the low end, we considered it a reasonable compromise between the time needed for independence and the time needed for a fine-grain analysis of space use.

After preliminary investigations in which we tracked a few squirrels almost continuously for nearly a week, we concluded that two to three days were all that was necessary to make an accurate assessment of space use, at least in a given season. Consequently, we chose to track each animal for three successive days from sunrise the first day to sunset the third. Locations were taken about every 90 to 120 minutes during all daylight hours, typically the only time diurnal tree squirrels are active.

The tracking procedure involved a rather simple process known as triangulation. At predetermined landmarks, distinguishable on aerial photographs of the study areas, we would determine the bearing for each radio-collared animal. Tuning to the exact frequency for a specific individual, we would listen carefully to the signal while moving the antenna in an arc parallel with the ground. The compass bearing of the strongest signal was then determined with a sighting compass and recorded along with the time, landmark, and activity of the animal. We then quickly drove to the next landmark and repeated the process for the same animal. By keeping bearing angles between 45° and 135° and using three or more bearings when possible, we could reduce error. Upon return to the lab after a tracking period we mapped the animals' locations by plotting each location on a map of the landmarks using the compass readings collected in the field. Once all the points were plotted for an animal we could then draw an X and Y axis, calculate the coordinates for each location, and enter these data into a computer. At that point we could calculate home range size and a variety of other measures of space use.

## HABITAT USE

Once the locations for a particular squirrel were mapped and entered in the computer, assessment of habitat use required only a few additional steps. The first step was to compare patterns of available habitat to that used by each animal. At each study area, the overall available habitat was delineated by a rectangle around the animals' home ranges in a way that no home range was closer to the edge of the rectangle than the longest

## Table 3.1
## Habitat Selection by Radiotracked Squirrels in the Southeastern Coastal Plain of North Carolina

| | Habitat Type | | | | | |
|---|---|---|---|---|---|---|
| Squirrel ID | Mature Longleaf (LL) Pine | Young Longleaf Pine | Hardwood (HW) Forest | Swamp/ Pocosin | Ecotone between HW and LL | Fields and Scrub Oak |
| Fox squirrels | | | | | | |
| 58 | — | — | O | O | + | — |
| 100 | — | O | O | + | O | O |
| 111 | O | + | O | — | O | — |
| 112 | — | O | O | + | + | O |
| 72 | O | O | O | — | O | O |
| 115 | O | O | O | O | + | O |
| 121 | — | — | O | O | + | — |
| 122 | O | — | O | — | O | — |
| 83 | — | — | O | — | + | — |
| 131 | O | O | O | — | + | — |
| 323 | — | — | O | O | + | — |
| 394 | O | — | O | — | + | — |
| 294 | — | — | O | + | + | — |
| | | | | | | |
| Gray squirrels | | | | | | |
| 172 | — | | O | O | + | O |
| 163 | — | | O | O | + | |
| 200 | — | | O | O | + | — |
| 162 | O | | O | — | O | O |
| 822 | — | | O | — | + | O |
| 530 | O | | O | — | + | O |
| 490 | — | | O | + | + | O |
| 540 | — | | O | — | + | O |

Note: The symbols — and + indicate significant avoidance or selection of the habitat, respectively. The symbol O indicates no difference between habitat use and habitat availability.

radius of that home range. In this way, we were able to survey the vegetation in the areas used by all tracked squirrels as well as the vegetation in the vicinity of, but not used by, these animals. To do this we relied on aerial photographs, followed by some ground-truthing in the field, to identify the major vegetation types (the dominant plant communities). In the lab we used the photographs to map and calculate the area of each major vegetation type available to each animal. In addition, following the lead of other studies in the Southeast (Ha 1983; Edwards 1986), we also defined and calculated the border, or ecotone, between bottomland hardwood forests and the upland pine stands by 164 feet (50 m) on either side of the two habitat types. Finally, using a number of statistical procedures (Neu, Byers, and Peek 1974; Byers, Steinhorst, and Krausman 1984; see also Edwards, Loeb, and Guynn 1998), we were able to compare the observed patterns of squirrel use of each habitat type with a pattern one would predict based simply on habitat availability. When use of a particular habitat exceeded availability, we concluded that the animal showed a preference for the habitat. By contrast, an animal was categorized as avoiding a particular habitat type when it was used less than predicted by its availability.

When the final results were in, the conclusions were clear but not what we expected. Despite the heterogeneity and patchiness of the vegetation and the opportunity for segregation between the two squirrel species, they showed considerable overlap in their habitat (Table 3.1). Yes—fox squirrels made extensive use of upland stands of longleaf pine as we expected. In fact, more than 50 percent of their locations were recorded in mature stands of longleaf pine forests (Weigl, Steele, et al. 1989). But these, along with most other habitat types, were used much less than predicted by their availability. Some fox squirrels at certain times of the year exhibited significantly lower use—even avoidance—of the pine forests. And even when individual fox squirrels made extensive use of pine forests, they were often retreating to the pine-hardwood ecotone to nest.

Gray squirrels, on the other hand, showed a clear avoidance of the longleaf pine stands and concentrated nearly all their foraging and nesting activity in the bottomland hardwood forests (>75 percent). Gray squirrels were bottomland residents, whereas fox squirrels moved between the two forest types. On two occasions we did observe gray squirrels nesting in open pine forests. But in each case they moved there from a nest cavity in bottomland hardwoods that was subsequently occupied by a fox squirrel (Steele 1988). Although we don't know for sure, it seems that the gray squirrels may have been displaced by the larger competitor.

How did these results compare with the published findings of other researchers? Previous studies point to distinctly different habitat preferences of the two species. Countless studies have noted that the midwestern fox squirrel prefers open forests with little understory, often selecting the ecotone between forest and field in which to nest and forage. Gray squirrels, in contrast, are residents of thicker forest patches with dense understory. In the East, similar differences have been documented between gray squirrels and the endangered Delmarva fox squirrel (G. Taylor 1976; Dueser, Dooley, and Taylor 1988).

Two important differences between the two species seem to best explain these contrasting habitat preferences but some fundamental similarities may help explain the enigma in our results. Failure to find significant differences in the way the two species process and use food led C. Smith and Follmer (1972) to conclude that this partitioning of habitats between the two was not based on food preferences or feeding efficiency as might be expected. Instead they argued that the heightened risk of predation on gray squirrels, as well as their greater agility in the canopy, provides this species with an advantage in thicker vegetation. Fox squirrels, in contrast, are free to access more open habitat and exploit areas that may be unsuitable to gray squirrels. Thus body size may in part explain the difference. Weigl, Sherman, et al. (1998) suggest that in the southeastern fox squirrels—the largest of all 10 subspecies—larger body size is a particular advantage for moving across open stands of longleaf pines and exploiting some of the resources in this habitat.

Why then do studies such as ours, where the two species occur together (sympatrically), report such extensive overlap in habitat use (Armitage and Harris 1982; B. Brown and Batzli 1984; Edwards, Heckel, and Guynn 1998)? There are some quantitative differences in the characteristics of nests and habitat used by the two species when they occur in the same forest (Edwards and Guynn 1995; Edwards, Heckel, and Guynn 1998). We, too, found similar evidence for habitat partitioning between the two species in our study. But despite these differences, overlap is extensive, even in the southeastern coastal plain. We suggest that even in this kind of environment, where opportunities for habitat partitioning are greatest, the two species frequently converge on patches of preferred resources over which they may interact and compete.

# 4

# The Diet

*There was no doubt about it; the oversized fox squirrel was eating for two or more. As she sat up on hind limbs to carefully husk each sunflower seed, her developed teats were obvious. Clearly she had a difficult time ahead of her. If she was lucky enough to see her pups through the next 13 weeks to weaning, she could expect further problems. While spring brings a reduction in thermoregulatory costs and a new flush of vegetation, it is still one of the toughest times of year for a tree squirrel. By then, her fall stores of seeds and nuts would be depleted. She would be forced to feed on spring buds, catkins, and the softer bark of some trees—all rather abundant—but notably poor in calories and rather costly to digest.*

More omnivorous than the casual observer expects, tree squirrels are truly opportunists in their quest for food. In addition to the nuts and seeds that are the mainstay of their diet, the animals often dine on a variety of budding leaves, catkins, and spring flowers. Although they may, at times, seem gluttonous, the tree squirrels are rather picky in their eating habits. Their ability to distinguish between different kinds of seeds—and even species and parts of acorns—elevates the tree squirrel to the rank of connoisseur.

The act of finding and consuming food often occupies the greatest amount of a tree squirrel's time; it influences nearly every aspect of its biology; and it is absolutely critical for its survival, growth, and reproduction. Couple this with the relative ease with which one can observe some foraging tree squirrels and it comes as little surprise that this subject has received the greatest attention from those studying the animals.

Quantifying, analyzing, and interpreting the feeding behavior of a tree squirrel can become a rather involved undertaking. Consider the diet of the gray squirrel. Its reputation as a granivorous (seed-eating) rodent, while generally accurate, is also somewhat misleading. Although the species has a strong predilection for seeds and fruits of a few primary trees, a complete dietary list for the species includes some 97 species of plants, many species of fungi, insects, bone, baby birds, and even other squirrels on a few occasions (Koprowski 1994a). Add fish and a few additional species of plants, fungi, and insects and you have a similar menu for the fox squirrel (Koprowski 1994b).

## INTRODUCTION TO FORAGING THEORY

Knowledge of what an animal includes in its diet is only the first step in understanding how feeding behavior influences its biology. How does one approach the study of foraging behavior in a systematic and quantitative way that provides something more than just a list of the dietary items? What are the interesting questions to address? Where does one begin? We open this chapter by briefly introducing the basics of foraging theory. This is an extensive field of study that provides a systematic framework and a specific set of predictions upon which to analyze and interpret the foraging behavior of any animal. In this chapter and the next we review the literature on the foraging ecology of tree squirrels within the context of this theory, while reviewing some of our own studies on various aspects of the foraging behavior of the squirrels.

The first lesson every student of ethology learns is that to study an animal's behavior requires that one break each complex behavior into its component parts—simple behavioral sequences and acts that can be observed, measured, and analyzed. Foraging behavior, for example, can be subdivided into behavioral sequences such as searching for, consuming, or digesting food. Each of these can be further divided into simple behavior acts, choices, even movements that can be quantified and compared under different situations. But in addition to just describing the behavior, a framework for asking the best questions is also necessary.

The field of foraging theory is based on an analysis of the costs and benefits of foraging, much the way an economist would analyze an investment. But instead of assessing a financial return, foraging theory is aimed at evaluating an energetic one. The currency is energy, and the goal is to maximize one's energy intake. It is also assumed that the animals are not making a conscious decision. Instead, as most behavioral ecologists agree, they have evolved simple behaviors that allow them to approximate optimal solutions to foraging problems (Krebs and Davies 1991). A second consideration of foraging models is the choices (decision variables) that nearly all animals must make when foraging. Although such behavioral choices vary, depending on how an organism makes a living, two are nearly universal to most species: what to eat (diet selection) and where and how long to forage (patch use). We address diet selection of the tree squirrels in this chapter and briefly discuss patch use in Chapter 5. We attempt to frame both these discussions in the context of a third important component of foraging models: the constraint variables. These are the variables that further limit what an animal is able to do to solve the foraging problems with which it is faced. For example, a foraging tree squirrel may choose not to feed on a more energetically profitable food item if by doing so its risk of predation increases. Predation in this case constrains the decision-making process and, as we discuss later in this chapter, changes the animal's behavior in some rather predictable ways.

## THE BASIS OF DIET SELECTION IN TREE SQUIRRELS

A systematic analysis of the diet choices of tree squirrels following the predictions and assumptions of foraging theory first requires a calculation of the total energetic costs and benefits of foraging on each available item. Although this may seem a daunting task, it can be simplified somewhat by restricting the analysis to items found at one particular time of the year or to those found in a particular location or habitat.

Suppose, for example, we want to analyze the quality of several species of tree seeds such as acorns, hickory nuts, walnuts, and

**Figure 4.1. An eastern gray squirrel eating an acorn at the entrance to its den. (Photograph courtesy of C. Salonick)**

pinecones—all common in the diet of most tree squirrels. Our analysis would begin with calculations of energy content (Table 4.1). First, it is necessary to measure the total dry mass of the consumable portion of each seed by husking the seed and drying the portion eaten by the squirrel. The energy content (calories per mass) of this consumable portion of the seed can then be measured in a device known as a "bomb calorimeter," which measures the energy released as the food material is burned in the calorimeter. An estimate of food quality may also require a calculation of the animal's digestive efficiency. For some foods, such as many types of herbaceous material, it may also be necessary to account for fiber, plant toxins, or both that may reduce the digestibility and quality of the food.

With the net value (energy content) of each item calculated, the next step is to measure the costs of eating each item, often referred to as handling costs. Handling costs represent the energetic costs to consume a food item. For a squirrel, such costs account for the time or energy to harvest and open the item (Figure 4.1). Often this is calculated only as handling

### Table 4.1
### Estimates of Mass, Energy Value, and Profitability of Various Squirrel Foods

| | | | | Profitability (cal/sec) | |
| Seed Type | Dry Mass (g) | Energy per Seed (Kcal/g) | Percent Consumable | Fox Squirrel | Gray Squirrel |
|---|---|---|---|---|---|
| Acorns | | | | | |
| Bur oak (*Quercus macrocarpa*) | 6.7 | 4.34–5.05 | 69.0 | — | 48.8 |
| Red oak (*Q. rubra*) | 3.2 | 5.45 | 55.4 | 58.8 | 30.8 |
| Shumard oak (*Q shumardii*) | 3.1 | 5.22 | 72.0 | — | 40.8 |
| White oak (*Q. alba*) | 0.8–1.4 | 4.17 | 70.1 | 42.9 | 25.8 |
| Hickory nuts | | | | | |
| Shagbark hickory (*Carya ovata*) | 3.0 | 6.57–7.56 | 33.0 | 29.3 | 17.8 |
| Mockernut hickory (*C. tomentosa*) | 6.3 | 7.92 | 21.0 | 21.0 | 11.8 |
| Shellbark hickory (*C. laciniosa*) | 12.0 | — | 23.6 | 6.0 | 11.8 |
| Others | | | | | |
| Black walnut (*Juglans nigra*) | 14.2 | 6.22–7.48 | 14.3 | 23.8 | 5.8 |
| Longleaf pine (*Pinus palustris*) | 101.9–168.3 | 6.50 | 2.0–2.5 | 7.6 | 5.8 |

*Source:* Adapted, by permission of the publisher, from Steele and Weigl 1993 and based on several sources cited therein.

time, but it is also possible to measure the exact energetic costs of feeding in a laboratory oxygen analyzer. Such a device allows one to measure directly the metabolic costs of a particular activity such as feeding.

The estimates for feeding costs in Table 4.1 are based on metabolic costs measured this way. Researchers at Wake Forest University trained lab-reared fox squirrels and gray squirrels to eat in a small chamber connected to an oxygen analyzer. The amount of oxygen used during feeding was measured and compared to that used during resting to calculate the exact metabolic costs to the animal during food consumption. This energetic cost of feeding (metabolic cost per time interval × time interval to consume an item) can then be subtracted from the total energy content of the seed (energy per mass × mass of consumable portion of the seed) to calculate the profitability of the food item. The food items in Table 4.1 are ranked according to these estimated profitabilities. From the table, for example, it is clear that although black walnuts contain far greater energy per seed (~15 kcal) than white oak acorns (~4 kcal), the acorns are far more profitable. This is due to the heavy hull of the walnuts, which can take a gray squirrel 15 to 20 minutes to open; an acorn, in contrast, can be eaten in as little as 2 minutes.

Knowing the profitability of a series of potential food items is only the first step in assessing a squirrel's diet choices. The next critical step is to gain some appreciation for the relative availability of each food item. According to foraging theory, an item that is high in profitability but rare in the environment should only be included in the diet as it is encountered. In other words, the high costs associated with searching for it should lower its rank as a preferred food; thus, the squirrel should not search specifically for this item. In contrast, less profitable but more abundant foods (i.e., those most profitable after search costs are considered) should rank highest in the diet.

In 1980 one of our colleagues, Allen Lewis, provided a nice demonstration of this for gray squirrels. He measured the density of various acorns and observed the animals as they foraged in winter and recovered items beneath the snow. By doing so he successfully demonstrated that squirrels spent more time searching for lower-quality acorns that occurred in higher density than they did for higher-quality acorns found at lower densities. His calculations revealed that in this particular situation gray squirrels maximized their foraging rate by feeding on the less-profitable acorns. This effect of food availability on foraging success and diet choices means that food preferences of squirrels may differ dramatically with location, season, or year as the relative abundance of various foods differs. It also illustrates just how efficient these animals may be at monitoring their resources and modifying their behavior in response to differing patterns of food abundance.

## FORAGING CONSTRAINTS FOR TREE SQUIRRELS

The squirrel's ability to behaviorally adjust to varying environmental conditions goes beyond responding to fluctuations in food abundance. Most animals are sensitive to a number of additional constraints that can greatly influence the outcome of each foraging decision. For tree squirrels, these confounding factors can take many forms, but three of the most critical appear to involve predation risks, plant defenses, and nutrient limitations.

## Predation Risks

An animal's ability to forage efficiently is only as good as its ability to avoid predators at the same time. The risk of predation is an important constraint that should greatly influence the outcome of many foraging decisions. But are animals able to assess such risks? Are they able to balance these conflicting demands? A growing body of research, led largely by the efforts of Stephen Lima, argues that indeed they are (Lima and Dill 1989). From countless studies with foraging birds and mammals, it is evident that the need for vigilance or the safety of cover during foraging shapes the outcome of many foraging decisions in ways that are not predicted by the early foraging models. Apparently many species regularly balance the trade-offs of efficient foraging against the probability of being eaten.

Two such studies with gray squirrels nicely illustrate this effect. Lima, Valone, and Caraco (1985) presented gray squirrels with small pieces of cookies at varying distances from forest cover. They found that squirrels were more likely to retreat to the safety of cover when the decision to do so did not greatly reduce their rate of food intake (foraging efficiency). Smaller cookies were eaten in the open more often than larger ones, and the probability of carrying any food item to cover decreased with the distance from cover. In a related study, Lima and Valone (1986) demonstrated that when exposed to predators, gray squirrels rejected smaller, more profitable food items (i.e., those with the highest calories per unit weight). Instead, they carried larger less profitable items to cover before consuming them because by doing so they could greatly reduce the time of exposure relative to the amount of food they retrieved. In neither study did foraging efficiency or sensitivity to predation risks alone explain the squirrels' behavior. Instead the animals' choices represented a compromise that balanced both demands.

## Plant Defenses

A number of plant defenses also shape the foraging behavior of tree squirrels. The most obvious of these are mechanical defenses. For squirrels, the most significant of these usually come in the form of protective seed husks or the heavy, sticky bracts of conifer cones. The evolutionary advantage for the plants is obvious: increased handling time and reduced profitability decrease the probability of predation. But most squirrel species are able to overcome such defenses. The squirrel's arsenal, however, extends well beyond simple morphological adaptations. When feeding on heavily armored conifer cones, for example, several squirrel species, including the European red squirrels, the pine squirrel, and the fox squirrel, are able to select individual cones based on cone hardness, number of seeds per cone, arrangement of cones on the branch, and the ratio of seed weight to cone weight (see Chapter 7). Such behavioral responses help squirrels circumvent many of these mechanical defenses. The result is continued selective pressure on the plants to evolve further defenses.

Chemical defenses of plants, although less obvious than many of the mechanical forms, exert an equal, if not greater, influence on the foraging decisions of squirrels. Plants in general possess a variety of compounds that reduce their digestibility and hence their usefulness as food to many herbivores (Howe and Westley 1988). Cellulose, hemicellulose, lignins, and tannins are all examples of typical plant compounds that inhibit digestion. Cellulose is a polysaccharide comprising up to 90 percent of the dry mass of many plant parts. Most herbivores require symbiotic organisms to aid in the digestion of cellulose, whereas many other species, including squirrels, are unable to digest this material at all. The overall effect for tree squirrels is that they are not able to make a living on leaves and stems but must restrict their diet to the more energy-rich seeds and nuts. On occasion, squirrels will consume tree buds, inner bark, and sap, but the digestive constraints imposed usually limit their use by squirrels to periods of nutritional desperation.

But even the seeds and fruits of most plants are not totally free of defense compounds. One group in particular—tannins—plays an important role in the foraging behavior of squirrels. Tannins are water soluble polyphenolic compounds found free-floating in the cytoplasm of plant cells. Common in many plants, seeds, and fruits, some tannins may have a metabolic function, whereas many others seem directed primarily at defense against herbivores. Condensed tannins, an especially important group of defensive compounds, interfere with digestion in three important ways. First, they bind to salivary enzymes and reduce the palatability of food. Second, they bind to proteins in the gut and interfere with digestion. Third, tannins will also bind to the proteins in the food and limit a squirrel's ability to digest them.

Although tannins are found at low levels in most seeds, they are particularly common in the acorns of oaks. And as we discuss later in this chapter and in Chapter 5, tannins exert strong direct and indirect effects on patterns of food choice and food hoarding by tree squirrels. Nevertheless a great deal remains to be learned about these important compounds and their influence on squirrel foraging. One especially puzzling enigma is why squirrels in the wild show a predilection for the high-tannin acorns of many oak species, when in captivity the same diet results in weight loss and malnutrition. One answer may be that in the wild squirrels rely on other sources for critical nutrients that are deficient in acorns.

### Nutrient Limitations

Just as some plants are laden with costly defense compounds, others lack critical nutrients that may further shape foraging behavior. While the nutrient content of most squirrel foods varies with species, season, location, and habitat (Gurnell 1987), several generalizations hold true. Studies on captive fox squirrels indicate that most seeds, such as acorns, hickories, and walnuts, are lacking in calcium and sodium (Havera and Smith 1979); others are deficient in phosphorous or nitrogen (Short 1976). The absence of such critical nutrients seems to exert two major effects on foraging decisions: it reduces the probability that the deficient food will be eaten, and when such foods are consumed the animal must supplement its diet with other foods rich in the deficient nutrient. Red squirrels in Scandinavia, for example, selectively consume the buds of individual Scots pine trees that are highest in nitrogen (Gronwall 1982). Although understudied, a number of other important behaviors including the gnawing of bones (Havera and Smith 1979), the licking of road salt (Weeks and Kirkpatrick 1978), and the consumption of weevil larvae (see Chapter 6) and fungi may all represent important ways in which squirrels balance nutrient deficits. Recent investigations also suggest that the use of fungi—especially that of the underground truffles (hypogeous fungi; Figure 4.2)—may be an important source of limiting nutrients (Weigl, Steele, et al. 1989).

## PINECONE SELECTION, BODY SIZE, AND PREDATION RISKS

We now return to the southeastern coastal plain of North Carolina to demonstrate how some of the above constraints can interact to influence diet selection. The pine forests of the Southeast represent a particularly harsh environment for tree squirrels (Weigl, Steele, et al. 1989). Although the diversity of seed- and nut-producing trees there is greater than one might expect, in some seasons and in some years finding food is not easy. Moreover, as we discuss in Chapter 3, the fox squirrels and gray squir-

Figure 4.2. Fruiting bodies of hypogeous fungi. These truffles are frequently retrieved from underground and eaten by tree squirrels in search of limiting nutrients. (Photograph courtesy of M. A. Steele)

rels that reside in these forests exhibit marked spatial and habitat segregation during much of the year but often converge on seasonally abundant resources especially during tougher times. The late summer crop of longleaf pinecones is one such resource that attracts the attention of both species. The ripening of the seeds inside the cones comes at a time when the animals have little else to eat (see Chapters 3 and 5). However, even when the animals are specializing on a single food item such as this, important diet choices must still be made.

Like the cones of other conifers in much of North America, longleaf cones are not fully mature until October. But long before maturity, the seeds inside the green, immature cones contain enough lipid for the animals to eat—and eat they do. By late July—a full two months before the cones dry, open, and disperse their seeds into the air (by early October)—the squirrels are busy stripping the sticky, green cones to get to the nutritious seeds inside (Figure 4.3). So busy, in fact, that they do little else at this time of year.

The process is pretty much the same for any squirrel attempting to eat a green female conifer cone. Starting at the base of the cone, the squirrel gnaws off one bract at a time, rotating the cone like an ear of corn.

Figure 4.3. A captive southeastern fox squirrel stripping the bracts of a longleaf pine to get to the nutritious seeds inside. (Photograph courtesy of M. A. Steele)

After removal of the first ten or so sterile bracts, each of the remaining bracts offers a small reward in the form of one or two high-energy seeds located at the base of the bract. In the case of longleaf pine, these seeds are of substantial size. The squirrel continues removing each bract and consuming each seed until all but the last few sterile bracts are removed. The animal then drops the cone axis to the ground, leaving behind an obvious record of consumption.

Because of the simplicity of this system, we decided a comparative study of cone selection by fox squirrels and gray squirrels seemed like a good place to begin an analysis of foraging and diet choice by the two species. The tremendous variation in size of longleaf pinecones (5.25–14 ounces [150–400 g]) meant we could evaluate diet choices among different items of the same food type. This would allow us to control for the many variables that so often occur between different species of foods. Such an analysis could be based almost entirely on the size, energy content, and handling costs of each cone size; other nutritional and chemical variables could be ignored or at least assumed negligible in their effect.

We also recognized an ideal opportunity to examine how body size might affect food selection in both these species. The extreme difference in body size between fox squirrels and gray squirrels in the southeastern United States is more exaggerated than anywhere else across their ranges. Here the two species differ in size by as much as 14 to 21 ounces (400–600 g); fox squirrels are 70 to 90 percent larger than gray squirrels. We hypothesized that this difference in body size might translate into different patterns of diet selection. Moreover, we anticipated, like many authors before us, that this difference would influence each species' sensitivity to predation risks. The smaller body size of the gray squirrel, thought to predispose the species to higher risk of predation, was considered a primary determinant of its more arboreal behavior and its predilection for denser vegetation (see Chapter 3).

We decided to wrap all these questions into one experiment. Our goal was to examine patterns of cone selection by both species under conditions of both high and low predation risk. A comparative study of diet selection by two similar species rather than one seemed like a more promising approach.

We first needed to know how cone profitability varied across cone sizes and between the two species of squirrels. We collected a range of cone sizes, from 5.25 to more than 12.25 ounces (150–350 g). As an extra comparison, we also collected the cones of the loblolly pine, which are far smaller than those of longleaf pine (<3.5 ounces [100 g]). We then timed captive squirrels as they fed on cones of different size, and we measured the total energy value inside the cones. Finally, we determined the profitability (calories/minute) of the cones by calculating the net energy each species could expect from cones of each size class. (See Chapter 5 for details on the procedure.)

These analyses provided us with a clear prediction. For both species, cone profitability increased with cone size. But the shape of this relationship was noticeably different for the two. For fox squirrels, profitability increased sharply from 100 calories per minute when feeding on the smallest cones to almost 700 calories for the largest ones. In marked contrast, profitability for gray squirrels ranged only between 200 and 350 calories per minute.

Armed with these data, we were ready to see if patterns of cone selection were consistent with our calculations. We chose our study areas carefully—several where only fox squirrels are known to occur and a single large forest tract in the small town of Hamlet, North Carolina, where only gray squirrels are found. We collected hundreds of fresh, immature cones that we cut directly from a few very productive trees. We then weighed each cone and separated the cones into eight size classes, one class for the small loblolly cones and seven others for those of the longleaf pine. In the apex of each cone we also placed a colored straight pin directly into the cone axis. Cones of each size class received a unique color. The cone cores left behind after a squirrel strips the cones' bracts represented a clear record of cone use. Thus we reasoned that by labeling each cone we could determine its fate even if it was carried off some distance by a squirrel.

Beginning in late August and continuing until the end of September, we presented free-ranging squirrels with small patches of these tagged cones. Each patch contained eight cones, one from each of the size classes. Patches were placed on the ground in areas where we could expect squirrels. To vary predation risks, we placed some cones in the open away from trees; others were placed at or near the base of a tree, usually under some additional cover. Following their placement, we periodically revisited the patches to record the animals' response. For each patch in which at least one cone was consumed by a squirrel, we recorded which cones were eaten, how far they were carried from their source, and whether they were eaten on the ground or in the tree.

This last variable was easily determined by the distribution of bracts around the cone core. If cones were eaten on the ground, a nice neat pile of bracts remained; if they were consumed in a tree, the bracts were scattered several yards from the cone core. And because we conducted the experiments where each of the species occurred alone, we knew who consumed each of the cones.

By the end of September the experiment was concluded and we tallied the data. The results were striking. Gray squirrels ate from all size classes and usually consumed all cones in a patch; fox squirrels clearly avoided the two smallest cone sizes. In some cases, fox squirrels only consumed the largest cones in a patch, ignoring all the others. These results were quite consistent with our estimates of profitability. What we didn't expect was what followed. Because cones were presented on the ground, fox squirrels consistently ate cones at their source and rarely consumed them in the tree. Gray squirrels did just the opposite, sometimes carrying cones 98.4 feet (30 m) or more to thick cover or to the lower branches of a nearby tree.

These results spoke volumes about the differences between these two species. Gray squirrels will readily consume the smaller loblolly cones, whereas fox squirrels clearly do not. Perhaps this is one reason why gray squirrels are able to reside in the bottomland forests where pondpine and loblolly pines grow (see Chapter 3). In addition, even in their own preferred habitat gray squirrels were feeding and behaving very differently from fox squirrels. Although these results do not demonstrate a causal explanation for habitat preferences, they do illustrate the close link between diet selection and the habitat in which a species resides.

# 5

# Patch Use

*It was late July, and the two fox squirrels we were tracking were on the move. It was quite a contrast to the previous tracking period (mid-June) when the two spent most of their time inactive in their nests. They also had shifted their home range and moved to a new primary nest. We were struck, too, by the pattern of movement. Most of their activity it seemed was in upland stands of longleaf pine, as compared with the pocosins used so heavily in June. The animals were never in one place for long. It all seemed to fit, with one nagging exception. It was time for the annual cone harvest. But why were the animals' movement patterns so erratic? Why did they seem to stay in one place for a short time before they moved on to another location?*

## THE CONCEPT OF PATCH USE

Equally important to the behavioral decision of what to eat is the consideration of where to eat and how long to eat in a particular location. Many tree squirrels, as well as other animals, are able to specialize on a single food item in certain habitats or at certain times of the year (Korschgen 1981; Steele and Weigl 1992). When they do, the decisions involved in maximization of feeding rate shift from what type of food item to eat (see Chapter 4) to what patches of the food item in which to concentrate feeding activity (MacArthur and Pianka 1966; Charnov 1976; Krebs and Davies 1993).

The importance of and study of the food patch were first introduced by Robert MacArthur and Eric Pianka in 1966 and later formalized by Eric Charnov (1976) in a classic paper that applied the marginal value theorem of economics to the problem of patch use by foraging animals. The premise behind this simple foraging model is that most resources in a habitat are distributed in a patchy or clumped manner (as opposed to an even or random one). It also assumes that natural selection will select for animals to forage most efficiently in these food patches. The marginal value theorem in essence predicts how animals should maximize their energy intake in a patchy environment.

To understand the model, it helps to visualize an animal arriving at a patch of food. As the animal begins to forage, it first experiences a high rate of energy intake. With additional time in the patch, however, the density of food items in the patch inevitably declines precisely because the animal is eating. Thus the animal's feeding efficiency declines over time. To maximize feeding efficiency the animal should stay in the patch long enough to pay the travel costs between patches but no longer, because it would then reduce the feeding efficiency. The specific optimum time is defined by the travel time between the patches in the habitat. If patches are widely spaced, the animal should stay longer in the patch; if the patches are dense and closely spaced the optimum time in the patch—the time that will maximize feeding efficiency—will be lower. Hence, for each patch and habitat there is a predicted threshold at which the animal should leave the patch in order to maximize its energy intake. If the patch density is below this critical threshold the animal should never even feed in the patch.

All this patch talk may seem too far removed from nature to have much relevance, but its utility in understanding foraging ecology is irrefutable. In countless studies, Charnov's marginal value theorem, as well as several more recent derivations of this first model (Stephens and Krebs

1986), have been remarkably successful at predicting the foraging decisions of a variety of animal species. The model has quite precisely predicted the actual behavior of animals. From the patch choices of nectar-feeding bats (Howell and Hartl 1977) to movement patterns of the horned lizard—an ant specialist that must decide when to leave an anthill when ant activity declines in response to the lizard's presence (Munger 1984)—the examples are many. Certainly these animals do not do the calculus to solve these problems, but as most behavioral ecologists agree, many species have evolved simple behavioral rules of thumb that allow them to approximate the nearly optimal solution to these rather complex problems (Krebs and Davies 1991).

## FOX SQUIRRELS AND LONGLEAF PINECONES

Our interest in foraging theory, in particular the ecology of patch use, goes back to the late summer of 1982 when Michael Steele was trying to decide on a project for his doctoral thesis and spent three days in the field with James Ha, a senior graduate student who was completing his research on fox squirrels. In addition to reviewing the radiotracking techniques and learning the unique vegetation of the coastal plain of North Carolina, Steele was hoping to catch his first glimpse of a southeastern fox squirrel.

Although we managed to accomplish a great deal in those three days, we never saw a fox squirrel. But, we knew they were there. As we made our way along the narrow, sandy fire lanes in Ha's aging Dodge Dart, we saw plenty of evidence of fox squirrel feeding activity. At the base of many of the longleaf pine trees were the fresh axes of green, immature longleaf pine cones, some eaten only a few hours earlier (Figure 5.1). As we learned later, the animals consume the cones directly in the trees and drop the remaining cone cores to the ground, where they provide an obvious record of cone consumption. The open habitat, with its widely dispersed longleaf pines, meant that cones were almost always eaten in the tree from which they were harvested. The open crown of longleaf pines meant too that the remaining cone cores usually fell to the ground. By the end of our short trip it was obvious that this was an ideal organism as well as an ideal habitat for a study of patch use. Perhaps, too, a study of patch use was an ideal way to study the behavior of the southeastern fox squirrels.

With other experiments and field studies to pursue, it was nearly two years before we found the time to test the idea. When we finally did, however, it was clear that we had stumbled onto an ideal system. In early Au-

**Figure 5.1. Evidence of recent cone consumption by southeastern fox squirrels. Note the scattered bracts and cone cores around the base of the longleaf pine tree. (Photograph courtesy of M. A. Steele)**

gust 1984 several of us were radiotracking an adult female fox squirrel at our Indian Camp study area. The squirrel, number 131, had been captured and fitted with a radio transmitter several months earlier during our spring nest box survey. We were now returning to conduct our third, three-day tracking session on the animal.

Lori Sherman, our research associate, assembled the handheld tracking antenna and plugged it into the receiver strapped across her shoulder. She then slipped the earphones over her head, connected them to the receiver, and tuned the receiver to 151.351 MHz, the frequency designated for animal number 131. As she turned on the power and pointed the antenna in the direction of where the animal's nest had been in June and July, she sighed as she detected a faint signal. The steady pulse meant at least that the transmitter was still in operation. The constant pitch of the signal also meant the animal was probably in a nest.

Holding the antenna overhead with her arm extended Sherman moved it smoothly in a 270° arc to locate the direction of the strongest signal. She then used a sighting compass to pinpoint the direction of the animal. We quickly headed to the next checkpoint to repeat the procedure and triangulate the animal's location. The second bearing confirmed our initial hunch: the animal had taken up residence in a new nest, some distance from the one it had occupied in early July. This midsummer shift in space use was a pattern we had now observed for several animals. In fact, if results from the previous summer were any indication, we could expect not only a shift and decrease in the animal's home range but also a marked difference in its fine-grain use of space within the range and an increase in daily activity as well.

The sharp shift in space use during June, often accompanied by long periods when the squirrels were inactive and remained in the nest, coincided with a period of extremely high temperatures and low food abundance (Weigl, Steele, et al. 1989). Weigl, Steele, et al. (1989) described the early summer

> as the period of the poorest food supplies of the year. The increasing temperature and aridity of the sandy habitats are associated with declining quantities of succulent plant parts and emerging insects. Old mast supplies [seeds of oak and pine] are exhausted, and the berries, fruits and fungi that are available are patchy in distribution. Squirrels are often thin and in poor condition at this time of year. This is the disappearance period.

With little to eat, and little reason to eat, the animals seem to shut down. But why does the rapid emergence from these summer doldrums occur in late July and early August when midday temperatures still frequently exceed 100°F (38°C)?

We knew that part of the answer was the ripening of the cone crop. But why such a change in space use? In a good mast year, cones were abundant and available in most trees. A fox squirrel could spend the entire day feeding in a single tree without moving far from the nest. But this was not at all what our telemetry data indicated.

Animal 131, we hoped, would help provide some of the answers. Usually we were tracking several animals at one time, which meant we were constantly on the move between checkpoints. This particular session, however, was devoted entirely to squirrel 131, so we decided to spend the extra time investigating the animal's home range for some explanation of this seasonal shift in behavior.

We first used the telemetry gear to verify that the animal was in fact in the new nest. We followed the signal to the ecotone between an open stand of longleaf pines and a small grove of blackjack oaks and there spotted an active twig and leaf nest in the crown of a mature longleaf pine.

The heavy *thunk, thunk* of the signal confirmed that the animal (or at least the transmitter) was in this tree. We then began to search systematically for evidence of feeding activity, first near the nest tree and then at the base of neighboring pines. At each of the first five trees, we found only a single cone axis (cone core) and a scattering of cone bracts, indicating that each of the cones was eaten in the trees not on the ground. Each of the trees also had several green cones still attached to its branches. About 328 feet (100 m) from the nest we spotted a longleaf pine with more than 200 green cones in the tree and a pile of cone bracts and cone cores at the base of the trunk. A careful count revealed a total of 70 cone cores, all of which appeared to have been eaten within the last week or two, some it seemed only hours earlier.

For the next three days, we recorded the animal's location every hour and then searched those portions of the range where we were least likely to disturb the squirrel. The squirrels' habit of leaving behind a record of their last meal meant we could accurately retrace their feeding behavior. We systematically searched the ground beneath each longleaf pine and carefully counted the cone cores at the base of each tree. By the end of the tracking session, we had tagged 65 trees: 28 in which only a single cone was eaten and 5 with more than 20 cones eaten. Most of the other trees had only a few cones eaten. Many of the trees in which only a single cone was harvested still had numerous green cones attached to their branches, suggesting that squirrels were possibly testing or sampling certain trees and then feeding in the best trees.

Over the next two years we devoted almost all our attention to the question of patch selection and patch use. By the autumn of 1986 we had recorded the patterns of cone use at more than 900 feed trees in eight study areas. For 590 of these trees, we established complete records of cone use through the entire foraging season from mid-July to early October when the cones open and release their seeds.

The procedure we followed was a simple but effective one. Beginning in mid- to late July we visited each study area and searched large tracts of open longleaf pine for evidence of cone use, tagged the trees from which cones were harvested, and recorded the number of cones eaten. We would then revisit the same areas every 7 to 14 days and repeat the procedure, revisiting all tagged trees and tagging any additional feed trees that had not previously sustained cone damage. We also found that cone cores could be aged based on the color changes that occurred as they dried. At the end of each season, just before the cones on the tree had fully matured and opened, we counted the number of green cones remaining in the canopy of each tree. This number, added to the number of cones eaten, provided a reliable measure of the cones available in each tree at the beginning of the season.

## PATCH DISCRIMINATION

To determine whether squirrels were selecting richer patches (trees) in which to feed, we first had to compare the number of cones in preferred trees with the number in those trees in which only a few cones were harvested. This comparison seemed to provide a quick end to the mystery. At most sites, cone densities were two to three times higher in the preferred trees (Steele and Weigl 1992), even though avoided trees had as many as 50 cones still remaining in their canopy at the end of the season. But while it seemed that animals were basing tree preferences solely on the density of cones in the tree, anecdotal observations at several sites suggested otherwise. At one site in particular a number of trees had only a single cone harvested, despite cone densities as great as those in preferred trees. Were these animals just sloppy foragers or were they basing foraging decisions on patch characteristics other than cone density?

A closer look was needed. We selected this and another site for a complete analysis of cone and seed quality. At each, we identified approximately 10 of the most heavily used trees and an equal, random sample of avoided trees (i.e., those visited only once by the squirrels). We then recruited a small army of friends, armed them with a 33-foot (10-m) pruning pole, a .22-caliber rifle, and rappelling gear, and headed off to the field to collect a sample of cones (5–7) from each of these trees.

After several grueling days of sticky, back-breaking work, all the cones were collected and returned to the lab. There they were weighed, measured, and analyzed for their energy content. With the help of a very patient undergraduate technician, each cone was painstakingly stripped, one bract at a time, and all its seeds removed. This process alone took about 30 to 60 minutes per cone but provided a wealth of information. For each cone, we determined the number of seeds, the proportion of viable seeds, and the proportion of insect-damaged seeds in each cone. A sample of 20 viable seeds were dried in a laboratory drying oven to determine their water content (a measure of their ripeness), and a portion of these dried seeds were analyzed for their caloric content by burning them in a device know as a bomb calorimeter. Together, these calculations provided several measures of cone quality, including the total dry weight of seeds per cone. This measure multiplied by the caloric value (per gram of seed) provided an overall estimate of the energy content in each cone.

But as anyone who studies foraging ecology knows, the energy content of a food item is only half the picture. To understand the relative value of the food, it is also necessary to calculate the cost to the animal when feeding on it. Longleaf pine cones, because of their large size (3.5–14 ounces [100–400 g]), are difficult for even a southeastern fox squirrel to handle. The largest cones are awkward to manipulate and therefore probably costly but they contain more seeds and thus more total energy. Smaller cones, in contrast, are easier to handle but contain less energy. How do energy costs vary with cone size? Which cones are the most profitable for the squirrels?

To address these questions we calculated the time and energy costs for a fox squirrel when feeding on longleaf pine cones. Feeding times were calculated directly with five adult fox squirrels that we maintained in separate large outdoor enclosures (8.2 × 8.2 × 8.2 feet [2.5 × 2.5 × 2.5 m]). Each animal was fed different-sized cones, and the time it took for each squirrel to fully consume each of the cones was recorded. Next, an estimate of the metabolic (caloric) costs for a fox squirrel feeding on longleaf cones was needed. These data were borrowed from researchers who measured the metabolic costs of a fox squirrel feeding on cones in a small chamber connected to an oxygen analyzer (see Chapter 4). These metabolic data (converted to calories), combined with the feeding times, provided a final estimate of cone profitability. It was no surprise that the largest cones were the most profitable, but the relationship between cone size and profitability (measured as calories/min) was not a linear one. Instead, profitability leveled off with increasing size of the cone.

With all the data in hand, it was now possible to compare the value of cones and trees at each of the two sites. As we started this analysis, an interesting difference between the two study areas caught our attention. At one site (Gardner Farms [GF]), there was a positive relationship between cone size (and therefore profitability) and the number of cones in the tree; here trees with the highest cone densities also contained the best cones. At the second site (Laurel Hills [LH]), where we had previously observed squirrels avoiding trees with high cone densities, we found just the opposite relationship: cone sizes here were negatively correlated with the number of cones. Here, the trees with the greatest number of cones contained the smallest, least-profitable cones.

At GF it seemed the animals' decision was an easy one: select the trees with the greatest number of cones and those with cones over a certain size. And the analysis verified that this was exactly what the animals were doing. The preferred trees contained the greatest density of cones and cones with greatest total seed weight per cone. At LH, though, the animals' preferences were quite different. Here, there were no discernible differences in either the cone density or any single measure of cone quality (e.g., cone size) except the total dry seed weight per cone and overall cone profitability. At LH squirrels based their tree preferences on neither the cone size nor the number of cones in the tree; instead they selected trees with intermediate cone numbers and cones of intermediate sizes. Perhaps squirrels were assessing their feeding rate in each tree and selecting those trees that provided the highest rate of energy return.

Intrigued by the animals' ability to make such fine distinctions between trees and cones, we were still curious whether these behavioral decisions required knowledge of both the density of cones in the tree and the quality of individual cones. Another way of asking this question is, do squirrels exhibit the same cone preferences once cones are removed from the context of the tree (patch)? We decided to test this at the LH study area by removing a sample of cones from both types of trees and presenting them to the squirrels at feeding stations on the ground.

In each of 20 trials, we presented free-ranging squirrels with eight cones: four from a preferred tree and four from an avoided tree. In 10 of the trials we paired cones of similar size; in the other 10 trials, we paired cones of contrasting size. We color-tagged the cones as we had before so we could verify their consumption (see Chapter 4). All we had to do was search the ground for the labeled cone cores to know which cones had been eaten.

The trials were completed in about one month, at the end of the 1986 foraging season. The animals showed a distinct preference, but not for the larger, more profitable cones as we expected. When we compared cone preferences with regard to cone size there was no significant difference in the number of cones eaten. Instead, the squirrels showed a preference for cones from preferred trees over those from avoided trees. Results of these trials—opposite of what we expected—were intriguing and raised yet another question. What cue were the squirrels using to distinguish between the two cone types? Were they able to recognize these as better cones?

We decided that chemical differences were worth exploring. Pines are laden with many chemicals, some of which are likely to be important in defense against tree squirrels (M. Snyder 1998). With cone season coming to an end, we quickly collected a single cone from each preferred and avoided tree. This time, though, we placed each cone in a sealed container. The volatile nature of many of the chemicals meant that chemical differences might disappear once cones were harvested. We arranged for a chemical analysis. A sample of air was drawn from each sealed container and analyzed with gas chromatography. While the compounds in the mix were many, two in particular differed significantly. Both were specific types of terpenes known as pinenes. But contrary to our predictions, the concentrations of both compounds were significantly higher in the preferred cones. To this day, we have not been able to fully resolve this rather unexpected result. Our best guess is that the compounds may have served as a cue to yet another cone characteristic, such as ripening or energy content, that differed between the two cone types.

These studies on southeastern fox squirrels demonstrate a strong preference for cones and trees that increase the animal's feeding efficiency. They are also consistent with observations from other species of tree squirrels. European red squirrels, for example, select individual trees in which to feed based on overall seed density and cone numbers (Mollar 1986). Similarly the pine squirrels are also quite selective with regard to cone characteristics when provisioning their winter middens (see Chapter 6). In the Pacific Northwest pine squirrels are also selective with regard to the tree species in which they feed. They first harvest cones from the tree species providing the highest rate of energy gain; they then switch to the conifer species providing the next highest energy value. They follow this pattern until all conifer cones in their territory are harvested (C. Smith 1970).

Together these studies support the notion that tree squirrels are making careful patch decisions in a way that maximizes feeding efficiency. They do not, however, really demonstrate the patterns of patch depletion predicted by the foraging models described earlier in this chapter. The patch depletion problem is perhaps not so well tested in our system. When fox squirrels find a preferred tree they often deplete the resource below that predicted by the patch models. This may have to do with the fact that the animals are exploiting these patches over several days or weeks. Other studies show that when fox squirrels are feeding in food patches that are both small and ephemeral, they do behave as predicted by the models. Joel Brown and his associates at the University of Illinois have used experimental seed trays in which free-ranging fox squirrels are forced to dig through sand to retrieve sunflower seeds. When seed densities are altered, the density of seeds at which the animals stop foraging (time in the patch) is easily predicted. Moreover, when seed densities are held constant and other variables, such as predation risks or habitat quality, are modified, it is possible to see how such factors influence patch decisions (J. Brown and Morgan 1995; Morgan, Brown, and Thorson 1997; Schmidt 2000).

## PATCH SAMPLING

Let's now return to the scenario and questions with which we opened the chapter. Why in late July were southeastern fox squirrels only eating one or a few cones from most of the trees they visited? Why didn't they just pick one tree and remain in it to reduce travel costs? Were they testing or sampling for the best trees? About the time we began to consider these questions, a new generation of foraging studies—many of a theoretical and mathematical nature—were beginning to emerge. Many predicted that sampling behavior should be common in nature. Several studies criticized the simplicity of the earlier models of foraging behavior and noted that both the diet and patch models assume that animals possess complete information in which to make foraging decisions. In other words they assume that the animal does not have to first experience available food types and patches in order to make decisions.

Of course, the assumption that animals possess complete information about all the foraging choices available to them is unrealistic. But documenting the occasions on which an animal is sampling a new food item or patch in the wild seems like an impossible task—unless of course you're studying a tree squirrel feeding on patches of extremely large and visible pine cones. Our system was an excellent one with which to address this question.

Throughout our fieldwork on patch use we suspected that the fox squirrels were in fact sampling trees. Indeed our comparison of preferred and avoided trees supported this contention. Our ability to identify trees that the animals visited once and then never revisited meant that we could be sure they had encountered the patches, a feature uncommon to most studies of this type. In effect, it suggested that these trees were tested and rejected by the animals. But by 1987, having accumulated several years of data on patterns of cone use and tree selection, we were able to look carefully for other evidence of sampling behavior.

We first decided on the consumption of a single cone per tree (per collection interval) as a conservative indication that the tree had been sampled. This excluded a number of observations in which animals consumed two to five cones per visit (and were also probably sampling), as well as those instances in which one or more squirrels repeatedly sampled only a single cone during a collection period. Nevertheless, several independent observations supported our argument that consumption of one or a few cones did in fact represent some form of sampling behavior. First, observations of captive fox squirrels revealed that a single animal could consume as many as 25 cones in a single two-hour feeding bout before showing any signs of satiation. Thus it was unlikely that a single cone would ever constitute a complete meal. Second, at some sites the proportion of bracts removed from individual cones at "sampled" trees was significantly less than that removed at all other trees in each study area. And three, at several of the sites the probability that sampled trees would be revisited (and sustain cone damage) by squirrels (<37 percent) was significantly lower than that for all other trees (>57 percent). This suggested that the animals were in fact basing their patterns of space and tree use on the information they learned from sampling.

According to our conservative definition of sampling, at five of the six sites studied sampling behavior occurred at more than 40 percent of the trees visited by the animals within any two-week collection period. Moreover, while sampling was more intensive early in the season (90 percent of trees at one site), it still accounted for 25 to 48 percent of the observations between mid-September and early October. Only at one site was sampling behavior consistently low during most of the season (12–30 percent of the trees); interestingly, this site had the highest cone densities during the entire study.

Thus it seemed likely that the animals were indeed sampling. But one question remained. Why did they continue to sample through the season? It seemed reasonable that intensive sampling would be important early in the season to identify the best patches, but once that was done why continue the effort? We were able to demonstrate that the onset of cone use at the end of July began just at the point in the cones' development when the fox squirrels were able to maintain a positive energy balance when feeding on the cones. We also noted that the highest period of cone use corresponded with the time at which the energy content in the seeds was highest (Steele 1988). Thus sampling behavior seemed to be important not only for patch selection but also for tracking development and energetic changes in the cone supply.

Our problem wasn't solved, however. Sampling continues even after the seeds in the cones are fully mature. In the end, we are able to offer one simple explanation for this. Like many other tree squirrels, fox squirrels exhibit overlapping home ranges. Thus while one animal is feeding in one part of its range, another may be depleting cones somewhere else. Constant monitoring of the resource by sampling is the only way to monitor resource depletion that results from the activity of other individuals. In this way fox squirrels can continue to make the best patch choices and feed in the most efficient manner possible.

# 6

# The Cache

*From our position behind the silver maple, we both watched through binoculars as Leila Hadj-Chikh, one of our research assistants, rolled a white oak acorn to the gray squirrel. The animal retrieved the acorn, retreated several feet from Leila, sat up on its hind legs, and rolled the acorn in its forepaws just below its nose. It then consumed the entire cotyledon of the seed, leaving nothing but a scattered pile of shell fragments on the ground. The animal immediately turned to Leila and waited for another handout, this time an acorn of northern red oak. The animal began again with the "rolling behavior," as we referred to it. But this time, it tucked the acorn in its mouth and headed across the park. As the squirrel approached the base of a beech*

*tree, about 100 feet (30 m) away, it began to dig.*
*Then it shoved its nose in the hole and covered*
*the hole quickly; the animal, it seemed, had*
*buried the acorn. But as we watched it move*
*several feet away and dig another hole, we spot-*
*ted the acorn still tucked away in its mouth. Fi-*
*nally the squirrel excavated a third hole with its*
*front paws, planted the seed firmly in the cache*
*site with four hard thrusts of the body, and cov-*
*ered the hole over with several quick passes of*
*its front paws.*

This scenario should be familiar to anyone who has taken the time to feed acorns to a squirrel. And at first glance it seems that the busy bushy tails are just a bit too randomly energetic for their own good. But those of us who have taken the time to look at this behavior more carefully know that tree squirrels are actually quite precise in their food-hoarding behavior. They make dozens of specific decisions each day about what to store, how to store it, where to store it, and when to store it (Figure 6.1). In fact, each of the behavioral acts described in the account above represents one of these decisions—behavioral choices that are critical for the provisioning, maintenance, and recovery of the cache and, ultimately, the animal's survival. In this chapter we discuss the various ecological and evolutionary constraints that have shaped caching behavior in tree squirrels, and we review a series of experimental studies that illustrate the specific behavioral decisions gray squirrels make when caching.

## INVESTMENT STRATEGIES OF SQUIRRELS: LARDERHOARDING VERSUS SCATTERHOARDING

The habit of storing food for later use, although certainly not unique to squirrels, is widely recognized by both causal observer and scientist alike as one of the most distinctive traits of the tree squirrels. This distinction is noteworthy indeed when one considers that food-hoarding is common

**Figure 6.1. Gray squirrel burying an acorn (Photograph courtesy of M. A. Steele)**

practice for members of more than 29 other families of mammals, 15 families of birds, and 20 families of arthropods (Vander Wall 1990).

Perhaps best known for their mastery of food-hoarding are the territorial pine squirrels (i.e., red and Douglas' squirrels). Common denizens of the conifer forests of Canada and the western and northern United States (Steele 1998, 1999), these small but highly aggressive and vocal squirrels store huge quantities of conifer cones that they vigorously defend against competitors (Gurnell 1987; Steele 1998, 1999). Such extensive hoards (or middens as they are sometimes called), easily recognized by their conspicuous piles of cone cores and bracts under which new cones are placed, provide a cool moist environment that is ideal for the storage of cones (C. Smith 1965, 1968). Most middens contain enough food to last one to two seasons, and they are often passed on through several generations of squirrels (Gurnell 1984; Lair 1985).

Food storing is also a critical survival strategy for many of the 100 or more species of tree squirrels distributed throughout the temperate and tropical forests of the world (Cahalane 1942; Thompson and Thompson 1980; Vander Wall 1990). But unlike the pine squirrels, the tree squirrels have adopted an entirely different approach to the problem of stockpiling their groceries. Members of this group are far less likely to store all their food in a single location. Instead, they place one or a few food items just below the ground surface in many—sometimes hundreds—of widely dispersed cache sites. The result is a spatial distribution of stored food that is impossible to defend against competitors, whereas the advantage is that competitors are less likely to pilfer the squirrel's "warehouse" (Steele and Smallwood in press).

Why the two different approaches? The nearly opposite food-hoarding strategies of the pine and tree squirrels—called larderhoarding and scatterhoarding, respectively—illustrate two extremes of a continuum of storing strategies employed by all food-hoarding animals (Vander Wall 1990). Most animals exhibit behavior well between the two extremes, and some vary their strategy with the environment, habitat, and conditions. On occasion, even pine squirrels will scatterhoard and tree squirrels will larderhoard depending on the availability and type of food (e.g., Hurly and Robertson 1986). But by and large the pine and tree squirrels each remain loyal to their adopted (evolved) strategy.

Most researchers believe that for food-hoarding animals in general the two strategies for storing food have evolved in response to one of four factors:

1. when the hoarder is active relative to potential cache robbers
2. the aggressiveness of the hoarder relative to robbers
3. the climate, which likely influences how well seeds will store and how easily they are recovered
4. the type of food that is stored (C. Smith and Reichman 1984; Vander Wall 1990)

Among the squirrels the fourth factor seems to have had an overriding effect. The larderhoard of pine squirrels provides a cool, moist environment that prevents cones from opening, thereby preventing cache losses to the many mammals and insects that are unable to open the cones and get to the seeds. The location of the midden, close to the center of the owner's territory, also makes it energetically defensible against neighboring squirrels that might otherwise glean a free lunch (C. Smith 1968).

But such a strategy would be ineffective for the nuts and fruits stored by many tree squirrels. The high energy value of these foods, easily consumed by many other species, would be virtually impossible to defend in an obvious larderhoard. The alternative is to secrete each item in an inconspicuous cache site and invest relatively little energy in defending it. Although the low density of food means it is probably indefensible, it is also less likely to be discovered by cache robbers (Stapanian and Smith 1978, 1984).

As we discuss in subsequent chapters, these two strategies for storing food have far-reaching effects on many other aspects of squirrel behavior. The defensible larderhoard of the pine squirrels contributes to its highly territorial social structure, which in turn dictates not only the animal's behavior but also many other aspects of its population biology. Similarly, for the tree squirrels, scatterhoarding allowed the evolution of nonterritorial behavior, overlapping home ranges, and a pattern of dispersal of the young that is very different from that of the pine squirrels. A full appreciation of the behavioral decisions involved in storing food is key to understanding many other important aspects of the biology of tree squirrels. In the remainder of this chapter we review a series of experimental studies designed to analyze the behavioral decisions that the tree squirrels make when storing food.

## EATING VERSUS CACHING DECISIONS

One of the immediate decisions that a food-hoarding squirrel must make is the choice of what food it should eat immediately and what food it should store for later use. The sheer range of food items that squirrels encounter and select for eating and caching make the potential outcomes of such choices endless—or so it seems. But a growing number of studies on gray squirrels are beginning to reveal that these animals make many fine distinctions between various food items when caching, and a few important criteria may override many others when making decisions about whether a food item is to be cached or eaten.

The studies of partial acorn consumption and caching of acorn fragments sparked our early interest in the subject of caching and suggested that perhaps a careful examination of the responses of gray squirrels to different acorn species was a good place to start (see Chapter 5). It was well known that characteristics of acorns vary in a rather consistent way. Perhaps tree squirrels show a similar consistency in their feeding and caching responses to these acorn traits (Table 6.1).

Most oaks, including all but one North American oak, belong to two subgenera: the white oaks (subgenus *Quercus*) and the red oaks (subgenus *Erythrobalanus*). Species of acorns within each of the subgenera exhibit similar characteristics. Acorns of red oak species have higher fat content,

## Table 6.1
## Summary of Acorn Characteristics and Responses
## of Squirrels

| Oak Group | Acorn Characteristics* | Predicted/Observed Responses of Squirrels to Corresponding Characteristics |
| --- | --- | --- |
| Red oaks | High levels of tannins | Store in autumn and eat in winter[a] |
| | High levels of lipid | Store in autumn and eat in winter[a] |
| | Delayed germination | Store in autumn[b, c, d] |
| | Higher tannin near embryo | Eat top half and store bottom half[e, f] |
| | Lower levels of insect infestation | Store mostly sound acorns[d] |
| White oaks | Low levels of tannins | Eat primarily in autumn[a] |
| | Low levels of lipid | Eat primarily in autumn[a] |
| | Early germination | Eat primarily in autumn[b, c, d, g] |
| | Rapid transfer of energy to radicle | Excise embryos if stored[h] |
| | High levels of insect infestation | Eat mostly infested acorns[d] |

* Sources for acorn characteristics are cited in the references below.

*Sources:* [a]Smallwood and Peters 1986; [b]Steele and Smallwood 1994; [c]Hadj-Chikh, Steele, and Smallwood 1996; [d]Steele, Hadj-Chikh, and Hazeltine 1996; [e]Steele, Knowles, et al. 1993; [f]Steele, Gavel, and Bachman 1998; [g]Barnett 1977; [h]Fox 1982.

which raises their energetic value. But they also contain higher levels of tannin, the nasty phenolic compounds known to reduce digestibility and palatability of plant material, including the acorns and leaves of oaks (see Chapter 4). Acorns of red oaks also enter a period of dormancy that usually requires exposure to cold in order for germination to begin. In contrast, acorns of white oaks exhibit lower levels of both tannin and fat, and they usually germinate immediately in the autumn soon after they fall to the ground, provided they have access to enough moisture.

While the differences between these two types of acorns seemed quite consistent, a quick review of the literature revealed that acorn preferences of mammals and birds were not so predictable. In fact, considerable confusion seemed to center on the type of acorns preferred by wildlife species. Smith and Follmer (1972) for example reported that captive gray squirrels and fox squirrels preferred species of red oak acorns over those of white oak. A. Lewis (1980) reported similar results for free-ranging gray squirrels in which he measured acorn preferences by recording acorn remains on the surface of the snow and comparing these records of food consumption to the density of various acorns on the forest floor. He concluded that squirrels feed in the most energetically dense patches of food and often select red oak acorns because of their high lipid content, a conclusion similar to that reached by Smith and Follmer (1972). But many other studies, on a number of wildlife species from deer to captive squirrels (Short 1976), concluded just the opposite: that acorns of white oak are preferred, probably because of their lower tannin levels.

In 1986 some of this confusion was resolved by our colleague Peter Smallwood of Richmond University. In a clever experiment (Smallwood and Peters 1986), conducted while still an undergraduate at Ohio State University, Smallwood directly tested the effects of both fat and tannin on food selection by presenting squirrels on the campus with artificial acorns to which he had added varying concentrations of both compounds. By grinding the cotyledon and endosperm of white oak acorns into a fine powder and adding either tannin (2 or 6 percent) or fat (10 percent) by weight he was able to construct artificial acorns (acorn doughballs) whose chemistry varied in a predictable and controlled way. He showed that added tannin significantly reduced both the probability that an acorn would be eaten by a squirrel as well as the amount of time spent eating, although this effect was greater in the fall than in winter. He also found that added fat tended to reduce the effects of tannin because of the higher energy it provided.

Recognizing that his results were inconsistent with much of the literature and the common assumption that animals should feed in a way that maximizes feeding efficiency, he suggested that studies of acorn preferences (including his own) failed to consider the importance of caching decisions on feeding preferences. He hypothesized that gray squirrels might selectively store acorns that were high in tannins (i.e., red oak acorns) and eat those with lower amounts (i.e., white oak acorns). In his initial prediction, Smallwood also pointed to another important difference between acorns of red and white oaks: contrasting germination schedules. The early rapid germination of white oak acorns, he suggested, might also lead squirrels to eat these acorns immediately and to store those of red oak for subsequent use.

The sensitivity of squirrels to differences in acorn germination patterns was already evident from an earlier study by John Fox (1982). He reported that gray squirrels sometimes cache white oak acorns, but when doing so they frequently excise the embryo, thereby killing the seed and preventing early germination. A few quick scrapes of their incisors and the seed is no longer able to germinate. One of our graduate students, Juan

Radillo, has demonstrated that in central Mexico the Mexican gray squirrel also excises the embryo of white oak acorns when caching.

Early germination in acorns of white oaks—generally interpreted as an adaptation to escape consumption by seed predators—involves rapid transfer of energy from the cotyledon to the emerging radicle (root tip) and results in a structure that is high in cellulose, less digestible, and less preferred as food by squirrels and other seed predators. In addition, many white oak species seem to show a more rapid pattern of seed fall than red oaks. They tend to shed their seeds over a shorter period of time, which may serve to satiate seed predators, providing more seeds than they could possibly consume. Thus some seeds germinate while animals are scurrying about to respond to this ephemeral abundance of food.

With the knowledge that gray squirrels can respond to the differences between the two groups of acorns, several of us, in collaboration with Peter Smallwood, tested the prediction that squirrels would selectively store acorns of red oak and eat those of white oak. We also hypothesized that while some white oak acorns may be stored for short-term use, gray squirrels would invest more time and energy in dispersing red oak acorns farther than those of white oak because of their greater value, perhaps by placing them in better cache sites.

We used two experimental approaches to test these questions. In the first, we observed the caching and feeding responses of relatively tame gray squirrels in a city park in Wilkes-Barre, Pennsylvania. We first presented individual squirrels with single acorns of either species and recorded whether the acorn was eaten or stored, the amount of time to eat or cache each acorn, and the distance each acorn was carried (dispersed) before being eaten or cached. The second approach involved labeling the seeds with small metal tracers, making them available to squirrels, then locating the seeds with a metal detector after the seeds were dispersed and either eaten or cached.

In both experiments the results supported our initial predictions and the patterns were obvious. Squirrels consistently stored the acorns of red oak and ate those of white oak. In autumn, when acorns of oaks are usually abundant, between 40 and 90 percent of red oak acorns were stored; acorns of white oak were almost always eaten (>90 percent of observations). In fact, only under certain conditions were white oak acorns stored and always at lower frequency than those of red oak. Quite frequently acorns of white oak also had the embryos excised as reported earlier by Fox (1982).

## PERISHABILITY AND CACHE RETURNS

Having established that gray squirrels preferentially disperse and store acorns of red oak, we were faced with determining the specific reason(s) for the response. The most plausible explanation was that the delayed germination of red oak acorns rendered them more suitable for caching. Perhaps, too, higher tannin levels meant that red oak acorns would store longer in the cache because of their preservative (antimicrobial) effects.

Maybe gray squirrels selectively store items that are least perishable and eat those that are less likely to store well. The idea that food-hoarding animals may be highly sensitive to the relative perishability of their food was well established by Jim Reichman and his graduate students at Kansas State University. Studies there on the food-hoarding behavior of woodrats and kangaroo rats suggested that these species always stored foods that would keep the longest in the cache (Reichman, Fattaey, and Fattaey 1986; Reichman 1988; Post and Reichman 1991).

If in fact squirrels were sensitive to perishability of their food stores, then a reasonable next question to ask was, how do they respond to insect-infested seeds? A variety of insects, from ants to moth and butterfly larvae, frequently rely on acorns for completion of part or all of their life cycle, often inflicting damage on or even complete destruction of acorns. One group in particular, the weevils, or snout beetles, after their formidable downward-curved beaks, seemed most relevant. This group of beetles includes in their family some of the most destructive insects known to humans (the boll weevil, the alfalfa weevil, the apple curculio, and the plum curculio), as well as several species of weevils that depend heavily on the nuts of many oak species for completion of their life cycles. Adult beetles typically feed on various fruits, seeds, and leaves, but it is the larvae that inflict serious damage to the acorns of oaks. During the summer, a few weeks prior to acorn maturation, adult female weevils will drill a small hole, excavate one or more nest chambers in the cotyledon of the acorn, and then turn and oviposit a single egg into each brood chamber. Within two weeks these eggs hatch into wormlike larvae that migrate through and feed on the cotyledon of the acorn, causing serious damage to individual acorns and infestation of as much as 90 percent of the crop of individual oak trees. When mature, the larvae cut a small hole and exit the acorn to complete their life cycle in the soil, where they pupate into adults (except in southern portions of North America where they overwinter and metamorphose within the acorn).

Infested acorns seemed to present an interesting problem for squirrels. Energy invested in storing infested acorns is likely to be wasted; the larvae will consume at least a portion of the seed, while its exit hole is likely to make the acorn more susceptible to damage by other insects and a variety of pathogens. But can squirrels detect infested acorns before the weevil has emerged? And more important—do they distinguish between infested and noninfested acorns when caching? We went first to the library and then to the park to answer these questions.

In the literature we found a bewildering array of conclusions about the responses of birds and mammals to insect-infested seeds. One thing though was definite: several species of birds and mammals can distinguish between infested and noninfested seeds. But for squirrels some studies reported that they could not distinguish between the two seed types, whereas others maintained that they could and that they often rejected them. One common omission of all these studies was whether squirrels were caching or eating the seeds. We hypothesized that squirrels might select the sound acorns for caching.

With the cooperation of a rather amused radiology staff at our local hospital, we x-rayed boxes of several hundred acorns to distinguish between noninfested seeds and those infested with weevils. We then presented the two types of acorns to our park squirrels. As we predicted they stored the noninfested acorns, but surprisingly, they ate the infested seeds, weevils and all. This observation was certainly consistent with the notion that squirrels are sensitive to perishability of their caches. But as our critics and reviewers were quick to note, we had not really demonstrated the specific proximate cue to which the animals responded, or that they had necessarily responded to the perishability of the seeds. Several other factors (i.e., acorn characteristics) may have coincidentally made it seem as though the animals were responding to perishability when in fact they were not. To test this we needed an additional experiment, one that controlled for these other alternative explanations.

One of those alternatives (and perhaps the most plausible) was first introduced in 1992 by Lucy Jacobs in a paper based on a portion of her doctoral research at Princeton University. Jacobs claimed that feeding or handling time, not perishability, was the primary factor driving caching decisions. She suggested that for food-hoarding animals, especially those faced with seasonally abundant foods such as an autumn acorn crop, the time available for hoarding should be the primary limitation to which they respond. If they did respond to such a time constraint, she reasoned, they should always cache the items that it takes the longest to eat (i.e., those with the longest handling time) and eat those that have the shortest handling time. Such a strategy of course makes good sense for a gray squirrel that must cache as much food as possible while it is still available. And in behavioral tests of her hypothesis, that is exactly what Jacobs found. Her captive gray squirrels consistently ate the smaller items regardless of their relative perishability.

Intrigued by her compelling argument and tantalizing results, we set out to test Jacob's handling-time hypothesis against our own hypothesis concerning perishability. One of our students, Leila Hadj-Chikh (now a graduate student at Princeton University where she is continuing her work on caching behavior of gray squirrels), suggested the perfect experiment: present individual squirrels with pairs of acorns that vary in either handling time or perishability due to differences in germination schedule (i.e., red oak versus white oak). With appropriate pairs it might be possible, she predicted, to see if one factor consistently determined the animal's behavior. For example, the perishability hypothesis predicts that when presented with acorns of red oak and pin oak the squirrels should store both seed types because both are red oaks and both show delayed germination and lower perishability. In contrast, the handling-time hypothesis predicts that the acorns of red oak should be stored and the smaller acorns of pin oak eaten because of their lower handling time (200 percent less than that of red oak acorns). Similarly, the handling-time hypothesis predicts that when presented with acorns of white oak and chestnut oak (both large white oak acorns with high handling times) squirrels should store both; consumption of both would follow from the perishability hypothesis.

Careful selection of six distinct experimental treatments—each one designed to test the animal's response to a unique pair of acorns—allowed us to tease apart the importance of each of the two factors as well as control for other variables that could arguably contribute to the animal's decisions when caching (i.e., tannin and fat levels). During each trial we presented each of 16 to 20 individual squirrels with a single pair of acorns and recorded whether the seed was cached or eaten and several other variables that described their feeding and caching behavior (e.g., caching or eating time, dispersal distance, dispersal time).

The experiment itself was a simple one but the results compelling. In every trial, the results statistically favored the predictions of the perishability hypothesis and at the same time negated those of the handling-time hypothesis (Hadj-Chikh, Steele, and Smallwood 1996).

## DETECTION OF SEED PERISHABILITY AND SEED DORMANCY

Perishability, at least in the context in which we examined it, exerted a primary influence on the animal's behavior; it satisfactorily explained 78 percent of the caching decisions. Why then were we not satisfied to stop there and conclude that perishability of the acorns was the primary proximate factor on which the animals base their caching decisions?

The answer to this followed from a simple nagging aspect of our study site in the park—one that had haunted us through many of our previous studies. Except for an occasional ornamental tree species, vegetation in Kirby Park is dominated by silver maples, red oaks, and pin oaks; not a single tree of any white oak species is found there. With an open field, a 109-yard-wide (100-m) strip of floodplain forest, and the mighty Susquehanna River on one side and extensive urban sprawl on the other, our study site and squirrels are isolated from the nearest white oak by a few miles. While gray squirrels will sometimes move several miles in search of suitable food sources, it was reasonable to assume that not many, perhaps none, of our animals had regular previous experience with acorns of white oak. How then could they so consistently distinguish between acorns of the two types of oaks? What cue could they possibly rely on to detect differences in germination schedules (perishability)?

Our first hunch, that gray squirrels can simply "see" the differences between the two types of acorns, followed from their reputation for keen visual acuity and their ability to detect color—a trait shared by few other mammals. However, as one colleague reminded us, this idea was not consistent with the position of their eyes, set wide apart on either side of the head, an arrangement ideal for stereoscopic vision but not for close-up work. This point, coupled with the animal's habit of inspecting the acorn by rolling it in the front paws just below the nose, meant there was little opportunity for visual inspection. In fact, it clearly suggested that the squirrels were relying on olfactory cues. These data made good sense given the importance of chemical cues in the behavior of most mammals. We further suspected that specific chemicals in the acorns, such as tannins, might be used as a cue to detect relative perishability. But results of our experiments were more consistent with the notion that the squirrels responded specifically to perishability, rather than tannin concentrations. Certainly squirrels cannot smell seed dormancy—or can they?

The next experiment, we decided, required a tad more ingenuity. We needed acorns that looked like one type (red oak or white oak) and smelled like the other. Such acorns simply do not exist, so we decided on the obvious alternative: we made them ourselves. By cutting acorns in half, carefully removing the cotyledon, grinding the cotyledon to a homogeneous powder, modifying the chemical content of the acorn powder, and then stuffing it back in the shell of the acorn, we found we could make just about any type of acorn we could imagine. The trick of course was to reconstruct an acorn that the squirrels recognized as a storable item, one that they didn't consider perishable because of a jagged or open seam. But after a few dozen practice acorns and preliminary tests over three field seasons, one of which was devoted entirely to developing a glue that did not affect the animals' behavior, we arrived at a reasonable approach. We decided the experiment would test whether caching decisions were based on external visual characteristics of the shell (pericarp) or specific, internal chemical cues, presumably detectable by olfaction. We also needed to control for other ancillary chemical cues in the shell. To do this, we simply soaked the empty shells in an acetone solvent to remove any such compounds.

Preliminary tests indicated that artificial acorns were frequently cached, and in formal tests in which we presented individual squirrels with red and white oak acorns that were just cut and glued, they consistently stored the red oak acorns and ate those of the white oak. We then proceeded with an experimental trial that examined the animal's response to two shells of red oak acorns, one containing the cotyledon of a white oak and the other filled with cotyledon of red oak. To our surprise, and contrary to our hypothesis, they ate both. And in several additional trials in which we modified the internal content of acorns of either red oak or white oak, we obtained the same results.

At first we thought the animals were recognizing the seeds as perishable items because of the seam. But these animals always ate from the basal end of the acorn first, rather than the seam, as those in our preliminary tests had when they were responding to what they likely viewed as damaged acorns. With additional trials we began to notice a pattern, one that we had not predicted or considered before. When we failed to soak the shells in the acetone, the squirrels stored the artificial acorns made with red oak shells, regardless of the internal composition of the acorns. This suggested that the animals relied on either a chemical cue in the shell, one that was removed with the acetone treatment, or that they were able to detect that the integrity of the shell had been compromised in some other way. Either way, it suggested that they might be able to determine if an acorn is dormant or not (Steele, Smallwood, et al. in press).

Two final trials in the experiment addressed this idea. First we presented each of our park squirrels with a pair of red oak acorns: one whole acorn that was still dormant and another that had emerged from dormancy and had begun to germinate. Not surprisingly, they stored the whole red oak acorns and ate or excised the embryo of those that were no longer dormant. They treated the germinating red oak acorns as they would those of white oak. What was surprising, though, were the results of the next experiment in which we presented each animal with a whole dormant red oak acorn and a one-year-old, nondormant red oak acorn without any external signs of germination. Again they stored the dormant acorn and ate the nondormant seed. Gray squirrels can detect whether acorns are dormant, and they respond by consistently caching the dormant seeds. At this point we don't know exactly how they do it, although it seems likely they may be able to detect a plant hormone or one or more by-products of a hormone released during germination. Ahh—a good experiment for the future.

## LONG-TERM AND SHORT-TERM INVESTMENTS: SEASONAL VARIATION IN CACHING AND FEEDING BEHAVIOR

The gray squirrel's keen sensitivity to seed perishability, while an interesting dimension of its caching behavior, points to an even broader perspective on the animal's biology and ecology. It suggests that in addition to making a number of immediate decisions about foraging and caching, gray squirrels are also balancing a variety of long-term constraints in order to ensure the greatest return from their food resources. The idea suggested to us that a complete understanding of the gray squirrel's foraging behavior meant that it had to be analyzed over a longer time period than that typical of most foraging studies.

This interest in long-term patterns of foraging and caching behavior was brought into focus when we began to notice significantly different feeding rates in autumn and winter. Typically we assessed feeding rate by first recording the time to eat part or all of the food item and then dividing this measure by the amount (mass) eaten. The amount eaten was calculated by simply subtracting the remaining weight of the food item from its original weight. In early autumn, feeding times averaged less than a minute, but by early winter these times doubled or tripled. An initial look at these data suggested that the gray squirrels were feeding far less efficiently in winter.

To make some sense of this shift in feeding strategy we decided to monitor the investment of energy in feeding and caching through an entire season. Periodically through the autumn of 1993 we presented approximately 20 individual squirrels per day with a single acorn and recorded whether each seed was cached or eaten, the time to cache or eat each seed, and the distance each seed was carried before it was cached. The results revealed several important changes in the animals' behavior through the course of the autumn as food availability and temperatures declined. As the season progressed, the probability of caching dropped and the time invested in eating or caching each food item increased. Later in the season seeds were carried farther before they were cached. Were the squirrels less efficient in winter? Such a result made little sense given the importance of feeding efficiency for winter survival. Perhaps our measures of efficiency were somehow inaccurate; but why did these estimates change through the season? After considerable deliberation, we decided the answer must lie with the squirrels and not in our calculations. At great risk of being labeled completely insane by the good citizens of Wilkes-Barre and even some of our colleagues, we returned to the park with a portable, handheld vacuum to collect all the small pieces of acorns dropped by the squirrels after they fed. The final results of this experiment are not yet in, but the initial findings make good sense. Early in the autumn the animals feed rapidly (and sloppily), dropping sizable fragments of cotyledon that we failed to account for in our initial measures of feeding efficiency. In winter they take their time, dropping very few small pieces or no pieces at all.

Our revised measures of feeding efficiency were now nearly similar for fall and winter. In autumn, it appears as though the squirrels minimize the time spent eating, perhaps so they can cache more of the food that is so abundant at this time. But in winter, when temperatures are low and the energetic costs of thermoregulation are high, they maximize their return by investing more energy in the eating and storing of each food item.

## PREVENTING CACHE ROBBERY

As we discuss in the beginning of this chapter, scatterhoarding allows animals to store food in a manner that reduces the impact of cache robbery by potential competitors. The primary advantage it confers is to reduce the high cost of defending stored food—an energetically expensive activity for any larder-hoarding animal and one that has virtually shaped the biology of the pine squirrels (C. Smith 1968, 1970; Steele 1998). However, is it reasonable to assume that the scatter-hoarding animals never invest energy in protecting their caches? Perhaps not. While little is really known about the fate of acorns cached by tree squirrels, pilfering does occur, sometimes frequently (Vander Wall 1990). The food caches of gray squirrels, for example, are frequently stolen by chipmunks, blue jays, and other gray squirrels, often immediately after the seed is cached. Are gray squirrels able to do anything to prevent such robbery, or is it a simple constraint with which they must live due to their lot as scatterhoarders?

Early in our studies of the caching behavior of gray squirrels at Wilkes University, we observed a particularly puzzling behavior that suggested a possible answer to this question. Our research students returned from the field a bit frustrated by their failure to recover cached food items. They reported that squirrels frequently excavated several holes before caching an acorn, sometimes covered empty caches with their front paws, and on rare occasions excavated and covered empty caches even after the acorn was buried. This behavior—eventually dubbed "deceptive caching" because we speculate that it reduces the probability of cache robbery—haunted us for several years, until the autumn of 1995 when a team of four students decided to tackle the question. Later we were joined by another team of researchers from Connecticut State University under the direction of Sylvia Halkins who were pursuing the same question.

We began by compiling three years of previous data in which we had made detailed notes on the behavior during other experiments. We then conducted more than 20 feeding trials focused only on this behavior. Although only descriptive, our initial results demonstrated the following. First, the gray squirrels excavated between two and nine cache sites in 30 to 40 percent of the occasions in which they cached an acorn. Second, they covered on the average 15 percent of these empty caches across all trials, and sometimes as many as 50 to 60 percent of the empty caches within a trial. And on a few occasions, they excavated and covered empty cache sites even after the acorn was stored.

Although the behavior was performed less frequently than we originally thought, it was clear that it was performed with some regularity; the behavior also was performed more often later in the autumn when availability of food was declining and more frequently in some years than others. We argued that the act of covering empty cache sites costs precious time and energy and must therefore serve some important function. The most obvious explanation was that the behavior distracts potential cache marauders by drawing their attention to an empty cache, while the squirrel moves on to bury the acorn undetected (Steele et al., unpublished data).

If this were the case, we predicted that the deceptive caching behavior should be performed more often when neighboring squirrels are nearby. In tests of this hypothesis, however, neither the number of squirrels within 22 yards (20 m) nor the distance to the nearest squirrel was strongly related to the occurrence of the behavior. Clearly we needed a more direct test of the ability of cache robbers to recover cached seeds. But observations of cache theft were relatively infrequent, possibly owing to our presence; so we accomplished this instead by using naive, human subjects as surrogate cache robbers. Volunteer college students, unaware of the questions we were addressing, were escorted to our field sites and charged with recovering acorns immediately after they were cached by the squirrels. To ensure that they had no previous experience, a new volunteer was used for each daily trial. Researchers watched and recorded the time it took to recover each cached acorn. Later we statistically compared the time required for the students to recover acorns when only one hole was excavated with the time for recovery when more than one hole was excavated. As predicted, significantly fewer acorns were recovered and it took significantly longer for recovery when at least two holes were excavated prior to caching.

Although further study on this behavior is still under way, the results above certainly suggest that interactions with potential competitors may influence how and where gray squirrels cache their food. Nevertheless, far more experimental work is required to fully demonstrate the tantalizing possibility that gray squirrels regularly engage in an act of deception in order to prevent cache losses. We predict that future efforts to decipher the full nature of this behavior will uncover exciting new insights into the complexity of the social behavior of these animals and its effect on strategies of food storing.

## CACHE RECOVERY AND CACHE MANAGEMENT

Once a squirrel has successfully stored an item in the cache, it is then faced with the obvious problem of returning to the cache and recovering the item. Unfortunately, at present, little is known about how this is done. A few years ago, if asked how tree squirrels recover food from their caches, a reasonable best answer and one that is still frequently given (although probably incorrect) is that they rely on memory to return to the general location of their caches and then use olfaction to locate specific items. Indeed, they use memory, perhaps more so than we ever thought possible. Recent pioneering work by Lucy Jacobs and her colleagues at the University of California is beginning to reveal that scatterhoarders such as gray squirrels may have the spatial ability to learn the specific location of stored food (Lavenex, Shiflett, et al. 1998). Although it is still unclear from studies on the gray squirrel brain how tree squirrels process so much spatial information (Lavenex, Steele, and Jacobs 2000a, 2000b), they do appear in this regard to be the mammalian equivalents of the jays and nutcrackers.

If we consider that for a larder-hoarding animal such as a pine squirrel, the ability to defend a central food hoard has virtually shaped its entire biology, it then follows that for a scatter-hoarding animal such as a gray squirrel, its biology should also be influenced by the habit of scatterhoarding. But unlike the territorial system of the pine or Douglas' squirrels, scatterhoarding is not so easily studied, which may explain in part why we still know so little and assume so much about their ability to locate, recover, and manage caches. We suggest that scatterhoarders such as gray squirrels do not simply stick their nuts in the ground and forget about them. Instead, they engage in a range of complex behaviors, moving and managing caches, much the way a financier will manipulate investments to maximize long-term returns. The tree squirrels, we may someday learn, are nature's ultimate bankers.

# 7

# Of Seeds and Squirrels

*Clearly, the gray squirrel was spending only a*
*few seconds on each acorn. The animal removed*
*the cap with its lower incisors, then proceeded*
*to chip away at the outer shell and the nutritious*
*kernel inside. But after a few seconds, the acorn*
*was discarded and the behavior repeated. This*
*continued a dozen times or more before the*
*shadow of a passing red-tailed hawk forced the*
*animal to seek thicker cover, and we were free to*
*move in for a closer look. When we did, our sus-*
*picions were confirmed. The ground was cov-*
*ered with thousands of half-eaten acorns; and*
*not one was eaten from anywhere but the top of*
*the seed.*

Why would any animal—especially one recognized for its ability to feed
so efficiently—waste time and energy, and risk predation, only to leave a
large part of each acorn uneaten? This simple question led to one of a se-

ries of experimental studies that are now beginning to unravel the complex interactions between tree squirrels and some of the plants on which they feed. The ecological and evolutionary interactions between squirrels and plants are complex. Indeed, Henry David Thoreau (1993) recognized the close interdependence of squirrels and plants more than a hundred years ago when he wrote: "Consider what a vast work these forest planters are doing! So far as our noblest hardwood forests are concerned, the animals, especially the squirrels and jays, are our greatest and almost only benefactors" (130).

Today, some of these interactions are obvious and well understood; others are not. Many, we are confident, remain to be discovered. Increasingly, though, a number of studies have begun to reveal an intricate web of interactions that are strongly suggestive of a coevolutionary relationship, one in which each player strongly influences the other. In this chapter, we review the evidence from both the literature and our own studies for this, sometimes subtle, ecological and evolutionary dance between tree squirrels and plants. We focus much of our discussion on two critical interactions: seed predation and seed dispersal. At the close of the chapter, we also briefly consider the importance of herbivory on ponderosa pine by Abert's squirrels.

## SEED PREDATION AND SEED DEFENSES

It is perhaps stating the obvious to say that when squirrels eat tree seeds they exert a strong selective pressure on the plant. Seeds of course are the plant's reproductive investment and the means by which its genes are passed on to the next generation. Consequently it follows that the activity of squirrels selects for specific seed traits that help protect or ensure their eventual germination. Squirrels on the other hand, adopt counterstrategies—through learning, evolution, or a combination of the two—that allow them to sometimes thwart these defenses (Gurnell 1987; Vander Wall 1990). Here we consider the characteristics of the seeds and those of the squirrels that are central to this interaction.

The plants exhibit a number of adaptations to prevent losses to seed predators such as tree squirrels. Whereas some may have evolved specifically in response to tree squirrels, others may have evolved to protect against entire assemblages of seed consumers. Still others may have evolved for entirely different reasons but function secondarily as protection against squirrels. Regardless of their origin, three general types of

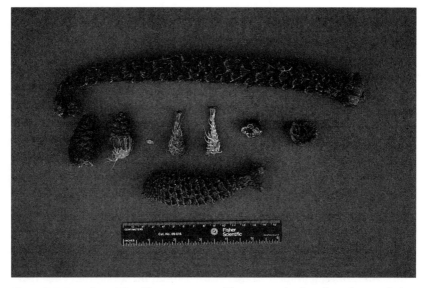

Figure 7.1. Remains of food items consumed by tree squirrels; rule at bottom is for size comparisons. Shown are *(top)* a cone core of a sugar pinecone eaten by a pine squirrel and *(bottom)* a cone core of a longleaf pinecone eaten by a fox squirrel. In the middle *(left to right):* a whole cone of red pine, a partially eaten (sampled) cone of red pine, a single red pine seed, two cone cores of red pine, a partially eaten shagbark hickory nut, and the remains of a mockernut hickory nut. These items were eaten by an eastern gray squirrel. Note the relative size of the pine seed to the cone from which it was extracted. (Photograph courtesy of M. A. Steele)

seed characteristics reduce predation by tree squirrels. We refer to these as physical, chemical, and numerical protection.

Many plants exhibit protective devices around their seeds that reduce the probability of consumption by tree squirrels (Figure 7.1). Obvious examples include the woody covering of some hickories and walnuts in which <20 percent of the nut's energy is devoted to the digestible kernel (Smith and Follmer 1972). Similar protection is common in conifers in which the small but nutritious seeds account for only a small portion of each cone. The remainder of the structure—as high as 99 percent by mass—is comprised of woody, sticky bracts that cover and protect the seeds (Elliot 1974; Steele and Weigl 1992). Such devices are not always successful against squirrels, but some are. The southern flying squirrel, for example, is able to open the heavy covering of walnuts, but the energetic costs for doing so exceed the energy acquired from the kernel; consequently, they avoid walnuts (Weigl, pers. com.). Many conifer cones are also arranged in clusters around tree branches in a manner that makes them difficult to harvest (Elliot 1974).

Chemical protection against seed predators and other herbivores comes in many forms (Abrahamson 1989). For tree squirrels a few compounds seem most critical. As we discuss later in this chapter, tannins are particularly important for protection of many squirrel foods, especially the acorns (Smith and Follmer 1972; Steele, Knowles, et al. 1993). Other compounds, such as lipids, carbohydrates, and proteins, vary considerably between various food items and are likely to affect food choices; yet, to date, the details of their influence are not well known (see Chapter 6). Conifers also often produce terpenes, which may deter squirrels from feeding on cones of a particular tree or tree species (Steele 1988).

Last, we consider numerical protection, that is, the abundance of seeds. The number of seeds produced by a tree, relative to other trees around it and to the number of seed predators, may greatly affect the probability of seed predation. Many seed trees, including the oaks, hickories, and beech that are so favored by tree squirrels of the temperate forests, often undergo tremendous yearly variation in seed crops. This phenomenon—known as masting—involves the periodic and episodic production of seeds in some years, followed by low or nonexistent crops in others (Lalonde and Roitberg 1992). Sometimes synchronized over large geographic areas, these boom-or-bust cycles can greatly affect the dynamics of forest communities (Ostfeld, Jones, and Wolff 1996; Wolff 1996; Jones, Ostfeld, and Wolff 1998). Although the mechanisms controlling these cycles are not yet understood (Sork, Bramble, and Sexton 1993), one potential explanation—the predator satiation hypothesis—holds that they evolved to satiate seed consumers in good mast years and cull their populations in poor years. And indeed it appears they may have this effect. Populations of tree squirrels and other small mammals frequently fluctuate wildly in response to these cycles in seed production (Steele and Smallwood in press).

## TREE SQUIRRELS AS SEED CONSUMERS

The ability of squirrels to thwart many of the protective traits of seeds and nuts supports the argument that tree squirrels have evolved to deal with many of these characteristics. Tree squirrels, of course, possess a number of general characteristics that predispose them to a granivorous lifestyle (see Chapter 1). But in some cases the evolutionary responses of squirrels to various plant defenses may be more specific and strongly suggestive of a close evolutionary relationship between squirrel and tree. Smith's 1970 study on red (pine) and Douglas' squirrels in the Cascade Range of southwestern British Columbia offers a good example of this. West of the Cascade Range, the wet maritime climate results in moist forests with few lodgepole pines, and forest fires are rare. Here the pines produce soft, symmetrical cones, with many seeds per cone. These cones mature in a single season and are shed to germinate at the end of the growing season. However, east of the range the forests are quite different. In the rain shadow of the Cascades, the dry continental climate produces dry forests of lodgepole pine where lightning strikes and low-temperature fires are common. On this side of the range, the common fire-adapted pines produce hard serotinous cones that remain closed sometimes for many years until the advent of fire stimulates them to open and release their seeds. These cones exhibit a hard cone surface, strong woody attachment to the branch, asymmetrical shape, and many fewer seeds per cone. The pine squirrels in these dry forests east of the range are well equipped to handle these hard serotinous cones. They are larger in size and equipped with strong jaw muscles and a more robust lower jaw that enables them to pry off the bracts of these hard cones. In contrast, the closely related Douglas' squirrels that reside to the west of the range are smaller in size and possess weaker jaw muscles and a weaker lower jaw (C. Smith 1968, 1998).

In addition to morphological characteristics, tree squirrels exhibit considerable behavioral flexibility in dealing with various seed and plant defenses. As described in Chapter 5, fox squirrels are quite efficient when feeding on cones of the longleaf pine despite the high costs of opening the cones (Weigl, Steele, et al. 1989). They sample cones from individual trees and then feed selectively in those trees that provide the greatest energy reward. Similar patterns of tree selection have been reported for the European red squirrel when feeding in a Scots pine forest in Scotland (Mollar 1986) and pine squirrels feeding on cones in North America (C. C. Smith 1968; Elliot 1988). Whereas such responses illustrate the squirrels' ability to circumvent some of these cone defenses, they also suggest that the tree squirrels may exert strong selective pressures on individual trees. Fox squirrels, for example, quite often consume the greatest number of cones and seeds in those trees that have invested the greatest amount in reproduction. As a result, where fox squirrels reside, those trees sporting only moderate cone crops early in the season often have the greatest number of cones surviving to maturation (see Chapter 5). Among pine squirrels, cone selection can also occur within a tree on the basis of cone characteristics such as number of seeds per cone, cone hardness, and the arrangement of cones on the branches (Elliot 1974).

Perhaps one of the most interesting behavioral adaptations for dealing with seed predation is the act of embryo excision of white oaks by some tree squirrels (see Chapter 6). Although the rapid germination of white oak acorns is likely to be a diffuse evolutionary response to escape a diverse assemblage of mammalian and avian seed predators, the squirrel's behavior of embryo excision of white oaks appears to be far more specific. To date, this behavior has been documented only for tree squirrels (Steele, Turner, et al. 2001), despite numerous studies and observations on other seed predators of white oak. This suggests that the behavior evolved only in tree squirrels. And although refined with learning, the behavior is present at an early age and is therefore likely to be partly genetically predetermined. However, studies of pine squirrels suggest that young squirrels may learn feeding techniques by observing the mother (Weigl and Hanson 1980). Clearly, some tantalizing questions remain about the genetic and evolutionary basis of embryo excision.

## TREE SQUIRRELS AS SEED DISPERSERS

Just as squirrels can exert a strong negative impact on plants by consuming large numbers of seeds, they can also serve to disperse seeds and facilitate their establishment and survival. In some situations they are essential to this process. Dispersal, or movement of young away from the place of birth, is an important stage in the life cycle of many organisms. Plants are no exception. For many plant species, the advantages of dispersal include a decreased chance of inbreeding, a reduction in competition with sibling and parent plants, and an opportunity to establish in sites more suitable for germination or growth. But because they are sessile, that is, not free to move about, most plants rely on the movement of a specific life stage, such as a seed, by some agent of dispersal (Pijl 1972).

Many avian and mammalian species of seed consumers—tree squirrels included—are critical for the dispersal of some plant species. This is especially true when the seed consumer caches the seeds in the ground and then fails to recover some of these stored reserves (Vander Wall 1990). By transporting and scatterhoarding acorns, hickory nuts, or walnuts to individual sites just below the leaf litter, many tree squirrels reduce the probability of seed predation, seed dessication, and seedling competition, and at the same time increase the chances of germination, root establishment, and winter survival (Steele and Smallwood in press). The cache sites of at least one species—the eastern gray squirrel—may even be optimal for germination, survival, and growth of oak seedlings (Smith and Reichman 1984; M. Price and Jenkins 1986).

Why select cache sites that are suitable for germination? Certainly it is not the squirrels' intention to actually plant the seeds. The squirrels' motives are purely selfish. Their objective, when scatterhoarding, is to place the food out of reach of competitors, in a microenvironment that prevents rotting or drying. By coincidence, these conditions are often quite similar to those required for germination. On those occasions in which the squirrels fail to recover the seed, a new seedling becomes established (Vander Wall 1990).

But just how often is the squirrel likely to overlook its food stores? How effective are squirrels at retrieving their caches? Although answers to these questions are still elusive, a few generalizations are possible. There is now strong evidence that squirrels may remember the specific location of caches using spatial information. They are, by most estimates, quite efficient at cache recovery, sometimes revisiting and managing their caches. In some situations they are thought to recover >95 percent of their stores (Steele and Smallwood in press). Under many other conditions, however, a great number of seeds are likely to become established from these caches. This is especially likely when seeds are abundant and the need for stored reserves is relaxed or when the squirrel dies or disperses from its caching area.

There is growing evidence, that this process is far more involved than the above description indicates. A closer look at the complex interactions between oaks and squirrels serves to illustrate this point. We return first to our observations at the beginning of this chapter of partial acorn consumption and an involved series of experiments that followed from our first sighting of the behavior.

## THE MYSTERY OF THE HALF-EATEN ACORNS

Early in winter of 1986, Michael Steele, along with fellow graduate student Travis Knowles, had just arrived at our Block O study area to begin the last of the winter nest box surveys. We decided to use the remaining hour of daylight to conduct a preliminary assessment of food abundance. We first checked the open, upland stands of longleaf pine; the mature cones in the treetops had opened and were barely distinguishable from the brown, faded cones of the previous year. Our earlier assessment of cone abundance from the summer survey was confirmed: the crop of longleaf

Figure 7.2. Acorns of willow oak following partial consumption by gray squirrels. Note that most of the acorns have more than 50 percent of their cotyledon remaining and that all were eaten from the top (basal) portion of the fruit. (Photograph courtesy of M. A. Steele)

cones was among the highest we had seen in two years. We made several quick counts, recorded the numbers on our data sheet, and headed down the hill toward the ecotone between the open, pine-oak forest and the dense pocosin in the ravine below.

As we neared the swamp, we entered a thick homogeneous grove of turkey oaks. There, we were immediately struck by the prodigious crop of acorns. Each of the approximately 13-foot-high (4-m) trees was packed with hundreds of the propagules. But as quickly as our attention was drawn to the acorns in the tree, it became focused on the equally dense blanket of acorns in the leaf litter. Turkey oaks, like many other scrub oaks in the Atlantic coastal plain, retain their acorns for months after maturation. Thus we thought it odd to find so many acorns on the ground. Closer inspection revealed how they got there. Each of the thousands of acorns was partially eaten, not in any haphazard way but neatly and consistently from the top or basal portion of the acorn—the end usually covered by the cap on the tree (Figure 7.2). Our initial suspicion that the incisor marks in the cotyledon were the work of gray squirrels was later confirmed by matching the marks with the incisors of museum specimens.

We were immediately struck by two questions that dominated our conversation for the remainder of the evening as we continued our nest box survey on into the night. The first of these followed from the rich literature on foraging behavior: why would any squirrel, or any animal for that matter, invest the energy to eat a small portion of a single food item, only to pick up another and repeat the process? It was clear from this literature that animals are amazingly efficient in their foraging abilities, and if an animal is discarding large quantities of food, there should be a good reason for it. We learned later that there were possibly several reasons for the behavior.

Our knowledge of acorn anatomy, although limited, was enough to pique our interest on the second question: could some of these acorns survive predation if eaten only from the basal portion of the seed? The acorn, technically considered a fruit, is comprised mostly of cotyledon that contains high levels of energy-rich lipid. This is the primary reason that acorns are prized foods for so many mammals and birds, including jays, woodpeckers, grackles, wild turkey, deer mice, white-footed mice, eastern chipmunks, white-tailed deer, black bears, and more than 140 other species of vertebrates in North America (Van Dersal 1940).

For the acorn, the cotyledon is essential for germination; it represents the young seed leaves of the germinating seed and contains the energy that allows the seedling to develop until it is able to sustain itself by means of photosynthesis. The embryo of the seed, located in the extreme distal end (or apex) of the acorn—the portion of the seed frequently not eaten—is extremely small and accounts for just a small portion of the dry biomass of the entire seed (Keator 1998). Perhaps then, partially eaten acorns could still germinate?

Before we were able to fully answer this question, our observations of partial consumption of acorns grew to include several other species of acorn consumers and several other species of oaks across a wide geographic area. In the autumn of 1986, while trying to complete work on several unrelated projects, we were distracted by a heavy crop of acorns produced by the 50 or so 70-year-old giant willow oaks on the campus of Wake Forest University in Winston-Salem, North Carolina. Each morning for several weeks that autumn, half-eaten acorns would literally rain from the trees, covering the ground beneath their canopies. The animals responsible for the early seed rain—eastern gray squirrels, blue jays, and common grackles—would converge on single trees in numbers as great as 50 animals, each eating only the top half of acorns.

That autumn we put much of our other research aside and spent several hours each day collecting partially eaten seeds, quantifying the rate at which seeds were eaten, and making detailed observations on the behavior of each of these three acorn consumers. Each of the three species used a different technique for opening the seeds, but all consumed cotyledon from only the top 30 to 50 percent of the acorn. Jays held the acorn against a branch with a foot while they stabbed the top of the seed with their bills. Grackles held the acorn in their bills and scored the middle of the seed, popped off the top half, and extracted the cotyledon with a quick flick of the tongue. Gray squirrels always spent several seconds rolling the acorn to position it so the basal end was upright; they then chipped away at the pericarp (shell) before consuming the cotyledon from the same portion of the seed.

During that same season we observed partial consumption of acorns by gray squirrels in several other species of oaks in the Piedmont and coastal plain of North Carolina. The total count now included six species: turkey oaks, willow oaks, northern red oaks, pin oaks, water oaks, and scarlet oaks, all belonging to the red oak subgenus of oaks. As we began to share our observations with colleagues around the country, many reported seeing the same behavior performed on acorns from Alabama, California, and Ohio, and one reported similar responses by white-footed mice in Pennsylvania.

Before continuing, it was necessary to turn to the literature in order to determine just how interesting or relevant these observations might be. We knew from a number of studies that many seed-eating mammals and birds can exert strong negative ecological and evolutionary effects on seed plants by consuming large numbers of their propagules (Abbott and Quink 1970; Elliot 1974). The response of squirrels to many of these traits of seeds and fruits supports the argument that squirrels have evolved specifically to deal with many of these characteristics. Tree squirrels in particular were reported to destroy thousands of acorns or conifer cones in the few short weeks of their maturation. Tree squirrels were also known for dispersing seeds, but it was assumed in the literature that successful dispersal and survival of these seeds only occurred when food-hoarding animals accidentally dropped seeds or failed to recover them from their caches (Howe and Westley 1988). After scouring several decades of published papers on seed dispersal and seed predation, we found only a few reports in which partial consumption of seeds actually resulted in seed survival (Vander Wall 1990). One such example, well known among most ecologists, involves the energy-rich elaisomes of ant-dispersed seeds. These tasty morsels attached to the seeds of many herbaceous species focus the ant's attention away from the important part of the seed, thereby allowing the seed to survive even after the ant has had its meal (Howe and Westley 1988).

The quick review of the literature gave us the direction we needed. We both agreed that the consistent and frequent behavior of partial consumption of acorns in itself was interesting. But we also knew that its significance depended largely on whether some of these partially eaten seeds could survive. The first step was to obtain acorns that were no longer dormant and test them for both metabolic activity and germination. Unlike the acorns of various white oak species, which usually germinate immediately in the autumn, those of the red oak group exhibit delayed germination and must first receive a stimulus (usually an extended period of cold) before they can germinate. So we stored partially eaten and whole acorns of turkey and willow oaks at 39°F (4°C) and returned to our other studies for six weeks.

At the end of this stratification period, as it is referred to by botanists and seed specialists, we tested a small sample for signs of metabolic activity and planted approximately 200 of the seeds in a greenhouse. The others we placed in plastic and stored in a dark cabinet. The metabolic test, a simple, standardized procedure for determining the viability of seeds, involves cutting a few seeds and placing and them in a small dish with tetrazolium stain. The formation of a pink and reddish color in the cotyledon and embryo of the half-eaten acorns told us immediately that our acorns were still alive and metabolically active, a good indication that they might still germinate. Our greenhouse experiments were not as successful as we hoped. A zealous greenhouse technician overwatered the seeds and caused most of them to rot and die. However, a few of both the whole and partially eaten seeds did germinate and produce young seedlings—at least enough to tell us that these partially eaten seeds are able to survive.

When we uncovered the stored seeds—both whole and partially eaten acorns from three willow oak trees—we discovered relatively high rates of germination of both. But when we looked closer, we found something we never expected. For two of the three trees, germination frequencies were significantly higher for partially eaten acorns than for the whole intact seeds. It was tempting to consider the possibility that partial consumption of the acorns actually facilitated germination, but we were fully satisfied that damaged seeds could at least survive. It meant, of course, that oaks might have evolved a particular characteristic that increases the chances that some of their seeds survive even after they sustain damage by seed predators. The next step was to identify the factors that caused squirrels and other seed consumers to eat only the top half.

## FACTORS CONTRIBUTING TO PARTIAL ACORN CONSUMPTION

Ideally, in a scientific study all potential hypotheses for a particular phenomenon are tested. When one produces evidence that supports one hypothesis and refutes the others, it is possible to make a strong case for the true explanation for the phenomenon. Such was our original goal in the pursuit of an explanation for partial acorn consumption. But as we soon learned this was not going to be an easy task.

The potential hypotheses for the observation were as numerous as the colleagues willing to offer them. One suggested it was the pericarp (the shell of the acorn), another the shape, while many argued that it had something to do with the chemistry inside the acorn. Initially it was the tannin hypothesis that caught our attention. Tannins are secondary plant products—a group of nasty-tasting, phenolic compounds—that are primarily important in the defense against the animals that eat plants (Robbins et al. 1987; Koenig 1991; Johnson, Thomas, and Adkisson 1993). It is still not fully known if tannins evolved as defensive agents against herbivores, but one thing is for sure, they certainly have this effect (Chung-MacCoubrey, Hagerman, and Kirkpatrick 1997). It has been shown, for example, that higher tannin levels result in reduced feeding, growth, and/or reproduction by many herbivores and that tannin levels often increase in plants in response to feeding by herbivores (Howe and Westley 1988). Tannins are also common in oaks and acorns, especially those of the red oak subgroup. So it seemed that the tannin hypothesis was a good starting point.

To address the tannin hypothesis, we enlisted a friend and colleague, plant physiologist Kenneth Bridle, who adopted a rather simple technique for quantifying the tannin levels in the top and bottom of the acorns. The technique, used by several investigators before us, relied on the natural tendency of the tannin compounds to bind to protein. This ability to complex with salivary and digestive enzymes (proteins) is how tannins elicit an astringent or bitter sensation in the mouth and interfere with digestion in the intestines of animals. The technique involves the use of a known quantity of protein (hemoglobin from blood) to gauge the amount of tannin in a sample. The color change that results from the hemoglobin binding to the protein is directly proportional to the amount of tannin in the sample—and readily quantified with a laboratory instrument known as a spectrophotometer.

Samples of acorns were collected from several trees of two species of oaks. Acorns were then cut in half to produce a top and bottom sample for each. After shelling the acorn halves, the remaining acorn cotyledon was dried in a laboratory oven and ground to a fine powder. A small sample of this powder was then tested for tannin concentration. In all, samples from 28 willow oak and 20 turkey oak trees were tested. In each sample, the tannin concentrations were highest in the bottom half where the embryo is located. The hypothesis was supported. Tannins were lowest in that portion of the seed eaten by the animals.

These initial results were compelling, but we had not come close to demonstrating a causal relationship between tannin levels and acorn preferences, nor had we ruled out any of the possible alternative explanations for the behavior. Beginning in 1991 two students at Wilkes University, Wendy Bachman and Kimberly Gavel, accepted this challenge. In a series of clever field experiments, they answered several important questions and at the same time raised several others that we had not yet considered.

Bachman began by presenting free-ranging gray squirrels with acorns of both pin oak and red oak. Early in the season, she found that the squirrels consistently ate a small portion of the acorns from just the top half of the seed, even when the pericarp (shell) was removed. Thus, contrary to the suggestion of one colleague that the pericarp is easier to open at the top, Bachman was able to show that this was not at all a factor influencing partial acorn consumption. She also found that the proportion of each acorn consumed increased through the season, and by late November the animals ate 100 percent of each seed. She also presented the animals with the top and bottom halves of acorns of both species, but found that the animals ate equal portions of both halves. This contradicted our tannin hypothesis, which predicted that more of the top of the seed should have been eaten. The observation was enough to convince Bachman that the animals were not responding to tannins directly. Instead, she suggested an alternative explanation. During her experiments, she frequently remarked the animals' rolling behavior and the considerable time they spent positioning the acorn upright before they began to feed. She attributed the response to the shape of the acorn.

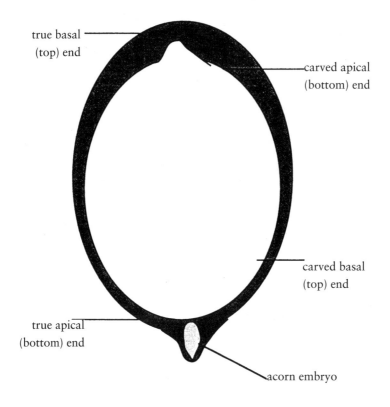

true basal (top) end

carved apical (bottom) end

carved basal (top) end

true apical (bottom) end

acorn embryo

**Figure 7.3. Diagram of whole, shelled acorn *(gray section)* and carved acorn *(white section)* indicating how acorn shape was modified to test its effect on gray squirrels. In this example, the basal end of the original acorn was carved so it appeared as the apical, or distal, end. The entire seed surface was scraped to control for any chemical changes that might occur when the exposed tissue oxidized. (Diagram drawn by M. Steele)**

Kimberley Gavel began the 1992 field season with a test of Bachman's hypothesis. In a carefully prepared experiment, she presented animals with whole unshelled acorns, whole shelled acorns, and shelled acorns in which the cotyledon of the acorn was meticulously carved so that the top appeared as the bottom and the bottom as the top. In effect, she reversed the shape of the acorn (Figure 7.3). The entire surface of the carved acorns was also scraped so that any changes in chemistry resulting from cutting the cotyledon was equally distributed across the surface of the seed. As before, gray squirrels consistently consumed only a small portion of both the whole and shelled acorns, and again always from the top. But when

Gavel presented the animals with the carved seeds, they frequently flipped the acorn and ate from the true bottom end, the portion now carved to appear as the top. She tricked the animals into consuming the bottom half of the acorn by changing only the shape of the acorn.

Did this mean that the shape rather than the tannin gradient explained the behavior? Gavel didn't think so. Although she was unable to quantify the amount eaten, she felt strongly that the animals ate much less of the bottom halves even though she was able to convince them that it was the top half of the acorn. We decided another experiment was needed. In late March and early April she returned to our study area to present the animals with nine types of acorns. These included whole acorns, as well as the bottom half of acorns of both red oak and pin oaks. In addition, following the lead of our colleague Peter Smallwood, Gavel made artificial acorns by grinding up acorn cotyledon and adding varying amounts of tannin. She included in her experiments acorn dough balls to which 0 percent, 2 percent, and 6 percent tannic acid had been added. She then presented each of the nine food items to approximately 15 to 20 squirrels.

Her initial results were disheartening, although not surprising. It was spring; there was little else to eat; and the animals consumed everything. But Gavel was quick to spot an opportunity. The previous autumn she had deduced that, in addition to other acorn characteristics, food availability might also influence the squirrels' behavior. Each week, during the month of September, she collected all the whole acorns and acorn fragments that had fallen under several pin oak and red oak trees. For each weekly interval, she weighed a sample of approximately 30 partially eaten acorns from each tree and determined the proportion of each seed eaten. She also determined the approximate number of acorns in the tree during each weekly interval by working backward from the acorns and acorn fragments she collected. Her observation: a strong negative correlation between the number of acorns in the tree and the amount of each seed eaten. It was clear that the availability of acorns had something to do with the squirrels' behavior.

Gavel decided she should repeat the feeding experiment, but only after she simulated conditions of high food abundance. To do this, she bought several large bags of sunflower seeds and combined them with what remained of our acorn collections from the previous autumn. Each day, for two weeks after the first feeding trial, we placed a pile of food at the base of each tree in the study area. Gavel then repeated her previous experiments as she continued to supplement the animals' food supply. The results were dramatic. The animals consumed much less of each of the food items presented, with the exception of those artificial acorns with little or no tannin added. The animals also spent less time feeding on the bottom halves of both species of acorns than they did the tops.

What did Bachman's and Gavel's work show? To our surprise it was not any one characteristic that induced the behavior, but probably a suite of traits and conditions. At least for gray squirrels, seed geometry, tannin levels, acorn abundance, and perhaps several other factors apparently interacted to cause partial acorn consumption. The only factor we could dismiss as a causal agent of the behavior was the shell of the acorn. But while these initial conclusions were tantalizing, we knew we couldn't stop there.

In the autumn of 1994 we sought to take a closer look at the relationship between acorn chemistry, partial acorn consumption, and acorn survival. We first collected large samples of acorns from 20 trees from each of three oak species: the white oak, the red oak, and the pin oak. We then divided our samples for each tree into two subsamples. One of these samples was processed for additional chemical analyses. The other was set aside for germination experiments, this time outside, under more natural field conditions. Our goal was to examine the concentration of various chemical compounds in acorns from each tree and then compare these levels with the germination success and seedling survival of both whole and half-cut acorns from the same tree.

The acorns collected for chemical analyses were shelled, cut in half, freeze-dried, and sent to the laboratory of Ted Stiles of Rutgers University. There, he and his technicians tested the tops and bottoms for protein, carbohydrates, and lipids (fats), while we kept a sample to determine tannin concentrations. Later that autumn, for each of the 60 trees, we planted 50 whole acorns and the bottom half of 50 acorns cut to simulate partial consumption. More than 5,000 acorns were arranged randomly, buried in a few centimeters of soil, then covered with leaf litter to simulate cache conditions. The plot was then fenced and covered with netting to prevent theft by any animals.

We returned in the spring, after most of the oak seedlings had emerged from the soil, and we excavated a sample of the seeds to determine frequency of germination and seedling emergence. We also followed a subsample through the summer to measure seedling growth. When the chemical analyses were complete we were able to compare the two sets of data. To our dismay there was little connection between the acorn chemistry and survival of whole and cut seeds, or the growth of seedlings. We did observe that for most trees a small percentage of the half-cut acorns were able to germinate, establish, and continue to grow through an entire field season. Moreover, a particularly striking result emerged from the chemical comparisons of the tops and bottoms of acorns. Although we again observed higher tannin levels in the two red oak species, the trend was not significant. This time, however, lipid levels differed between the top and bottom. But unlike tannin levels, lipids were significantly higher in the top of the seeds, the part preferred by the animals. They were lowest in the half containing the embryo. This indicated that the top of the acorn was not only more palatable but also higher in energy— perhaps more utilizable energy, too, because of the lower tannin levels.

These data added a completely new dimension to our interpretation. The tannin gradient observed earlier in our study may have evolved for a number of reasons, such as a need to protect the embryo from fungi and bacteria. At best, we could conclude that the animal's behavior may have only represented a response to existing tannin gradients that evolved for another reason. But the evidence for a lipid gradient suggested a closer link. It argued that these chemical gradients may reflect adaptations specific to the animals that feed on the acorns. In fact, collectively our experiments and observations suggest that an entire suite of characteristics may have evolved to promote partial acorn consumption and subsequent survival of the seed. Perhaps we are beginning to actually determine at least one reason *why* acorns look and taste like acorns.

## TREE SQUIRRELS AND THE DISPERSAL OF OAKS

Much remains to be done to fully unravel the mystery of the half-eaten acorn. The experiments to date are strongly suggestive of a complex relationship between the oak and the squirrel, and this relationship extends well beyond the small acorn fragments that initially captured our interest in this subject. Shortly after we completed our first experiments on partial acorn consumption we launched our studies on caching by eastern gray squirrels (see Chapter 6). Slowly, between 1991 and the time of this publication, with the help of colleague Peter Smallwood, several other critical links between the squirrels and the oaks began to emerge.

To put these discoveries into proper context we first introduce the concept of the dispersal syndrome. As its name suggests, dispersal syndromes are suites of characteristics of seeds or fruits that increase the probability of dissemination and establishment by particular dispersal agents (Howe and Westley 1988). The characteristics that potentially promote partial consumption and survival of these damaged acorns comprise just one component of a much more extensive oak dispersal syndrome. Other components follow from the differences in the characteristics of the white oak and red oak acorns (see Chapter 4).

From the squirrels' perspective, the contrasting tannin and lipid levels of the acorns of the two oak groups certainly influence feeding decisions at different times of the year (Smallwood and Peters 1986). A third characteristic—the germination schedule and resulting perishability of the acorns—seems to have the greatest relevance to oak dispersal. Results of our caching studies show why. Gray squirrels readily distinguish, possibly by chemical cues in the shell, between the dormant species of red oaks and the rapidly germinating white oak acorns. They selectively disperse and cache the former and eat the latter. In those situations in which they cache white oak acorns, they usually first excise the embryo, killing the acorn before it is stored, sometimes for up to six months (Fox 1982; Steele, Turner, et al. 2001). Gray squirrels also selectively cache sound red oak acorns over those infested with insect larvae. Together, these responses, coupled with the behavior of partial acorn consumption as well as recent evidence that several other species of acorn consumers may exhibit similar responses, led us to one inevitable hypothesis, now dubbed the differential dispersal hypothesis (Steele and Smallwood in press).

Collectively our results suggest markedly different dispersal syndromes for the two oak groups. On the one hand, it seems that an entire constellation of acorn characteristics, including shape, shell, delayed germination, and chemistry, aid and even promote the dispersal of red oaks. On the other hand, white oaks possess characteristics that instead render them highly susceptible to seed predation. If we are correct that tree squirrels, and perhaps other acorn consumers, serve as important dispersal agents of red oak species and equally devastating predators of the white oaks, two important questions logically follow. How do these behavioral responses influence the spatial distribution of the oaks in the forest? And how are white oaks dispersed, if not by the animals that eat their seeds?

Although the second of these remains an enigma, we were afforded a preliminary answer to the first in a study that Michael Steele and two others coauthored with Peter Smallwood (Smallwood et al. 1998). Under Smallwood's able leadership it was predicted that if this characterization of red oak and white oak dispersal holds, then young red oak seedlings should be widely dispersed at greater distances from parent trees, whereas seedlings of white oak should be clumped, close to parental sources. To test this we needed a mature forest dominated by several species of oaks, where oak seedlings were common. Smallwood found such a site at the George Washington National Forest near the Smithsonian Research Station in Front Royal, Virginia. There, he and a group of volunteers organized by Smithsonian staff scientist William McShea carefully measured the distribution of four oak species along two forest transects. The oaks studied included two red oak species (the black oak and the northern red oak) and two white oak species (the white oak and chestnut oak). Smallwood and his small army of assistants first mapped all the seedlings of each species along each transect. At each of these sites they also identified and mapped the distribution of all adult oak trees (all trees more than 5.85 inches [15 cm] in diameter) occurring within 98.4 feet (30 m) of each side of the two transects.

Using a computer model developed by botanist Eric Ribbens (Ribbens, Silander, and Pacala 1994), Smallwood then calculated the best-fit distribution of seedlings around parent trees, a distribution known as the seedling shadow. The seedling shadow follows from the term "seed shadow," first introduced by ecologist Daniel Janzen (1971). A seed shadow describes the distribution of seeds around a parent tree after they fall from the tree. Janzen argued that the seed shadow of most trees will be characterized by a high density of seeds close to the tree and decreasing densities at greater distance from the tree. The seed shadow can also account for the distribution of the seeds after they are dispersed but before they germinate. In a similar way, the seedling shadow considers the distribution of young seedlings around the parent tree after seed dispersal, seed mortality, and seed germination. The computer model developed by Ribbens uses a rather involved statistical procedure to work backward from the distribution data of seedlings to calculate a best-fit seedling shadow for each species under consideration.

The result is primarily a theoretical one, but this analytical approach allowed an independent test of our differential dispersal hypothesis. The outcome was striking. As predicted, the two white oak species exhibited truncated seedling shadows, whereas those of the two red oaks were distributed three to six times farther, with many fewer of their seedlings expected to occur near the parent (Smallwood et al. 1998). Much can happen between the time of seed dispersal and seedling establishment, thus distorting the seedling shadow in a way that does not at all reflect patterns of seed dispersal. Nevertheless it is quite interesting that the seedling shadows observed are consistent with our predictions that red oaks should be widely dispersed and white oaks clumped near their parents. This of course is not the final word. The next step, which we are currently pursuing, is to determine the precise seed shadows by using DNA fingerprinting of seedlings and parent trees to establish true parent-offspring relationships. Ultimately our goal is to test the hypothesis of differential dispersal in several oak forests to determine if other scatterhoarders of acorns, in addition to the eastern gray squirrel, exert a similar influence on the structure of oak forests.

If we are correct about the differential dispersal of red and white oaks, several differences in seedlings and perhaps adult trees are likely to follow. Howe (1989) argued that scatter-hoarding birds and mammals are likely to contribute not only to the dispersal of seeds but also to a range of demographic and genetic traits as a result of the animals' influence on the spatial arrangement of plants. For the two oaks, several consequences are likely to follow the contrasting dispersal patterns. Indeed, preliminary evidence from the forestry literature points to higher establishment of red oak seedlings in more exposed sites away from parents, greater clumping of white oak seedlings, higher shade tolerance in white oaks, and the ability of red oak seedlings to withstand low soil moisture. Ultimately, the squirrels' decision of what to eat and what to cache may determine the structure, composition, and population biology of our oak forests.

## HERBIVORY AND TREE SQUIRRELS

Throughout this chapter we allude to the mounting evidence for the close evolutionary relationship between squirrels and the plants on which they depend for food and other resources. We now close with a few remarks on the nature of this relationship and the question of whether it fits with the concept of coevolution. Coevolution, first described for butterflies and plants by Ehrlich and Raven (1964) and further articulated by Janzen (1980) and many others, occurs when the trait of one species evolves in response to that of another species, which itself evolves simultaneously in response to the trait of the first. For tree squirrels and plants the evidence for the reciprocity and simultaneity of genetic changes needed to satisfy this rather restrictive definition of coevolution is clearly lacking. Nevertheless, we submit that there is a reasonable, if not compelling, argument that tree squirrels and plants exhibit characteristics that have specifically evolved in response to one another.

Although we have reviewed a number of such interactions, one that we have not yet considered may be most central to this discussion. It is the close ecological and evolutionary relationship between the Abert's squirrel of southwestern North America and the ponderosa pine. The distribution of Abert's squirrel is restricted primarily to stands of this one pine species in areas of Colorado, New Mexico, Arizona, and southern Wyoming in the United States, and three northern states of Mexico, Chihuahua, Sonora, and Durango, in the Sierra Madre Occidental.

As described in detail by Marc Snyder (1998) nearly all aspects of the squirrel's ecology are tied in one way or another to this one tree species. Interestingly, this dependence by the squirrel seems to have exerted a strong selective force on the tree. Active year-round, Abert's squirrels rely on ponderosa pine for nest sites, sanctuary from predators, and most of their food. From late summer to fall, Abert's squirrels feed heavily on the seeds of developing and mature cones of the ponderosa pine, an important energy and nitrogen source (Keith 1965). But this food source is temporally limited, even in high mast years when cones are abundant. Once cones open and seeds are dispersed, the Abert's squirrels switch to feeding on the tissues of the inner bark of ponderosa pine— mostly cambium and phloem—which they strip from the terminal twigs (M. Snyder 1998).

Although an extremely important food source, this inner bark is a nutritionally poor food, low in calories, protein, carbohydrates, and most minerals (M. Snyder 1992). Nevertheless, this is the mainstay of the animal's diet through most of the year (E. Hall 1981). Moreover, these squirrels show a strong preference for the cambium and phloem of individual trees, similar to the preference for cones of specific longleaf pine trees shown by southeastern fox squirrels (see Chapters 4 and 5). But unlike fox squirrels, Abert's squirrels return year after year to the same trees. Other trees are consistently avoided (Farentinos 1972b; M. Snyder 1992). Compared with these avoided trees, preferred, or "target," trees show lower concentrations of several chemical compounds in the xylem, higher levels of sodium and specific carbohydrates in the phloem, and lower levels of iron in the phloem (M. Snyder 1992).

The potential for a strong evolutionary relationship, however, goes much further than this. Herbivory by Abert's squirrels causes a significant reduction in growth, a reduction in the numbers of cones and seeds normally produced, and a dramatic change in the architecture of the trees, all of which in turn reduce the overall genetic fitness of the preferred trees (M. Snyder and Linhart 1993). As M. Snyder (1998) also points out, many of the characteristics that distinguish these target trees are under tight genetic control—possibly determined by one or a few genes. Thus it follows that the Abert's squirrel, so closely dependent on the ponderosa pine, is also exerting a strong directional, evolutionary force on the tree (M. Snyder 1998).

Two other herbivores, the porcupine and mountain pine beetle, and one parasitic plant, the dwarf-mistletoe, also select certain ponderosa pine trees in which to feed. But tree preferences of each species are based on different chemicals, so each species exerts a different selective pressure on the trees. Consequently, this community of specialized herbivores, which includes the Abert's squirrel, act to produce multidirectional evolutionary pressures that may help to maintain, rather than reduce, genetic diversity in the ponderosa pine (M. Snyder 1998).

We suggest that the importance of tree squirrels in some biomes or ecosystems may be significant enough to elevate them to the status of keystone species. As defined by Powers et al. (1996), keystone species are those whose impact in an ecosystem exceeds that which would be predicted simply from their relative abundance. For tree squirrels, the specific data needed to make such an assertion are clearly lacking. Yet there are some tantalizing systems to consider. The oak forests of eastern North America, the ponderosa pine forests of the West, the boreal coniferous forests, and the southeastern forests of longleaf pine are all ecosystems in which tree squirrels are critical and dominant players. In some, they act as important agents of seed and fungal dispersal; in others they cause significant damage as seed predators or herbivores. We predict that with additional research it will become increasingly evident just how great an influence tree squirrels have on ecosystems in which they live.

# 8

# Reproduction

*The female, a two-year-old in her first attempt at mating, will only be receptive for about six more hours, and she has already mated once today. She will not be receptive again for at least another 3.5 months and more likely an additional year. It will be a long day for the female, being pursued by a dozen desperate males, and for the males that will compete vigorously, most of whom will come away with torn ears, dislocated tails, or bite marks on the haunches and only a few of which will successfully mate.*

Reduced to the most basic level, the name of the game of life is the propagation of one's genetic information—that is, to reproduce. Charles Darwin, in *The Origin of Species*, recognized the drive to reproduce as a major force shaping the biology of living organisms. The drive to reproduce can be seen throughout the ecology of tree squirrels. Because tree squirrels are endotherms, they live a high-energy lifestyle in which at best 5 percent of the energy that is ingested is available for reproduction; the vast majority of energy simply goes to maintain the tissue and routine functions. Success ultimately depends on efficiently "shunting" the energy requirements of day-to-day life into reproduction.

To study reproduction in a natural setting, biologists must repeatedly sample from a population, preferably by capturing individuals, marking them so that they can be recognized, and recapturing them repeatedly. Male reproductive condition is typically scored as abdominal or scrotal, depending on the location of the testes. The testes descend into the scrotum when capable of producing sperm, whereas nonfunctional testes recrudesce, or shrink, and ascend through the inguinal canal into an abdominal location. The difference between these two conditions can easily be assessed visually or verified by palpating the testes to be certain of their location. The assessment of female reproductive condition is a bit more complex. Females can be considered nulliparous (never having reproduced), postreproductive but not currently lactating, or presently lactating (milk can be expressed from the teats). When a female nurses a litter of young, her teats become distended, fur is lost from the area surrounding the teat, and the teats become pigmented with black, and this coloration is retained for at least several years (Figure 8.1). In addition, the late stages of pregnancy can be detected by palpating the stomach. These methods have been used to determine most of what is known about reproduction in fox squirrels and gray squirrels.

## WHEN TO REPRODUCE?

The first problem that squirrels face is when to reproduce. We explore the timing of reproduction from two perspectives: when to reproduce during the annual cycle and when to reproduce in one's lifetime. Not surprisingly the answer to the first question is related to the timing of energy availability and costs during the annual cycle (Gurnell 1987).

The emergence of young in the dead of winter, with numbing temperatures and a dearth of food, would be disastrous for the offspring and a wasted attempt at reproduction by the parent. Such frivolous expenditures of energy available for reproduction would result in greatly reduced fitness—individuals that time their litters so poorly will not leave offspring.

Due to the seasonality of tree reproduction across the majority of gray and fox squirrel ranges, energy is most available during fall, followed by spring (Figure 8.2). Although hoarded food helps sustain squirrels in winter, this is typically a time of relative dormancy for trees. This is espe-

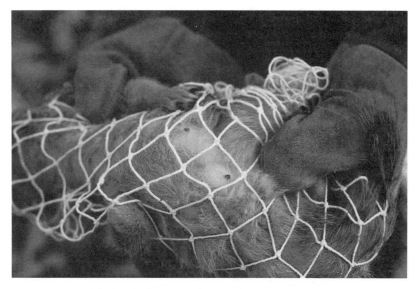

Figure 8.1. An adult female fox squirrel. Note the pigmentation on the teats that clearly denotes past reproduction. (Photograph courtesy of J. L. Koprowski)

cially true for deciduous trees that shed their leaves as they are hormonally commanded to cut their losses in winter; however, even evergreen species invest very little in growth and reproduction during the shortened daylight hours from which they draw energy. This period of short days, cold temperatures, and at best slow plant growth is an energetically challenging period for tree squirrels. In a Virginia woodlot, available energy levels were shown to dip well below the minimal requirements necessary for squirrels to maintain their basic bodily needs (Montgomery, Whelan, and Mosby 1975). Higher thermoregulatory costs coupled with declining food reserves make winter a difficult time. The bleakness of winter typically is broken in February or March as temperatures increase and the first leaves and flowers begin to appear from buds on deciduous trees. People often take solace in the first tints of green on branches as harbingers of the coming spring; to a squirrel this growth must be rather like a lifesaver tossed to a waterlogged shipwreck victim weary of treading water. The following weeks see an incredible growth of new plant tissues often well endowed with proteins and other nutrients (but also highly protected by plant defense compounds, for these reproductive tissues are valuable to the tree). The cornucopia of food that becomes available results in an early spring feast for squirrels, and available energy levels quickly exceed the

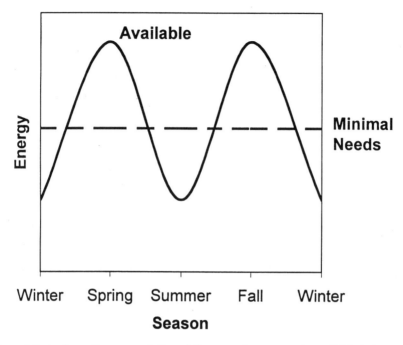

Figure 8.2. A schematic representation of the annual energy cycle available to tree squirrels. (Drawn by J. L. Koprowski)

squirrels' maintenance needs (Montgomery, Whelan, and Mosby 1975). This time of plenty may last through summer and fall as trees begin to generate edible fruits and seeds. Early seeds are produced by maples, mulberries, and cherries, followed later by the seeds of oaks, hickories, walnuts, and pines. Not surprisingly, tree squirrel reproduction is usually timed to coincide with the seasons of energy abundance.

Young of fox squirrels and gray squirrels are typically born beginning in February or March (L. Brown and Yeager 1945; J. Moore 1957). On our study site in Kansas, where both species were found, the mean estimated birth date for 13 litters of fox squirrels was 11 February, compared with 27 February for 27 litters of gray squirrels. We do not know the reason for this difference in birth dates; however, we hypothesize that the larger fox squirrel may require more time for young to grow, which is permitted by the half-month head start (Koprowski 1996). The timing allows females to take advantage of the flush of energy that is just beginning to hit the forest. But this seemingly exquisite timing means females must mate and endure pregnancy during a period of extraordinary resource shortage. The gestation period for gray squirrels is 44 days (Webley and Johnson 1983) and 44 to 45 days for fox squirrels (Flyger and Gates 1982a). As a result, female fox squirrels must mate in late December or early January; gray squirrels, in mid-January (L. Brown and Yeager 1945; Koprowski 1993a, 1993b). They must weather the period of food shortage on reserves of fat, cached foods, or both. Given that litter size averages two to three young and that each offspring is about 2 inches (5 cm) long and weighs 0.46 to 0.63 ounces (13–18 g; D. L. Allen 1942), females must produce 5 to 10 percent of their body weight in newborn mass. This is equivalent to the size of a human newborn—quite a production when one realizes that the female is pregnant while trying to cope with a serious energy shortage.

Although litter size for both fox squirrels and gray squirrels averages about 2.5 young per litter across a large range of geographic regions (Koprowski 1994a, 1994b), the variation in litter sizes is considerable. Some females will only produce a single offspring during a reproductive event, whereas the record litter size for fox squirrels was 7 fetuses found in a female from Colorado (Hoover 1954) and a gray squirrel in North Carolina produced 8 young (Barkalow 1967). This level of productivity suggests that a female of average size would produce young that account for about 20 percent of her body mass. One needs only to imagine a human baby on the order of 25 pounds (11.4 kg) to realize the immense investment such a litter represents. In addition to such high single reproductive events, females are capable of producing two litters in the course of a year, although the incidence of producing more than once in a year is apparently low. Ralph Harnishfeger, John Roseberry, and Bill Klimstra (1978) studied a population of fox squirrels in Illinois that were not hunted and found that during the eight-year study only 2 percent of the females repeated reproduction within a given year; however, 27 percent of female gray squirrels in Ohio produced twice in a year (Nixon and McClain 1975). In other studies nearly 90 percent of female fox and gray squirrels reproduced only once during a year (Nixon and McClain 1975; Weigl, Steele, et al. 1989). Following a year in which tree seed crops fail, >90 percent of females in a population may forego reproduction, and litter sizes decrease to less than 2 squirrels (Barkalow 1967; Nixon and McClain 1969; Weigl, Steele, et al. 1989). Most certainly, reproduction is timed to capitalize on the availability of energy. Furthermore, year-to-year fluctuations in seed availability (i.e., mast cycles) clearly influence productivity.

The other question about timing concerns when during her lifetime a female should reproduce. The earlier the better one might argue, for this would provide a female the greatest number of reproductive active opportunities over the course of her lifetime. The vast majority of females do not reproduce until somewhere between their first and second birthdays (Harnishfeger, Roseberry, and Klimstra 1978; Nixon and McClain 1975) and <5 percent of gray squirrels in Ohio reproduced before their first birthday (Nixon and McClain 1975). In nearly 20 years of research, we have never seen a fox or gray squirrel produce a litter before her first birthday; however, it is somewhat common to see individuals produce as yearlings. And reproductive maturity appears to be very responsive to available food resources as precocious reproduction following record tree seed crops has been observed as early as 5.5 months in gray squirrels (N. Smith and Barkalow 1967) and 8.0 months in fox squirrels (McCloskey and Vohs 1971). Bearing young early in life can certainly increase the potential number of opportunities to reproduce over a lifetime, but not if such an early start decreases life span or future reproductive success. The influence of early reproduction on residual reproduction is not known in squirrels. We do know that the reproductive longevity of tree squirrels can be exceptional for a medium-sized mammal. A female gray squirrel in North Carolina lived and reproduced into her twelfth year (Barkalow and Soots 1975), and we observed a female fox squirrel in her twelfth year of life that was still vigorous and had recently reproduced (Koprowski, Roseberry, and Klimstra 1988).

Our reference to only females up to this point in this chapter is not an oversight. Only female tree squirrels care for young. Male and female fox squirrels and gray squirrels do not form a pair bond or in other ways associate after mating (Koprowski 1993a, 1993b; Thompson 1977b); the investment in parental care comes exclusively from the female. As a result, we focus primarily on females in this chapter. To answer the question of when should males reproduce, the simple reply is, whenever females are receptive. We have found male fox squirrels and gray squirrels to exhibit enlarged testes, and thus a readiness to mate, in all months of the year. However, most males are reproductively active from November until August each year—a much longer range of reproductive activity than females. Needless to say, male tree squirrels appear to be opportunistic.

Young are born, like many rodents, naked (except for the vibrissae, or whiskers), pink, and with closed eyes. At 0.46 to 0.63 ounces (13–18 g) and about 2 inches (5–6 cm), newborns are poorly developed and completely dependent on their mothers for survival. We have observed that fe-

**Figure 8.3. Female fox squirrel carrying a young nestling to a new nest. (Photograph courtesy of J. L. Koprowski)**

males nest alone with young prior to their weaning but will rejoin nesting groups after young are weaned. Prior to weaning, females may change nests, especially following disturbance of a nest. To move a litter, the mother carries her young in her mouth by grasping the excess skin on their abdomen. The juvenile responds by wrapping its legs around the head of its mother (Figure 8.3). We once watched a female fox squirrel transport her litter of 5 nearly weaned young, estimated to be 6.3 to 7.0 ounces (180–200 g), a distance of about 109 yards (100 m), and the complicated process took 1 hour to complete. Young will weigh approximately 8.75 ounces (250 g) when weaned at 8 to 12 weeks of age, which represents a 16-fold increase in size over slightly more than 2 months. This growth is indeed impressive. In humans, this would equate to an 8-pound (3.6-kg) newborn reaching a body size of 130 pounds (59 kg) by the end of the second month. What's in that milk? A squirrel mother's milk is exceptionally rich in fat (up to 25 percent) and protein (up to 9 percent; Nixon and Harper 1972) and serves as the sole source of nutrients for the young until shortly before the time of weaning.

At 7 to 10 days after birth, hair begins to emerge on the back; by three weeks the tail becomes covered with fur, ears open, and incisors begin to erupt. By the fifth week of life, the eyes open, and soon after the cheek teeth begin to come into the jaw. Weaning often begins in the seventh week. Juvenile dispersal from the natal site can occur anytime after weaning; however, some individuals remain in their birthplace and exhibit natal philopatry (Koprowski 1996, 1998; Thompson 1978a) that results in the formation of social groups that help each other build nests, defend a core area, and keep warm.

## HOW TO FIND MATES

The final question related to reproduction is how males and females locate each other. Earlier, we noted that the separation of the sexes was the rule throughout much of the year, and in this chapter we have dealt with the reproductive cycles of the sexes independently. Obviously, though, for reproduction to occur the sexes must come together to copulate. The necessity of interaction between the sexes is probably even more complex as it turns out; adult males apparently need to be present in order for females to mature to reproductive age (Webley and Johnson 1983). During the last 15 years we have examined the mating system of fox squirrels and gray squirrels through detailed observation of uniquely marked animals in order to assess the tactics used by males and females to successfully reproduce. By following individuals over time, we have been able to examine the importance of factors such as age and dominance rank in achieving success.

How difficult can it be for males to find females? In humans, females may be receptive to mating at any time during their near month-long menstrual cycle but this is quite exceptional among mammals. Females in the vast majority of mammals are only receptive during a relatively short period during their reproductive cycle. In fact, when a male squirrel approaches a female of reproductive age outside of the breeding season, he is quickly and quite effectively rebuffed by a swat to the face with four sharp claws and a snap from the female's ever-dangerous incisors. This reduced period when females are willing to couple in most species decreases the availability of mates significantly. The ratio of males in reproductive condition to receptive females is known as the operational sex ratio. A 1:1 ratio would mean that for every female that is receptive there would be a single male that is also reproductively active. Such a ratio might be expected in a species with a monogamous mating system. For tree squirrels, however, operational sex ratios typically are on the order of 5:1 to 20:1. Such male-biased ratios typically indicate a mating system in which males must search and fight for females. Thus finding females can be a remarkable challenge. As if the odds are not long enough for most males to pass on their genes, gray squirrel and fox squirrel females are only in estrus and receptive to males for about eight hours on a single day during the reproductive season (Thompson 1977b). Because females typically do not breed more than once each year, males must respond quickly to the presence of a receptive female in a population.

What strategies are used by male and female squirrels to achieve reproductive success? While adaptations that increase survival are obviously important, those that are directed specifically at increasing the number of mating opportunities are often under the greatest pressure from natural selection. Males that do not detect a female during her eight-hour estrus have missed their only opportunity to mate with her for at least several months and very likely an entire year. We predicted that males must track the reproductive condition of females on a daily basis if they are not going to miss a mating opportunity.

Do males use tactics to maximize their likelihood of detecting receptive females? Not surprisingly the answer is yes. Male tree squirrels of nearly all species range widely in their daily activities, covering significantly more area than females—usually 1.5 to 2.0 times greater (Koprowski 1998). This occurs despite the fact that males and females do not differ in size. If male needs were greater and they required more food than females, we might rightly expect a difference between the sexes, or sexual dimorphism, in home range size. What explains the difference then? Robert Kenward (1985) cleverly manipulated food reserves by adding food to his study area and by removing females. Although food did influence ranging patterns of male squirrels somewhat, males ranged more widely when females were less common. When we examined the activity budgets of males during the breeding season from November until August, the pattern was clear. The day in the life of a male is quite predictable. After awaking in the morning, males spend the first few hours of each day visiting the nests and home ranges of adult females. In Kansas we watched males leave their dens and followed their behavior during the rest of the day. On average, males interacted with 5.8 (±1.2) females within the first 3 hours of activity. Males clearly attempt to seek out females. When a male encounters a female during his travels, he approaches deliberately but slowly and follows the female from behind. While he does so, he smells her genitalia by cautiously leaning forward. If the female is not in or approaching estrus, the meeting is a brief one lasting just a few seconds. Males demonstrate remarkable tenacity in following a female when she is within about 5 days of estrus (Thompson 1977b), and females become quite aggressive in repelling males that are too persistent in their approach. As a result, females approaching estrus attract considerable attention from numerous males by the day of estrus. Thompson (1977b) reported that many males are drawn from as far away as 546.8 yards (500 m), and we observed a male travel 929.6 yards (850 m) to join a mating chase in Kansas—this represented a straight-line distance of about half a mile. Clearly males are extraordinarily diligent in their monitoring of female reproductive condition and invest considerable time and energy in this process. Male body masses plummet markedly during this period as fat reserves are quickly tapped to provide the energy for increased movement and interaction. Scott Howe and Matt Woolsey, undergraduates at Willamette University, applied the same technology used to estimate the percentage of fat in ground meat at the grocery store to determine that male fat levels are significantly higher than females just before the breeding season but significantly less during the breeding season. Nothing demonstrated this to us more graphically than when we watched a rather groggy adult male fox squirrel emerge in the early morning hours and fall dead to the ground. Upon conducting a necropsy of this individual, we observed that he had 14 wounds from other squirrels and no visible body fat stores. He had died primarily of malnutrition. However, he had copulated five times during that breeding season, third most among males in the population. Though his death clearly indicates failure on one level, his performance during the breeding season suggests success in the game of life.

By the day of estrus, males have been following the female for several days, and a number of individuals leave the nests before sunrise and travel in the faint dawn light to the nest of the estrous female. Because many of the mating chases of fox squirrels and gray squirrels occur in winter, the early morning darkness is typically characterized by temperatures well below freezing and often with wind-chills below –4°F (–20°C). Not only are the male squirrels faced with these conditions but also the researcher interested in squirrel mating systems. Male squirrels and researchers await the exit of the female. Males continue to congregate and begin jockeying for a position in proximity to the female's den entrance. A clear, well-defined linear dominance hierarchy occurs even before the female's emergence. The quiet still of the morning air is periodically defiled by the bark and squeal of the female inside her den as the most dominant males attempt to enter and are foiled. Typically, just after sunrise the female exits her nest and attempts to feed but quickly attracts the atten-

Figure 8.4. Typical posture for copulation. Here both the male and female gray squirrels have been marked for identification using freeze marks that result in the unique patterns of white hair. (Photograph courtesy of J. L. Koprowski)

tion of the assembled males—she will have little time to feed until her eight-hour period of estrus is over. To the casual observer, what ensues is probably best described as pure and unadulterated chaos. Our goal was to systematically observe and quantify this chaos and detect patterns in the tactics used by the male and female participants in the mating bouts by observing uniquely marked animals throughout the mating season. We capitalized on the behavior of males to assist in predicting which females were most likely to be in estrus.

The mating bout lasts for much of the day. Copulation occurs when the male mounts the female (Figure 8.4) and lasts for only 20 seconds, after which both the male and female groom their own genitalia. The male continues to guard the female for about 20 minutes and then the pursuit continues. The mating bout finally terminates in midafternoon as males begin to lose interest in the female; pursuit wanes and numbers dwindle. By the end of the mating bout females have usually mated with two to four males, which means the vast majority of males do not mate during a single mating bout.

Mating bouts are incredibly intense. As many as 34 males have been reported to participate in mating bouts (P. D. Goodrum 1961), and we have observed 22 male gray squirrels chasing a single estrous female. Because the estrous female represents an ephemeral resource that is directly related to the reproductive success of the male and the operational sex ratio is heavily skewed toward males, competition for females is fierce. Fighting between males is common, and during peak activity more than 2,000 interactions occur each hour as males attempt to gain access to the female. The female typically moves to the end of a branch or hides in a den cavity, which elevates the level of aggression among males.

A dominance hierarchy is well defined and obvious. The most dominant individuals are the older males, although they may not be the largest of the participants, and more order exists during mating bouts than may be apparent at first glance. As we continued to quantify the mating bouts, we realized that something subtle was occurring. We were most interested in learning why subordinate males continued to participate in the mating bouts even though they might be ranked tenth or fifteenth, with extremely low chances of accessing the female. What is the incentive to expend energy and time?

We decided to look more closely at the tactics of individual males and quickly realized that two different tactics were being used by individuals within a mating chase. About 40 percent of the males in the mating bout are actively involved in attempting to access the female and attempt to gain proximity to the female by forcefully exploiting their dominance rank. We named this technique "active pursuit." The remainder of the males that participate in the mating bout do so in a much less overt manner. The more passive "satellite male" tactic is adopted by the majority of males and consists of individuals that sit on the periphery of the mating bout and forage for food. At first glance these apparently disinterested individuals appear to be females because they are not participants. In actuality, these satellite males are young, low-ranking males that are quickly rebuffed if they attempt to challenge one of the older, dominant active-pursuit males. Yet satellite males remain in the vicinity of the mating chase. Why? As we began to look at the summary statistics we generated, it became clear that the satellite males were able to accrue copulations. This explained why the satellite males continued to remain involved in the mating bout. But how were these subordinate animals able to overcome the numerous dominant, active-pursuit males that literally stood between them and the estrous female? The answer lies in the female's behavior. During the mating chase, active-pursuit males attempt to sequester the female on a branch and copulate. This is a sensible tactic for a dominant because it allows the male to take advantage of his strengths by rewarding despotic behavior. The female, however, often sprints from the position of restraint in what we call "breakaways." The breakaway most frequently results in a single file of males in hot pursuit of the female. The train of males that follows the female includes the satellite males that immediately drop whatever they were doing and join in the pursuit. Within seconds, satellite males change from apparently disinterested and distracted squirrels that are in the vicinity of the mating bout only because of happenstance to keenly interested males with the opportunity to increase their reproductive success.

In some of the breakaways, the active-pursuit males are so distracted by the intense interindividual interactions that the female is actually able to lose the males. The "desperation" that appears to occur among males can only be conveyed with a bit of anthropomorphism. A frenzy of activity ensues as males crisscross the female's home range uttering a call that sounds much like a high-pitched sneeze. Although scent is a fine indicator of the location of the estrous female in the calm of the morning, her odors are now found throughout her home range, and the only useful sensory information is visual. Anything that moves can be a female. Males will chase any individual that moves in the canopy or underbrush—whether male, juvenile, or nonreproductive female. In fact, any object about the same size as the female may be followed. Some of our more humorous moments in the field have included watching males attempt to follow blue jays *(Cyanocitta cristata)*, crows *(Corvus bradyrynchus)*, and cottontails *(Sylvilagus floridanus)* in their fervor to find the female. On one occasion, outside a study area at a city park in Lawrence, Kansas, we introduced a large softball into a mating bout. Following a breakaway in which the males frantically searched for the lost female, we rolled the ball along the ground, through the middle of the mating chase. Six males quickly pursued the ball until it stopped and settled into the grass. Desperate measures indeed.

Breakaways provide the opportunity for satellite males to achieve reproductive success. Following a breakaway, the female finds a secluded position that is close to the ground and mates with the first male to find her. The criterion on which success depends changes from dominance rank to the ability to locate the female. The rivalry shifts from "contest competition," where the actions of a despot are rewarded as males fight to maintain access to the female, to "scramble competition," where different skills are effective. We never observed satellite males copulate except following a breakaway. Their entire success is dependent on the behavior of the female. After a breakaway, success is randomly distributed among the males using the two tactics: active-pursuit males, which account for about 40 percent of the population, locate and mate with the female in proportion to their abundance (Koprowski 1993a, 1993b). The cost of a breakaway significantly decreases the success rate of active-pursuit males to the benefit of the satellites. These dynamics during the seemingly chaotic mating bout clearly explain why so many satellite males continue to participate. But why go through the incredible aggression that occurs in actively pursuing the female? When we tallied the number of copulations that each male achieved, we noted that the average number of copulations among active-pursuit males was twice as great as that of satellite males; active-pursuit males accrue mating from both breakaways and dominant behavior. Active pursuit is an advantageous strategy, and we can see this clearly in the age distribution of males that pursue the two tactics. Males under the age of 3.25 years old never used the active-pursuit strategy, which was the exclusive tactic of males older than 3.25 years. Only individuals between 3 and 3.5 years used both strategies during different chases in the same year, suggesting that the tactic is age-related and dependent on the composition of the mating chase. If you are only borderline in your dominance rank, you adjust your tactic depending on who shows up for that day's mating bout. A pretty sophisticated approach for a rodent. This type of tactic is referred to as a mixed evolutionarily stable strategy or mixed ESS (Krebs and Davies 1993) because the two types of tactics found in a population do not change. But individuals may mix these tactics between mating bouts depending on the other individuals involved. The tactics are termed "evolutionarily stable" because they yield predictable levels of success and cannot be invaded by other strategies. For instance, a one-year-old male could not enter the population and use the active-pursuit strategy to reproduce successfully. Individuals without the appropriate characteristics are quickly lost from the mating population.

An argument often posed is that the most dominant individuals carry the best genes. So we were curious as to why females would avoid the older, dominant active-pursuit males. By actively avoiding such genetically well-endowed males, females would seem to be risking the quality of their offspring and therefore their own reproductive success. A poor choice? Maybe not. The female may benefit in several ways. In Abert's squirrels, females appear to actively solicit copulations from subordinate males during mating chases in what may be a subtle form of mate choice (Farentinos 1980). Perhaps some characteristic of this male is appealing and recognizable at a young age. We have not been able to test this idea in any convincing fashion. However, we do know that in gray squirrels and fox squirrels the chance for solicitation of individual males is minimal because females mate with the first male to find them following a breakaway. What females do appear to most definitely gain from the breakaway is the ability to mate in a specific type of location. Copulations following breakaways occur in sites lower to the ground and with a decreased likelihood of interruption by other males. By "interruption" we mean a pair of incisors plunged directly into the hindquarters or a sidelong ramming that dislodges the male from the female and often both members of the copulating pair from the tree. When mating takes place some 33 feet (10 m) or more above the ground, the possibility of a three-story fall must be considered a significant risk. In fact, fully 20 percent of copulation attempts by males are terminated by the attack of another male. What females clearly gain from a breakaway is the possibility to mate in seclusion, near to the ground, with the decreased chance of attack resulting in less likelihood of physical injury. For the female, who is just beginning her annual reproductive attempt and has much time and energy yet to be invested in her offspring, an injury here would be critical. The males' investment in reproduction is nearly complete, so their aggressive tactics are less likely to have a negative impact on their own reproductive success. Interestingly, the flip side of such a successful maneuver is that the female may lose *all* the males when conducting a breakaway—and this is not good either! Although this could clearly be a significant cost of breakaways for females, it is a rare occurrence. We have observed it on only nine occasions (Koprowski 1993c), and in each case the female first remained motionless in an appropriate location for mating and then began to chatter and yelp in a call that sounded very similar to the alarm call used when startled. Males immediately responded, and the first male to locate the female mated with her.

Outside of well-known instances of female choice, females are often considered to be relatively uninvolved in controlling mating patterns. This is not strictly true for the tree squirrels. In many rodents, including most tree squirrels (Koprowski 1992), the semen of the male coagulates and hardens into the copulatory plug, a white, opaque, waxy-to-rubbery obstruction that is molded within the vagina of the female. This copulatory plug is about the size of the tip of a person's little finger. Its function is probably to impede copulation with and sperm transfer from another male. Following copulation, females always groom their genitalia. And the female may then remove and consume the recently deposited plug, which has an extraordinarily high protein content. About half the females consume the plug; the other half simply discard the proteinaceous plug. Removing the plug may simply dislodge an awkward or uncomfortable structure, but it also allows the female to mate with another male, which may ensure that her eggs are successfully fertilized and increase genetic variation of her offspring. Although the reason for removal is not clear, what is clear is that female gray and fox squirrels do have reproductive agendas that may conflict with those of individual males. Female tree squirrels manipulate a number of different aspects of the mating behavior of males that demonstrate they are not merely passive observers in the mating game. Females break away from males, select mating locations, mate with multiple males, call when males are unable to locate them, and remove copulatory plugs—all behaviors that are detrimental to the reproductive success of individual males. Such behaviors highlight the subtle ways the reproductive process has been shaped by natural selection to maximize efficiency and capitalize on even the most minuscule of advantages.

# 9

# Social Behavior

*A boisterous chatter from inside the cavity pro-*
*vides only a brief warning to the yearling as two*
*adult females and three young of the year ex-*
*plode from inside the cavity and initiate pursuit*
*to a cacophony of chatters and squeals. The*
*yearling drops the leaves from its mouth, makes*
*a spiral retreat down the length of the tree trunk,*
*and sprints across the forest floor. After briefly*
*sniffing each other's faces, the victorious resi-*
*dents spend a few minutes grooming each other*
*with teeth and claws and then retreat to their*
*nocturnal nest.*

Such is the life of a squirrel and many other mammals. The majority of
mammals live solitary lives; estimates suggest that at least 85 percent of
mammals can be classified as asocial animals (Waser and Jones 1983) that
aggregate only briefly at a seasonal food source or to mate. A plethora of
reasons exist for not living in groups (reviewed in Krebs and Davies 1993),
and an investigation of why squirrels are solitary animals has been the

focus of much of our research. Members of the same species are extremely good competitors for critical resources, such as food, dens, or mates, that determine an individual's fitness. In addition, living in groups increases the chance for disease and parasite transmission and visibility to predators. Food, dens, and mates are important resources for tree squirrels, and a great diversity of predators and parasites depend upon tree squirrels. As a result, most of these costs and benefits of living in groups are applicable to fox squirrels and gray squirrels. In this chapter, we describe the social organization and communication of squirrels.

## COMMUNICATION IN SQUIRREL SOCIETIES: MODE AND CONTEXT

Within any social system, individuals must be able to communicate a wealth of information. Effective signals convey messages with minimal cost and over an appropriate time period. Tree squirrels rely on three major modes of communication: sight, hearing, and smell. Here we explore the use of these senses in the context of the squirrel's social world.

The use of displays and other visual cues in communication between squirrels is rather poorly described in tree squirrels. However, we can make a few general statements about communication through visual cues (Gurnell 1987; Horwich 1972; McCloskey 1975; McCloskey and Shaw 1977). The tail and body hair become erect (piloerection) prior to aggressive interactions and when squirrels are disturbed. Most observers have noted the apparently chaotic tail flicking from fore to aft that often grades into a rapid flagging of the tail depending on the degree of alarm or aggression. During a mating bout, this flagging often slows as the male approaches the female. Hind foot stamping also increases as the level of aggression or alarm heightens. Low-ranking "subordinate" individuals may use a slinking body posture and groom themselves to indicate submission. Jan Taylor (1969) hypothesized that the highly visible white on the tail, back of the ears, and around the eye emphasized the signals from these important body regions to other squirrels.

Smell, or olfaction, is important in many aspects of the life of a squirrel, ranging from locating caches and fruiting trees to detecting receptive females nearly a kilometer distant. Scents are deposited by squirrels in at least two ways. Fox squirrels and gray squirrels urinate at traditional sites (Koprowski 1993d; Taylor 1969, 1977). Marking sites are usually found in protected locations that probably maximize the length of time the scent mark remains detectable to other squirrels. Most often these sites are under major branches, on the underside of a tilted trunk, or on the leeward side of large-diameter trees (Koprowski 1991a; Taylor 1977). Once we learned what to look for in scent marks and where to look, we realized that traditional areas, distinguished by years of bark chipping and incisor indentations, are quite common. We have seen them in every location we have studied or visited. In addition, glands on the inside of the lips are used in a behavior called face-wiping or cheek-rubbing. Individuals wipe each cheek along the substrate when depositing scent (Benson 1980; Koprowski 1993d; Taylor 1977). For the naturalist ambitious enough to take a sniff, a musky odor awaits. To humans, this odor says not much more than an animal was here; substantially more information may be conveyed to squirrels by such scents. Oral marking can occur at dispersed sites throughout the home range, where it appears to function in both sexes to mark pathways (Benson 1980; Koprowski 1993d). From 1987 until 1991 we studied the use of traditional marking sites and discovered that only male gray squirrels used oral marking at these locations (Koprowski 1993d). Females were quite interested in this scent and frequently visited and investigated the marking locations—raising the question, what information is conveyed at marking sites?

Oral marking is positively correlated with age and high ranking; dominant individuals mark more than low-ranking animals (Benson 1980). We have observed adult males attack other males that are in the process of oral marking at traditional marking sites and then immediately mark the spot that the displaced male was attending. At the start of the active day, males visit and mark sites in rapid succession (3.1 ± 0.7 sites within the first 2 hours; n = 9 males), whereas females do not mark any such sites. All these observations support the important role of olfactory communication within the social system of tree squirrels.

Auditory cues are used in alarm calls in response to predators and in a variety of social situations. The calls of gray squirrels typically consist of four notes referred to as *buzz, kuk, moan,* and *quaa* that can be modified depending on context (Lishak 1982a, 1982b, 1984), and those of fox squirrels, although less studied, appear to be similar (Zelley 1971). Young nestlings use calls to initiate contact with their mother and in instances of distress, and many of these same call characteristics can be found in adult calls associated with mating, alarm, and aggression (Table 9.1). Aggressive encounters typically involve a great deal of tooth chattering that escalates in frequency and intensity with heightened levels of conflict.

## Table 9.1
## Vocalizations of Adult Squirrels

| Species | Call Type | Context When Given |
|---------|-----------|--------------------|
| Fox squirrel | Bark | Mild distress |
| | Chatter bark | Startled or agonistic chase |
| | Low-frequency groan | Restrained or confined |
| | Grunt | Males in mating chases |
| | Scream | Severe distress |
| | High-pitched whine | Females in mating chases |
| Gray squirrel | Buzz | Startled or distressed |
| | Kuk | Mild distress |
| | Quaa | Startled or distressed |
| | Tooth chatter | Agonistic chases and distress |
| | Moan | Startled or mild distress |
| | Scream | Severe distress |
| | Grunt | Males in mating chases |
| | High-pitched whine | Females in mating chases |

## THE SOLITARY LIFE OF SQUIRRELS: AGGRESSIVE INTERACTIONS

For many years, fox squirrels and gray squirrels were believed to exhibit a solitary existence common to many mammals. When foraging throughout the day, individuals occasionally may be seen in association with others at a local food source such as a tree with ripening nuts. The rare anecdotal accounts of animals nesting in groups were attributed to mothers with young (more on this later). However, most often individuals are observed conducting their behaviors in solitude. Aggressive interactions are the most common interactions between individuals (Thompson 1978b; Koprowski 1996). These interactions can range from an aggressor staring at another animal, stomping its feet, waving its tail, and chattering its teeth to physical combat. Our research suggests that aggressive interactions most often involve these ritualized displays or perhaps a short chase over a distance of 16.4 to 32.8 feet (5–10 m) and only rarely escalate into physical combat (<4 percent of 776 aggressive encounters; Koprowski 1996). The settlement of disputes without a fight is common among animals, for conflict escalation carries with it significant costs. Behavioral ecologists have adapted a technique known as "game theory" used by economists and social scientists to demonstrate that escalation to physical combat should only occur when the potential combatants are evenly matched and the value of the contested resource is high. Such is the case with the intense aggression that occurs among males in pursuit of an estrous female. But in most situations, such as traveling or food-gathering, squirrels have other options, so less risky means of settling disputes are used. If combat does ensue, tree squirrels are particularly well equipped to participate. The squirrels' agility and the sharp recurved claws that aid arboreal travel do double duty, providing lethal weaponry in combination with the always dangerous paired incisors.

Aggressive interactions can have deadly consequences. R. F. Holm (1976) observed an adult eastern gray squirrel in Chicago that chased, bit, killed, and cannibalized a young conspecific. But such lethal results are rare. Most often the aggressor will bite ears or grab the tail during a scuffle. For gray squirrels, we found that about 32 percent of adult males and only 2 percent of adult females possessed torn ears. Fewer fox squirrels seem to experience damage to ears (7 percent of males, 13 percent of females), and males and females sustain similar levels of damage. Tails also make an easy target. In November 1990 we watched a vicious chase between two adult male gray squirrels. At a height of 30 feet (9 m) in a mulberry tree (Morus alba), a male grasped the base of the tail of the overtaken rival with his mouth. With the motion of a cowboy throwing a lasso, the aggressive male tossed the second male from the branch. The subordinate male retreated to his den along the ground with a tail that dragged limply behind the body and possessed an obvious kink. The distal portion of the tail wasted away over the next two days and fell off, leaving a 2-inch (5-cm) stump. This kind of physical confrontation seems to be somewhat common and equally so among the sexes. At our Kansas study site 10.4 percent of 96 gray squirrels and 18.2 percent of 22 adult fox squirrels had tails that were either dislocated or shortened.

## DETERMINANTS OF DOMINANCE: SPATIAL AND TEMPORAL VARIATION

The most common approach to determine what leads to one individual's dominance over another is to monitor interactions between a number of individuals that have been uniquely marked and are recognizable at a distance. The interactions can be monitored in a field setting, a captive arena, or at an artificial food source, and each animal's rank within the pecking order determined. Behaviorists who have used these techniques have typically found that sex and age are the principal determinants of dominance

(Allen and Aspey 1986; Benson 1980; Bernard 1972; Pack, Mosby, and Siegel 1967). Males dominate females of similar age, and adults dominate younger animals. Surprisingly, Doug Allen and Wayne Aspey (1986) at Ohio State University determined that body mass alone does not correlate significantly with dominance. Factors such as experience that correlate with age may be important in determining dominance relationships, but those kinds of particulars are extremely difficult to measure. Clearly though, the interactions between individuals are not cut and dried in natural settings where the playing field is rarely level. In the field a curious phenomenon called "residence dominance" often occurs in animal populations: the owner of a piece of real estate has significant advantage over an intruder, and the dominance relationships seen at a neutral site do not apply. This home field advantage is obvious among weaned juvenile gray squirrels that are still in their natal area—residents win almost every encounter with similarly aged juveniles when in their own home range (Koprowski 1993c). Immigrants of any age are frequently the targets of aggressive chases and attacks, thereby making it difficult for individuals to recruit into a local population (Koprowski 1996; Thompson 1978a, 1978b). One's low dominance rank can also be substantially enhanced through group associations. Adult males often dominate females in artificial settings and during the intense mating bouts. But with the assistance of female associates, 27 of 44 adult female gray squirrels evicted from the female's den tree adult males that had chased them previously in the field.

Adult females that are lactating prefer to nest alone, are particularly aggressive, and possess few rivals of either sex or any age. After marking and releasing juveniles, we have been attacked by the juvenile's mother on three separate occasions. Although the attacks did not quite instill the fear that a charging black rhino might, the mother's message was clear and we hastily retreated. Several ingenious studies have revealed the important role that adult females play in the regulation of populations in both fox squirrels and gray squirrels. Stephen Havera, a doctoral student at the time, and his adviser, Charles Nixon, reported that adult females tend to remain evenly spaced within a woodlot during the winter breeding season (Havera and Nixon 1978b). This finding led several researchers to manipulate densities of adult males and females (Brown and Batzli 1985a; Hansen and Nixon 1986). By moving individuals of either sex from a woodlot to another site, the importance of the removed individuals to the local population's social organization could be assessed by monitoring the rate of immigration and survival following removal. The results indicated that adult females but not adult males were important in deterring individuals from establishing residence. Robert Kenward (1985), working in England, also used removal experiments to demonstrate that female gray squirrel distribution was quite influential to the distribution of males. Males ranged more widely when adult females were removed, whereas similar manipulations of the distribution of food did not have the same effect. Males clearly focused on females, not on food, which is consistent with the differences in the resources that limit each sex's reproductive success. Despite their apparently low dominance rank, adult females play an integral role in the social organization of tree squirrels.

## SOCIALITY IN FOX SQUIRRELS AND GRAY SQUIRRELS

Aggressive interactions were clearly the most frequent interaction among squirrels (between 62 and 67 percent; Koprowski 1996), and even to most trained and keen observers, tree squirrels appear relatively asocial and solitary. However, as we sought a focus for our research on social organization, we were puzzled by the fact that numerous biologists had reported, either in publications (Christisen 1985; Kenward 1985) or in conversation, tree squirrels nesting in groups. And these observations agreed with our own. Not something one would expect from an asocial animal. Some of these nesting associations were clearly the result of mothers nesting with young of the year, but some associations had several adult-sized animals and involved both sexes. Were these nesting associations simply ephemeral gatherings or were they indicative of an underlying level of social complexity that was masked by the solitary diurnal habits of squirrels seeking a well-dispersed food source? We suspected the latter but had no evidence. Not until we obtained a copy of Jan C. Taylor's 1969 University of London dissertation did we receive information that verified our suspicions. Working over several years in an urban park in London, England, Taylor reported nesting groups that were clearly composed of at least some related individuals. The suggestion that kinship was involved pointed toward a very different system of social organization.

In the early 1960s William D. Hamilton postulated the revolutionary idea of inclusive fitness to explain why social insects such as honeybees and ants obtain individual benefits even by forgoing reproduction and serving only as workers. His "Genetical Evolution of Social Behavior" (1964) suggested that an individual's success at passing on genes to the next generation (an individual's inclusive fitness) was composed of two components: direct fitness, where genes are passed on through one's direct descendants, and indirect fitness, where one's genes could also be passed along by assisting indirect descendant relatives or collateral kin. Although a revolutionary idea at the time, the idea of inclusive fitness was well received for it focused evolutionary thinking at the level of the individual and permitted a framework in which most puzzling cases of altruism could be logically explored. In short, when relatives are interacting, many things are possible.

How important is kinship in squirrel populations? It depends on what species you study and perhaps in what habitat you are observing the species. In fox squirrels, kinship does not appear to be important at all. Although individuals do occasionally nest in groups (<5 percent of nests checked by Christisen 1985) that range from 2 to 5 adults and are most common during the cool months of winter and spring (Koprowski 1996), the nesting associations are almost exclusively of adult males (72.9 percent of 48 nesting assemblages). Mixed-sex (27.0 percent) and all-female groupings (10.4 percent) are uncommon (Koprowski 1996). However, most important, no fox squirrels remain in their natal area (0 of 21 juveniles; Koprowski 1996), so nesting groups based upon relatedness are not possible. This lack of sex bias in the dispersal patterns of juveniles is consistent with that found in most solitary mammals (Waser and Jones 1983). The primary advantage of group nesting in fox squirrels appears to be one of thermoregulation during extreme cold. Fox squirrels nest alone during the torrid summer months and shift into nesting groups occasionally during cold winter nights. The only times (n = 5) that we have observed adult female fox squirrels nesting in groups occurred when nocturnal temperatures dipped below $-4°F$ ($-20°C$).

Eastern gray squirrels possess a radically different pattern of group nesting and natal dispersal. While nesting groups do vary with season and peak in the cold winter months, gray squirrels are found in groups ranging from 2 to 9 individuals during all seasons, including the hot summer months. The nesting assemblages also suggest significant sexual segregation as in fox squirrels; thus female gray squirrels are commonly found in single-sex groups.

Nesting groups are impressive to watch coalesce. Two hours before sunset, our research teams would sit about 27 yards (25 m) from the nest and record individuals returning to the nest. Just a few minutes before sunset, individuals would begin their return to the nests. Although returning from nearly all directions, squirrels would usually travel via the interwoven tree canopy (86.8 percent of 735 returns) and most often along ex-

**Figure 9.1. Adult male fox squirrels grooming each other (allogrooming). (Photograph courtesy of J. L. Koprowski)**

actly the same branches as the other individuals with whom they would nest. Individuals would pause briefly at the nest entrance to vocalize, sniff the snout of any individuals that responded to their call, and then enter headfirst. The entrance was usually followed by some low-level chattering and obvious repositioning of the occupants. Sometimes (11.8 percent) the returning squirrels carried nesting material back to the nest, and occasionally (4.0 percent) groups of individuals would remain outside the nest to allogroom (i.e., groom each other), play, or collect nesting materials en masse. For someone accustomed to the relatively solitary appearance of these squirrels, these few moments are the only glimpse one gets into the social life of eastern gray squirrels. While the collective return to the nest spans a period of no more than 15 minutes (7.8 ± 2.1 min), the exit from the nest in the morning occurs almost simultaneously. Individuals exit the nest in quick succession, bask in the sun, and allogroom before descending to the ground (Figure 9.1). But the amicable social interactions that began with nightfall end quickly in the morning, thus offering the evidence of the solitary life of gray squirrels that was commonly accepted until recently.

Not every squirrel is permitted to enter a nest that contains a group of individuals. The nesting assemblages do change, especially among all-male and mixed-sex groups, but all-female groups are remarkably consistent and cohesive, with only pregnant females leaving the assemblage. When males or immigrants attempt to enter the nest, a series of squeals and chattering echoes from inside the nest. This usually deters the visitor, but if the individual continues to seek entrance, the entire nesting group exits the nest and sets chase. Individuals will often descend the tree, collect nesting material, and attempt to gain entrance again. Only on extremely cold winter nights (32°F [<0°C]; n = 17) are new individuals permitted into a nest, and they are always evicted in the morning, suggesting that they were essentially used for their body warmth and then cast out. On two occasions, we observed an individual that was denied entrance to a nest spend the night in the crotch of a tree curled into a ball with the tail strewn over the face. Given that a single fox squirrel raises the temperature of a nest more than 72°F (40°C) (Havera 1979), a quality nest cavity probably conveys significant survival value to its inhabitants, particularly in the winter months.

The finding that female gray squirrels nest in stable groups suggests that kinship may influence social dynamics. The nesting groups are composed most often of related females (82.7 percent of 52 nesting groups with >1 adult female; Koprowski 1996). The relationships occur because female gray squirrels remain in their natal area and exhibit natal philopatry (Cordes and Barkalow 1972; Koprowski 1996); 37 percent of 43 females in our Kansas study were philopatric, whereas only 2 percent of males remained near their birth site. These two males remained only after the death of their mother. Most males established residence 0.7 miles (1.10 km; range 0.24–2.0 miles [0.38–3.23 km]) from their birth site. The pattern of male natal dispersal and female natal philopatry is common among social mammals (Clutton-Brock 1989).

As a result of this female-biased pattern of natal philopatry, gray squirrel populations exhibit significant substructure that is based upon kinship. The stable female groups are composed of individuals with a coefficient of relatedness (the proportion of shared genes) that is equal to 0.50. In other words, on average, each individual in a group shares about 50 percent of its genes with every other individual, about the same degree of relatedness shared between a mother and daughter. Based upon W. D. Hamilton's concept of inclusive fitness we expected that individuals within the population would benefit the most by assisting individuals with whom they shared the greatest proportion of genes, that is, close relatives.

Two patterns of kin differential behavior have been documented. Some species demonstrate a pattern in which individuals with a decreasing proportion of shared genes are treated with a similar decrease in the frequency of amicable behavior (proportional altruism; Bennett 1987). This seems logical but requires a great deal of discriminatory ability between individuals to assess who is a close relative and who is a more distant one. Other species direct amicable behaviors only toward close relatives and treat distant relatives as unrelated animals (Armitage 1989). The latter appears to be the case for gray squirrels, with adult mother-daughter and sister-sister dyads (which share 50 percent of their genes by descent) treated amicably >75 percent of the time while more distant levels of relatedness such as grandmother-granddaughter and aunt-niece were most often treated agonistically (>60 percent of the time), much like unrelated animals would be.

What benefits, if any, do individuals in these kin clusters receive? The amicable treatment (communal nesting, greeting, allogrooming, play) that is directed toward close relatives apparently does result in payoffs for the recipient's fitness. Remember that immigrants are the targets of high levels of aggression (Koprowski 1996; Thompson 1978a, 1978b). Recruitment in gray squirrel population appears to be primarily through natal philopatry when related females are found in the natal area (88.9 percent of 18 cases of successful recruitment in which females established residence in the population for >2 years). The benefits of establishing residence translated into 75 percent of these females mating and 50 percent producing a litter in the population.

Males are not often discussed in the social organization of the squirrels described above, and this is not unintentional. Because male fox squirrels and gray squirrels disperse from their birth sites, kinship does not influence interactions. Furthermore, because male groupings are not cohesive and stable, and many males nest alone, social interactions are less frequent and less important. While females appear integral to the regulation of densities, males remain relatively segregated within both fox squirrel and gray squirrel populations. In fact, the social systems of males and females seem remarkably isolated, with males and females interacting in the field with much less frequency than expected. Same-sex individuals, however, interact both amicably and agonistically more frequently than expected. Males are effectively removed from interactions with females throughout much of the year except for the breeding season; this is the only time in which the sexes truly need to interact. As we mention in Chapter 8 with respect to reproductive behavior, home ranges of male tree squirrels are typically at least 1.8 times greater than those of females despite the lack of a sexual dimorphism in body size (Koprowski 1998). Much of a male's social life is spent roaming widely in search of females.

The social organization of fox squirrels and gray squirrels demonstrates the differences between the sexes and the indifference of the sexes toward each other during most of the year. Female sociality is focused on procuring, defending, and bequeathing a small home range that encompasses quality food and den resources. Male sociality is focused on ephemeral associations during cold weather, establishing and maintaining dominance over rivals, and monitoring females as a fitness-limiting resource that is only available for a few hours each year.

# 10

# Population Ecology

*We see the quick flash of an orange tail across the opening of the den cavity. We are not prepared, for the sight we see next. The female pokes her head out of the nest and attempts to exit the den. Her face is nearly hairless and the eyes are almost completely closed; a yellowish fluid oozes from the surrounding tissue. Gruesome. Her body is only 40 percent covered by fur, with the remaining skin dry and flaking. Suddenly her grip loosens and she plummets to the ground without flailing. Her stiff body lies at the base of the cottonwood tree. She is dead. After transporting her body back to the laboratory, we collect skin scrapings with a scalpel and place them in a potassium hydroxide solution on a microscope slide for examination. Just as we suspected, we see the small burrowing mites that*

*are characteristic of a mange outbreak.*

Over the coming month, nine adult squirrels would disappear, and all 13 litters that were expected to emerge in just a few weeks would die from an outbreak of mange, a condition resulting from high levels of parasitism by mange mites from the genera *Notoedres, Sarcoptes,* or *Cnemidoptes.* The near paralysis, hair loss, and scaling of skin are characteristic signs of an infection (D. L. Allen 1942; Kazacos, Kazacos, and Demaree 1983). This is one of the more dramatic mortality factors found in tree squirrels and perhaps the most lethal. It is only one of the numerous challenges that must be overcome in order to survive in the often harsh environment of the forest. In this chapter, we focus on population level processes and examine the factors, including human, that influence mortality.

To study the ecology of populations, biologists rely heavily on live trapping and marking individuals for recognition at a later time. By trapping with the same degree of effort, in similar locations over time, one can obtain a good record of the lives of individuals within the population. From the massive data sets that often result from these long-term efforts, individual histories of age and reproductive performance can be assembled. These records then permit patterns of reproduction and survival to be assessed. Most often animals are marked with metal ear tags on which a unique number has been stamped. Other methods that have been used include ear tattoos, toe-clipping, fur dye or freeze marking with unique spots on the pelage, colored collars, and more recently the use of subdermal implanted passive integrated transponders (PIT tags). The goal of each method is to mark individuals so they can be recognized. The data that we and others have gleaned from using these techniques have provided us insight into important population processes. Chapter 8 deals with the process of reproduction; in this chapter we focus on other aspects of population ecology.

## SQUIRREL POPULATIONS

Populations of tree squirrels can vary greatly in their size and density (number of individuals per 2.47 acres [individuals/ha]), depending in part on the quality of the habitat. Fox squirrels appear much less dependent on forests than gray squirrels (B. Brown and Batzli 1984; Nixon and Hansen 1987), and viable fox squirrel populations can exist in the fingers of woodland that extend into prairie grasslands. Fox squirrel ranges are expanding along riparian corridors of cottonwood (*Populus deltoides;* Knapp and Swenson 1986) and even fencerows of relatively small trees (Packard 1956) such as Osage orange *(Maclura pomifera).* While driving in central South Dakota in October 1996, we observed a subadult male fox squirrel running on the road and followed him for 0.3 miles (0.5 km). After surveying the surrounding grassland, we determined that the nearest trees from which the animal could have traveled were fully 4.5 miles (7.2 km) away. Chris Smith at Kansas State University and others postulate that the relatively large body size of fox squirrels may be influenced by the antipredator benefits that could be provided while foraging on the ground. Densities in such marginal habitats can be excessively low and even approach zero. However, high-density populations of squirrels are found in isolated urban woodlots. Lafayette Park, located just across the street from the White House in Washington, D.C., has the highest reported density of gray squirrels with >21 squirrels per 2.47 acres (1 ha; Manski, VanDruff, and V. Flyger 1981). From 1968 to 1985 we studied fox squirrels on a campus in the southern Illinois town of Carbondale as part of a long-term project of the Cooperative Wildlife Research Laboratory. The population was located in a protected woodlot, and the density of fox squirrels on this study site reached 12 squirrels per 2.47 acres (1 ha; Koprowski 1985), the record density for this species. The density of squirrels can vary considerably between habitats and regions. Annual fluctuations are also evident, such as at the southern Illinois site; however, long-term average densities tend to remain constant (Gurnell 1987). A negative relationship exists between woodlot size and density: the smaller the woodlot, the greater the density of squirrels. The increase in density probably occurs as a consequence of home range compression and perhaps increased overlap (Don 1983). In addition, mast trees in these edge habitats may exhibit higher seed production due to reduced competition for resources such as light.

Population growth and decline are related to several factors. At the most basic level, only two values need to be known to conclude the trajectory of the population. If the number of additions to a population by birth and immigration exceed the number of losses from the population due to emigration and death, a population is on the increase. Should fortunes change and the relationships be reversed, the population will be in a decline. Increasing populations are characterized by an enlarged proportion of young animals (>50 percent; Barkalow 1967; Mosby 1969;

Thompson 1978a), early reproduction (as early as 5.5 months; Smith and Barkalow 1967), and high annual survivorship of juveniles and adults (>60 percent; Hansen, Nixon, and Havera 1986). Such conditions are common when a flush of young animals results from an abundance of food. In southern Illinois, three major (>50 percent over three years) increases in fox squirrel populations were composed of >50 percent of yearlings or juveniles in each instance, whereas we observed that decreasing populations were composed almost exclusively of only a few adults (Koprowski 1985). Similar age structure has been reported during a population decline of the gray squirrel (Nixon and McClain 1969). Interestingly, sex composition within a population rarely diverges from a 50:50 ratio of males to females, and such changes are not related to population trends (Koprowski 1994a, 1994b). What are the major influences on survivorship that ultimately influence population size?

## PATTERNS OF SURVIVORSHIP

If the currency of success in an organism is the number of offspring that are produced, then longevity can have a profound impact on lifetime reproductive success. Each additional year that an individual survives means one or two more breeding seasons in which to pass on copies of its genes. To understand patterns in survivorship, biologists frequently use a technique called a life table analysis. The life span of each individual is entered into the database, and this accumulation of individual life histories is used to detect the age groups that are most vulnerable and those that are least susceptible to mortality. The pattern that emerged from life table analyses of fox squirrels in southern Illinois that were first captured as juveniles is that survivorship is extremely poor in the first year of life. Thereafter, the probability of survival is relatively high and constant for both males and females. An identical pattern occurs in gray squirrels (Barkalow, Hamilton, and Soots 1970; Mosby 1969; Thompson 1978a). The probability of survival during the first year of life is often well below 50 percent followed by high (>70 percent) survival throughout adulthood (Barkalow, Hamilton, and Soots 1970; Hansen, Nixon, and Havera 1986; Mosby 1969; Thompson 1978a).

Surprisingly, despite numerous long-term studies, no seasonal patterns or weather variables are correlated with survival of juveniles or adults (D. S. Allen 1982; Hansen, Nixon, and Havera 1986; Thompson 1978a). Once a gray squirrel or a fox squirrel survives to adulthood, the probability for numerous reproductive events is high due to relatively high adult survival. In fact, we recorded the maximum ecological longevity for fox squirrels as 12.6 years for females and 8.3 years for males in Illinois (Koprowski, Roseberry, and Klimstra 1988). One male survived for 13 years in captivity (Flyger and Gates 1982a). In gray squirrels, ecological longevity reaches 12.5 years for females and 9.0 years for males (Barkalow and Soots 1975) with life in captivity extending more than 20 years (Barkalow and Shorten 1973). Not too bad for a medium-sized mammal.

## MOVEMENTS BETWEEN POPULATIONS

Another means by which squirrels can enter or exit a population is by movement. Ingress, or immigration, refers to movement into a population; egress and emigration denote movement out of a population. In the chapter on reproduction, we examine the importance of natal philopatry in gray squirrels. What is the fate of natal dispersers, those individuals that leave the area in which they are born? Unfortunately little is known about dispersing individuals because they are remarkably difficult to locate. In Kansas we were able to locate seven males and one female as adults after they had dispersed from their natal area. The distance from natal areas to new home range centers varied from 0.09 miles (0.15 km) for the female to 2.17 miles (3.5 km) for males, with an average dispersal distance of 1.16 miles (1.8 km) for males (Koprowski 1996). These may seem rather impressive distances for a 21-ounce (600-g) mammal; however, the record movement for a fox squirrel is 39.9 miles (64.4 km; D. L. Allen 1943), and a gray squirrel moved 62 miles (100 km) (W. M. Sharp 1959). Individuals have been known to return home from a distance of 2.8 miles (4.5 km) after experimental displacement (Hungerford and Wilder 1941). Such a scale of movement clearly shows a need for studies of movements at a landscape level if we are to truly understand the process of dispersal. The majority of dispersal movements occur in April and May or July through October as young of the year and yearlings move (Kenward 1985; Thompson 1978a). In many popular accounts as well as the scientific literature, the late summer and autumn movements have taken on the quaint name of the "fall shuffle." Aggression also peaks at this time and may be influential in the decision to emigrate (Adams 1984; Thompson 1978a).

Historically, both fox squirrels and gray squirrels have been reported to make massive migrations in which sometimes *millions* of animals were believed to be on the move. Schorger (1949) provides a wonderful summary of these historical accounts from western explorers and naturalists of the 1700s and 1800s. Some migrations reportedly extended over more

As diurnal medium-sized mammals, squirrels are the perfect size for many aerial predators and the major terrestrial carnivores as well. Some species, such as the goshawk *(Accipiter gentilis)*, may make squirrels a staple in their diet (Toyne 1998), but for most species tree squirrels are only an occasional food source. The predictable array of predators such as bobcats, foxes, hawks, and owls have been reported to feed on tree squirrels (Koprowski 1994a, 1994b), as well as more unusual ones, including black rat snakes *(Elaphe obsoleta)* and bullsnakes *(Pituophis melanoleucus)* that climb trees to eat nestlings; timber *(Crotalus horridus)* and diamondback rattlesnakes *(C. admanteus)* that take adults on the ground; and our personal favorite, the largemouth bass *(Micropterus salmoides)* in Florida that was found with an adult squirrel in its stomach. Predators clearly play a role in regulating squirrel populations, but given the prodigious ability for compensatory reproduction in tree squirrels, the role appears to be relatively minimal under most circumstances.

Parasites are another influence on the populations of squirrels. Fox squirrels are known to harbor 55 species of parasites, and gray squirrels have an even more impressive total of 104 species (Koprowski 1994a, 1994b). The diversity of parasites is also quite impressive. Fox squirrels have 5 protozoans, 12 tapeworms, 10 roundworms, 17 mites and ticks, 3 lice, 7 fleas, and 1 botfly. Gray squirrels have 6 protozoans, 2 flukes, 10 tapeworms, 1 acanthocephalan, 23 roundworms, 37 mites and ticks, 7 lice, 17 fleas, and 1 botfly. Though the species richness of parasites in squirrels is impressive, few of these parasites cause pathology. As mentioned at the beginning of this chapter, mange mites can be devastating to squirrels and result in alopecia, paralysis, and death; populations seem particularly susceptible during harsh winters (D. L. Allen 1942, 1943). Perhaps the most visible parasite is the botfly *(Cuterebra emasculator)*, which lays its eggs in the skin of fox and gray squirrels. The larvae, also known as "warbles," parasitize squirrels primarily in the fall. After hatching from the egg, the larvae can grow to 1.17 inches (3 cm) in length and form a cystlike myiasis in the skin usually around the neck or shoulders. The larva continues to move in its cutaneous home and eventually emerges through a small hole to complete its life cycle. Although the pathological consequences are minimal, the larvae are common and infest 5 to 50 percent of the individuals in some populations (Jacobson, Guynn, and Hackett 1979; Jacobson, Hetrick, and Guynn 1981). So common, large, and to many hunters grotesque are botfly larvae that stories of rather incredible effects are often promulgated. Much like the scientific name *emasculator* might suggest, many lay persons incorrectly ascribe the lack of pendant testes found in some males to the wanderings of the botfly larvae; we now know that the abdominal condition of testes is common outside of the breeding season and explains this phenomenon.

Squirrels also have other afflictions that can lead to their demise. We have documented the deaths of two juvenile fox squirrels from rather unusual causes. One juvenile male died from complications related to a massive granuloma on its liver that increased the size of the liver by 50 percent. Another juvenile male was found in a honeybee *(Apis mellifera)* hive at the base of his nest tree on the first day in which he was known to have left the nest. He had apparently stumbled into the hive and was covered with what we estimated to be several hundred stings. Accidental road kills, fatal falls (Thompson 1976), congenital narrowing of the aorta (Phillips and Dubielzig 1980), tumors from pox virus (Flyger and Gates 1982a), and cancerous mammary tumors (Shivaprasad, Sundberg, and Ely 1984) are other unusual causes of death in squirrels. In addition, although incidences are extremely rare, several diseases that are important to humans have also been detected, including toxoplasmosis (Roher et al. 1981), tularemia, plague, encephalitis, ringworm, leptospirosis (Flyger and Gates 1982a), and the rare case of rabies (Cappucci, Emmons, and Sampson 1972; Pritchett 1938). Incidences of direct natural transfer to humans of any of these diseases are extraordinarily rare, and generally speaking squirrels are relatively free of human pathogens.

# Appendix: An Overview of the Tree Squirrels of North America

Although we have devoted the majority of this book to fox squirrels and gray squirrels—our personal research focus and two of the most common species of tree squirrels in North America—we often refer to other species. Here we provide a brief account of all the species of tree squirrels native to North America north of Mexico, beginning with the eastern gray squirrel and the fox squirrel. Range maps for all but two of these species (the Arizona gray squirrel and Mexican fox squirrel) are shown in Figure A.1.

## EASTERN GRAY SQUIRREL (*SCIURUS CAROLINENSIS*)

The eastern gray squirrel—referred to as the gray squirrel in this book—is a medium-sized tree squirrel (10.5–24.5 ounces [300–700 g]) common throughout mature deciduous forests of the eastern United States (see Figure 1.1). Due to introductions, the species also has become established in several areas of the western United States and Canada (Flyger and Gates 1982a), as well as England, Italy, Scotland, and South Africa (Millar 1980; Lloyd 1983; Koprowski 1994a; Currado 1998). The species is predominantly grizzled gray with a whitish belly, but sometimes has a tawny or rust wash throughout the fur. Both melanism, which results in completely black animals, and albinism occur throughout the species' range, although melanistic populations are more common in the north. The "black squirrels" of northern Michigan and the all-white squirrels of Olney, Illinois, are simply color variants of the eastern gray squirrel (Koprowski 1994a).

The gray squirrel is noted for its habit of storing food in individual, widely spaced cache sites just below the ground surface (Vander Wall 1990; Steele and Smallwood 1994). Known as scatterhoarding, this behavior is a critical survival strategy that allows gray squirrels to remain active through the winter and spring. In addition to storing pine seeds, acorns, beechnuts, walnuts, and hickory nuts, gray squirrels also feed on a variety of other plant and animal material, especially during periods of food shortage in winter and summer. It is not uncommon for the gray squirrels to rob bird nests for eggs or young or to eat insects to obtain limiting minerals. And depending on the habitat or season, they may also feed heavily

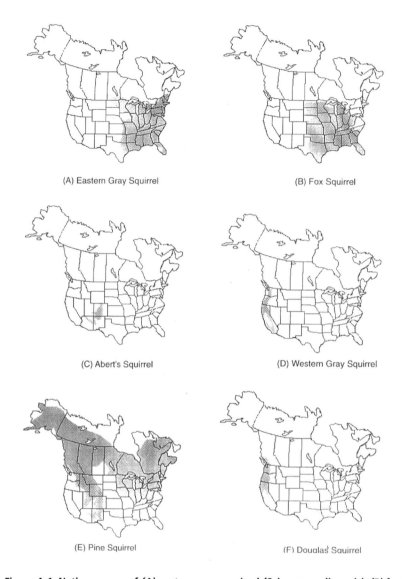

**Figure A.1. Native ranges of (A)** eastern gray squirrel *(Sciurus carolinensis);* **(B)** fox squirrel *(S. niger);* **(C)** Abert's squirrel *(S. aberti);* **(D)** western gray squirrel *(S. griseus);* **(E)** pine squirrel *(Tamiasciurus hudsonicus);* and **(F)** Douglas' squirrel *(T. douglasii).* **(Maps drawn by B. Sefchik, courtesy of M. A. Steele)**

on tree buds and flowers as well as bark and cambium (inner bark), which they strip from the trunks and limbs of trees (Kenward 1983).

Although some authors consider the gray squirrel asocial, several studies suggest a complex social system for gray squirrels (Thompson 1978a, 1978b; Koprowski 1991b, 1993a). Group nesting is common, and amicable behavior is directed toward close kin (Koprowski 1991b). Males are dominant over females; adults are dominant over subadults (immature individuals); and pregnant and lactating females are solitary and aggressive toward all (Koprowski 1994a). Social interactions are facilitated by scent marking from oral glands (Koprowski 1993c) and vocalizations (Gurnell 1987).

Home ranges of gray squirrels overlap considerably, and there is no evidence of true territoriality in this species (Don 1983) although core areas are sometimes defended (Kenward 1985). Home range size is usually <12.35 acres (5 ha; Flyger and Gates 1982a), and densities of gray squirrels range from <3 squirrels per 2.47 acres (1 ha) to sometimes well over 20 per 2.47 acres (1 ha) in urban parks or on college campuses (Manski, VanDruff, and Flyger 1981). Gray squirrels are also noted for migrations that may extend over large geographic areas (Schorger 1949; Flyger and Levin 1969). Such events most likely represent widespread, localized dispersal in the face of autumn food shortages when they occur.

Gray squirrels nest in tree hollows, especially in colder months, and in nests that they construct of leaves, twigs, and shredded plant material (Flyger and Gates 1982a; Koprowski 1996). Breeding occurs regularly between December and February and again during the summer (L. G. Brown and Yeager 1945). From 1 to 5 young are born, pink and hairless, 44 days after conception. Development of the young occurs over 8 stages, and weaning usually takes place 70 days after birth. Gray squirrels can live up to 12 years in the wild, but annual mortality rates are quite high in the first year of life (Koprowski 1994a).

Selected references for the gray squirrel are L. G. Brown and Yeager 1945; Currado 1998; Don 1983; Flyger and Gates 1982a; and Levin 1969; Gurnell 1987; Kenward 1985; Koprowski 1991b, 1993a, 1993c, 1994a, 1996; Lloyd 1983; Manski, VanDruff, and Flyger 1981; Merritt 1987; Millar 1980; Nixon and McClain 1975; Schorger 1949; Steele and Smallwood 1994; D. Thompson 1978a, 1978b; Thompson and Thompson 1980; and Vander Wall 1990.

## THE FOX SQUIRREL (*SCIURUS NIGER*)

The fox squirrel is a medium- to large-sized tree squirrel (19.25–31.50 ounces [550–900 g]) common throughout open and mature deciduous and mixed forests of the midwestern and eastern United States and extending into the Prairie provinces of Canada and to northern Mexico (see Figure 1.2). Due to introductions, the species is also established in the western United States including New Mexico, Colorado, Washington, Montana, Oregon, Idaho, North Dakota, Texas, and California, and into Ontario, Canada (Flyger and Gates 1982a). Fox squirrels are quite variable in coloration depending on which of the 10 subspecies is being viewed. Most are predominantly grizzled brown to gray on the back with an orange to whitish underside. Partial and total melanism occur throughout the range but are most common in southern localities, a trend opposite that of gray squirrels (Kiltie 1989; Koprowski 1994b).

A classic scatterhoarder, the fox squirrel is noted for its habit of storing food just belowground in individual, widely spaced cache sites (Cahalane 1942; Stapanian and Smith 1984; Vander Wall 1990). This characteristic behavior is an important survival strategy that permits fox squirrels to be active throughout the winter and forgo hibernation. Fox squirrels have a diverse diet that includes the seeds of pines, oaks, beech, walnut, pecan, and hickories as well as insects, eggs, birds, and fish (Koprowski 1994b).

The social system of males and females is relatively separate (Koprowski 1996). Communal nesting occurs but nesting groups are typically unisexual in composition (Koprowski 1996). Like gray squirrels, males dominate females; adults are dominant over subadults; and pregnant and lactating females are solitary and aggressive toward all (Koprowski 1998). Scent markings from oral glands (Benson 1980; Koprowski 1993d) and vocalizations (Zelley 1971) facilitate social interactions.

Fox squirrel home ranges overlap greatly, although core areas are defended by resident females (Havera and Nixon 1978b). The removal of adult females from a population results in increased ingress and survival, suggesting that females play an important role in the regulation of density (Hansen, Nixon, and Havera 1986). Home range size is usually <19.76 acres (8 ha; Flyger and Gates 1982a); however, in many of the uncommon subspecies in the southeastern United States home ranges are >37.1 acres (15 ha; Koprowski 1994b). At least four subspecies in the southeastern United States receive some legal protection. Densities are often well below 1.0 individual per 2.47 acres (1 ha) in these regions; densities in the midwestern United States may reach 12 squirrels per 2.47 acres (1 ha; Koprowski 1985, 1994b).

Fox squirrels nest in cavities in tree hollows and in nests they construct of leaves, twigs, and shredded material (Flyger and Gates 1982a; Stoddard 1919). Most breeding occurs between December and January and again in late spring or early summer (L. G. Brown and Yeager 1945). From 1 to 7 young are born, pink and hairless, 44 or 45 days after a mating bout; young leave the nest at about 8 weeks of age and are weaned by 10 weeks (Koprowski 1994b). Juvenile mortality is exceptionally high during the first year of life but is followed by relatively high survivorship in adulthood (Hansen, Nixon, and Havera 1986). Fox squirrels can live up to 12.5 years in the wild (Koprowski, Roseberry, and Klimstra 1988).

Selected references for the fox squirrel are Benson 1980; L. G. Brown and Yeager 1945; Cahalane 1942; Flyger and Gates 1982a; Gurnell 1987; Hansen, Nixon, and Havera 1986; Havera and Nixon 1978b; Kiltie 1989, 1992; Koprowski 1985, 1993d, 1994b, 1996, 1998; Koprowski, Roseberry, and Klimstra 1988;

Nixon and McClain 1975; Stapanian and Smith 1978, 1984; Stoddard 1919; Vander Wall 1990; Weigl, Steele, et al. 1989; and Zelley 1971.

## WESTERN GRAY SQUIRREL (*SCIURUS GRISEUS*)

Western gray squirrels are large-bodied tree squirrels, with adults ranging from 24.5 ounces to more than 35.0 ounces (700–1,000 g; Carraway and Verts 1994). Aptly named with the specific epithet *griseus,* which means "gray," this squirrel is a silvery gray, grizzled on its back with black from nose to tail. The local nickname in Oregon is the "silver gray squirrel." This squirrel lacks the brown coloring that is often found in the coats of the eastern gray squirrel. The underside of the body is a creamy white that stands in stark contrast to the back and sides. Found in the western mountains of Washington, Oregon, and California, this species appears to thrive in mature mixed oak forests on the western "rainy" side of the mountains, as well as in pine-dominated forests found on the dry eastern sides of the mountains of the western coast of North America (Carraway and Verts 1994). The species is generally absent from pure conifer stands.

Western grays feed heavily on tree seeds, including various oaks, pines, and firs throughout their range; the species also eats a variety of fungi and insects (Stienecker 1977; Stienecker and Browning 1970). Nesting occurs in cavities as well as the leafy bolus nests in branches (Ingles 1947). Sociality of western gray squirrels is not well understood; however, a well-defined dominance hierarchy occurs at concentrated food sites (Cross 1969). The action-packed, half-day mating chases similar to those found in other tree squirrels occur primarily in December and January, with young appearing outside the nest in late April or May. Litter sizes range from one to five young, and the vast majority of females produce only a single litter each year (Carraway and Verts 1994). Young mature between one and two years of age. One individual in captivity lived at least 11 years (Ross 1930). Western grays range over areas from 1.95 to 13.73 acres (0.79–5.56 ha; Carraway and Verts 1994; Cross 1969); little is known of their sociality and their proclivity to overlap. At a concentrated food source, Stephen Cross (1969) noted a relatively clear dominance hierarchy among residents. Western gray squirrels are hunted for food in Oregon and California (Carraway and Verts 1994). The Puget Trough population in Washington is imperiled and the species receives legal protection as threatened wildlife (Ryan and Carey 1995).

Selected references for the western gray squirrel are Carraway and Verts 1994; Crase 1973; Cross 1969; Ingles 1947; Maser, Mate, and Franklin 1981; Ross 1930; Ryan and Carey 1995; Stienecker 1977; Stienecker and Browning 1970; and Verts and Carraway 1998.

## ABERT'S SQUIRREL (*SCIURUS ABERTI*)

The Abert's squirrel is a large-bodied (21.0–31.5 ounces [600–900 g]) tree squirrel found in western North America. *Sciurus aberti* is also commonly known as the tassel-eared squirrel in recognition of its conspicuous ears that are adorned with lengthy tufts of hair, especially in winter (Keith 1965). The typical Abert's squirrel is a light to slate gray on the back with a brilliant white underside (Nash and Seaman 1977); however, complete and partial black, or melanic, forms are known (Allred 1995; Ramey and Nash 1971, 1976) from throughout the species range in the lower Rocky Mountains from Wyoming, Utah, Colorado, New Mexico, and Arizona, and extending southward into Mexico (Nash and Seaman 1977). Though originally considered a separate species, the Kaibab squirrel found on the north rim of the Grand Canyon in Arizona is now recognized as a subspecies of the Abert's squirrel (J. Hall 1981). Despite the Kaibab squirrel's black underside and almost fully white tail, the genetic differences between this isolated population and other nearby populations are minimal (Lamb, Jones, and Wettstein 1997; Wettstein et al. 1995).

Abert's squirrels feed heavily on the tissues of ponderosa pine *(Pinus ponderosa)*. Although this squirrel eats a variety of fungi and tree seeds (Keith 1965; D. Brown 1984), in many populations Abert's squirrels depend heavily on the cambium (inner bark) of ponderosa pine. The preference of Abert's squirrels for certain ponderosa pine trees is related to the chemical characteristics of the tree (M. Snyder and Linhart 1994, 1998). A tell-tale sign of this tree squirrel is clippings of ponderosa pine twigs (3.1–3.9 inches [8–10 cm] long) strewn about the ground (Keith 1965). The considerable herbivory of Abert's squirrels upon ponderosa pines can significantly decrease cone production (Allred and Gaud 1994; Allred, Gaud, and States 1994). Large dreys (leaf nests) are often found in the branches of trees or in witches' broom caused by mistletoe infections (Farentinos 1972a; Halloran and Bekoff 1994). Mating chases for Abert's squirrels are similar to those described for other tree squirrels (Farentinos 1972c); most mating seems to occur in February and March, with young born 40 to 46 days later (Farentinos 1972b; Keith 1965). Young typically mature at 1 to 2 years of age (Allred and Pogany 1996). Although found predominantly in forests dominated by ponderosa pine, Abert's squirrels also occur in mixed forests (D. Brown 1984; Nash and Seaman 1977). Home ranges in these habitats average 17.29 to 19.76 acres (7–8 ha) during summer but are greatly reduced (to about 4.94 acres [2 ha]) in the heavy snows of winter (Keith 1965; Nash and Seaman 1977). Abert's squirrels are hunted and have been released in many areas thereby increasing the range of the species (D. Brown 1984).

Selected references for the Abert's squirrel are Allred 1995; Allred and Gaud 1994, 1999; Allred, Gaud, and States 1994; Allred and Pogany 1996; D. Brown 1984; Farentinos 1972a, 1972b, 1972c, 1974; J. Hall 1981; Halloran and Bekoff 1994, 1995; Keith 1965; Lamb, Jones, and Wettstein 1997; Nash and Seaman 1977; Ramey and Nash 1971, 1976; M. Snyder and Linhart 1994, 1998; and Wettstein et al. 1995.

# PINE AND DOUGLAS' SQUIRRELS (*TAMIASCIURUS HUDSONICUS* AND *T. DOUGLASII*)

*Note:* Designation of *T. mearnsi* as a separate species from *T. douglasii* based on comparisons of size and shape of the skull (Lindsay 1981; Hoffman et al. 1993) is now in question due to recent genetic comparisons (Arbogast, Browne, and Weigl in press). We therefore recognize only two species of *Tamiasciurus*.

The pine and Douglas' squirrels are two similar species of diurnal tree squirrels that are easily recognized by their small body size (<10.5 ounces [300 g]), deep reddish or chestnut coloration, white eye ring, and aggressive, territorial behavior (J. Hall 1981; Flyger and Gates 1982b; Gurnell 1987). In the Pacific Northwest, where the range of the two species overlap, they are distinguished by color of pelage; the belly of *T. douglasii* is reddish or rust colored, whereas that of *T. hudsonicus* is white or faint yellow. Tail hairs of the Douglas' squirrel have white tips with a black band; those of the pine squirrel are rust colored with black bands. The pine squirrel ranges across most of boreal Canada and the northern United States southward across the mountains of the western and southwestern United States and the Appalachian Mountains of the East. The range of Douglas' squirrel is limited to the Pacific Coast and the Sierra Nevada and Cascade ranges of the Pacific Northwest (Steele 1998, 1999). A zone of contact, where the two species are sympatric, occurs in southern British Columbia, northwestern Washington, and eastern Oregon (C. Smith 1965, 1970, 1981; Lindsay 1981).

Both species commonly inhabit coniferous forests, although hardwood forests often support pine squirrels, especially in the southern portion of their range. Both species are noted for their territorial behavior. Territories, which are centered on the midden or larderhoard (of conifer cones), usually average less than 2.47 acres (1 ha) in size and are actively defended by individuals against conspecifics and a range of other competitors (C. Smith 1968, 1981; Rusch and Reeder 1978). A complex array of vocalizations are an integral part of territorial defense and other social interactions (C. Smith 1978). Territory size appears to be inversely related to food abundance, and territory quality is closely linked to survival. Bequeathal of territories by mothers to young at the time of dispersal is important for juvenile survival (K. Price 1992; K. Price and Boutin 1993; Larsen and Boutin 1994).

Like other tree squirrels, pine and Douglas' squirrels prey on a variety of plant and animal material and are even known to eat other squirrels on occasion (Steele 1998). However, throughout most of their range they specialize on the seeds of conifer cones, which they stockpile in centralized larderhoards. Both species are highly efficient at harvesting cones, making careful decisions about the tree species, trees, and cones on which to feed. Cone and tree selection are based on the energy per cone, cone hardness, the arrangement of cones on branches, and how far from the midden cones are harvested (C. Smith 1970; Elliot 1974, 1988).

Female pine and Douglas' squirrels are receptive on one day during the reproductive period. Up to 2 litters per year are produced: one in spring and another in late summer. Gestation is 33 days, and litter sizes vary from 1 to 8 young per litter. Young are born hairless, are active outside the nest by 7 weeks, and are weaned by 8 weeks (Steele 1998, 1999).

Selected references for the pine squirrel and the Douglas' squirrel are Ackerman and Weigl 1970; Aleksiuk 1970; Arbogast, Browne, and Weigl in press; Bakko 1975; Boutin and Larsen 1993; Boutin and Schweiger 1988; Boutin, Tooze, and Price 1993; Bovet 1984, 1991; Clarkson and Ferguson 1969; D. W. Davis 1969; D. W. Davis and Sealander 1971; Dempsey and Keppie 1993; Dippner and Armington 1971; Dolbeer 1973; Elliot 1974, 1988; Fancy 1980; Ferner 1974; Ferron 1975, 1981; Ferron and Prescott 1977; Ferron, Ouellet, and Lemay 1986; Flyger and Gates 1982b; Gurnell 1984; J. Hall 1981; Halvorson and Engeman 1983; Heaney 1984; Heinrich 1992; Hoffman et al. 1993; Hurly 1987; Hurly and Robertson 1986; Kemp and Keith 1970; Kilham 1954; Klugh 1927; Koford 1992; Kramm, Maki, and Glime 1975, 1985, 1990; Larsen and Boutin 1994; Layne 1954a; Lindsay 1981, 1982; Mahan and Yahner 1992; Mahan, Yahner, and Stover 1994; Mossman 1940; B. Nelson 1945; Obbard 1987; Pauls 1978, 1979; K. Price 1992; K. Price and Boutin 1993; K. Price, Broughton, et al. 1986; Pruitt and Lucier 1958; Rausch and Tiner 1948; Reitsma, Holmes, and Sherry 1990; Reynolds 1985a; Riege 1991; Rothwell 1979; Rusch and Reeder 1978; Sherburne and Bissonette 1993; A. Smith and Mannan 1994; C. Smith 1965, 1968, 1970, 1978, 1981; M. Smith 1968; Steele 1998, 1999; Sullivan 1990; Sullivan and Klenner 1992, 1993; Sullivan and Vyse 1987; Svihla 1930; Weigl and Hanson 1980; Wunder and Morrison 1974; and Yahner 1980, 1986, 1987.

## ARIZONA GRAY SQUIRREL (*SCIURUS ARIZONENSIS*)

Arizona gray squirrels are relatively large-bodied tree squirrels (about 21.8 ounces [624 g]; D. Brown 1984) and are restricted almost exclusively to the forested mountains of Arizona, although the range of the species extends barely into New Mexico and northern Sonora, Mexico (Best and Riedel 1995; Hoffmeister 1986). The grizzled gray back and tail of the Arizona gray squirrel contrasts with the tawny underside (Best and Riedel 1995). Arizona grays are poorly studied and little is known of their ecology. Like most tree squirrels they appear to feed heavily on the mast (fruits and seeds) of oaks, pines, firs, junipers, and walnuts (D. Brown 1984). Truffles, mushrooms, and other fungi provide a substantial dietary supplement to tree seeds (D. Brown 1984; Hoffmeister 1986). Cavity nests are used predominantly for nurseries; however, conspicuous bolus leaf nests are constructed in the branches of trees (D. Brown 1984; Hoffmeister 1986). Females can reproduce after their first birthday, with peak breeding activity occurring in April and May; litters that average 3.1 individuals per litter are reported from June through October (Best and Riedel 1995; D. Brown 1984). Nesting groups do occur (Hoffmeister 1986). Beyond the fact that the Arizona gray squirrel must range widely to find food in hostile oak-pine scrub little else is known about the movements of this uncommon squirrel (Best and Riedel 1995; D. Brown 1984). The population in the Santa Catalina Mountains near Tucson, Arizona, is considered to be imperiled (Best and Riedel 1995).

Selected references for the Arizona gray squirrel are Best and Riedel 1995; D. Brown 1984; Hobbs 1980; Hoffmeister 1986; Lange 1960; and Theobald 1983.

## MEXICAN FOX SQUIRREL (*SCIURUS NAYARITENSIS*)

Mexican fox squirrels are strikingly colored, large-bodied tree squirrels of about 24.5 ounces (700 g; D. Brown 1984). Found only in the Chiricahua Mountains of extreme southeast Arizona within the United States, the grizzled brown-and-black back hides a bright yellow to rust-colored underside (Best 1995; Hoffmeister 1986). The tail is substantial and generally black, frosted with a creamy white or buff (Best 1995). Mexican fox squirrels are found in the montane islands that rise from the Sonoran and Chihuahuan deserts of Mexico (Hoffmeister 1986) with oak-pine forests apparently the preferred habitat (D. Brown 1984). Tree seeds from oaks, pines, walnuts, and junipers, in addition to fungi, are the most common foods of *Sciurus nayaritensis* (D. Brown 1984). Dreys and tree cavities are used for nesting (Hoffmeister 1986), and we have observed as many as six individuals nesting together. From our studies, nursing females appear to use nest cavities in trees almost exclusively. No evidence exists to indicate that females can produce two litters in a single year as occurs in some of the other tree squirrels. Most litters in Arizona are born in April (Cahalane 1939); young emerge in May and June, suggesting a birthing season about the same length as other tree squirrels. We have, however, observed six mating chases in July, which indicates an extended breeding season and highlights just how little is known about this uncommon tree squirrel. In nearly six years of study, we have never observed a litter size larger than two, although two hunted females were reported to carry three embryos (Anderson 1972; Mearns 1907). The Mexican fox squirrel is protected in the United States due to its uncertain conservation status (Best 1995).

Selected references for the Mexican fox squirrel are Anderson 1972; Best 1995; D. Brown 1984; Cahalane 1939; Hobbs 1980; Hoifmeister 1986; Kneeland, Koprowski, and Corse 1995; Lee and Hoffmeister 1963; and Mearns 1907.

# References

These references include literature cited in the text and the appendix and additional relevant literature.

Abbott, H. G, and T. F. Quink. 1970. Ecology of eastern white pine seed caches made by small forest mammals. *Ecology* 51:271–278.

Abbott, R. J., G. P. Bevercombe, and D. M. Rayner. 1977. Sooty bark disease of sycamore and the grey squirrel. *Transactions of the British Mycological Society* 69:507–508.

Abrahamson, Warren G. 1989. *Plant-animal interactions*. New York: McGraw-Hill, 391 p.

Ackerman, R., and P. D. Weigl. 1970. Dominance relations of red and gray squirrels. *Ecology* 51:332–334.

Adam, C. I. G. 1984. The fox squirrel in Saskatchewan. *Blue Jay* 42:241–246.

Adams, C. E. 1976. Measurement and characteristics of fox squirrel, *Sciurus niger rufiventer*, home ranges. *American Midland Naturalist* 95:211–215.

———. 1984. Diversity in fox squirrel spatial relationships and activity rhythms. *Texas Journal of Science* 36:197–205.

Adler, B., Jr. 1988. *Outwitting squirrels*. Chicago: Chicago Review Press, 169 p.

Ahl, A. S. 1987. Relationship of vibrissal length and habits in the Sciuridae. *Journal of Mammalogy* 68:848–853.

Aleksiuk, M. 1970. The occurrence of brown adipose tissue in the adult red squirrel *(Tamiasciurus hudsonicus). Canadian Journal of Zoology* 48:188–189.

Allan, P. F. 1935. Bone cache of a gray squirrel. *Journal of Mammalogy* 16:326.

Allen, A.W. 1982. *Habitat suitability index models: Gray squirrel*. Washington, D.C.: U.S. Department of the Interior, Fish and Wildlife Service, FWS/OBS-82/10.19, 11 p.

Allen, D. L. 1942. Populations and habits of the fox squirrel in Allegan County, Michigan. *American Midland Naturalist* 27:338–379.

———. 1943. Michigan fox squirrel management. *Michigan Department of Conservation Game Division Publication* 100:1–404.

Allen, D. S. 1982. Social status and survivorship in a population of eastern gray squirrels *(Sciurus carolinensis)*. Ph.D. diss., Ohio State University, Columbus, 132 p.

Allen, D. S., and W. P. Aspey. 1986. Determinants of social dominance in eastern gray squirrels *(Sciurus carolinensis):* A quantitative assessment. *Animal Behaviour* 34:81–89.

Allred, W. S. 1995. Black-bellied form of an Abert's squirrel *(Sciurus aberti aberti)* from the San Francisco Peaks area, Arizona. *Southwestern Naturalist* 40:420–420.

Allred, W. S., and W. S. Gaud. 1994. Effects of Abert's squirrel herbivory on foliage and nitrogen losses in ponderosa pine. *Southwestern Naturalist* 39:350–353.

———. 1999. Abert's squirrel *(Sciurus aberti)* as a soil excavator. *Southwestern Naturalist* 44:88–89.

Allred, W. S., W. S. Gaud, and J. S. States. 1994. Effects of herbivory by Abert's squirrels *(Sciurus aberti)* on cone crops of Ponderosa pine. *Journal of Mammalogy* 75:700–703.

Allred, W. S., and G. Pogany. 1996. Early estrus in a female Abert's squirrel *(Sciurus aberti aberti)*. *Southwestern Naturalist* 41:90–91.

Anderson, S. 1972. Mammals of Chihuahua: Taxonomy and distribution. *Bulletin of the American Museum of Natural History* 148:149–410.

Applegate, R. D., and R. C. McCord. 1974. A description of swimming in the fox squirrel. *American Midland Naturalist* 92:255.

Arbogast, B. S., R. A. Browne, and P. D. Weigl. In press. Evolutionary genetics and Pleistocene biogeography of North American tree squirrels. *Journal of Mammalogy.*

Arden, G. B., and P. H. Silver. 1962. Visual thresholds and spectral sensitivity of the grey squirrel *(Sciurus carolinensis leucotis)*. *Journal of Physiology* 163:540–557.

Armitage, K. B. 1989. The function of kin discrimination. *Ethology, Ecology, and Evolution* 1:111–121.

Armitage, K. B., and K. S. Harris. 1982. Spatial patterning in sympatric populations of fox and gray squirrels. *American Midland Naturalist* 108:389–397.

Atkeson, T. Z., and L. Givens. 1951. Gray squirrel parasitism by heel fly larvae. *Journal of Wildlife Management* 15:105–106.

Audubon, J. J., and J. Bachman. 1849. *The viviparous quadrupeds of North America.* New York: V. G. Audubon, 383 p.

Bachman, J. 1839. Monograph of the species of squirrel inhabiting North America. *Proceedings of the Zoological Society of London* 1838:85–103.

Baker, R. H. 1944. An ecological study of tree squirrels in eastern Texas. *Journal of Mammalogy* 25:8–23.

Bakken, A. 1952. Interrelationship of *Sciurus carolinensis* and *Sciurus niger* in mixed populations. Ph.D. diss., University of Michigan, Ann Arbor, 252 p.

———. 1959. Behavior of gray squirrels. *Proceedings of the Southeastern Association of Game and Fish Commissioners* 13:393–406.

Bakko, E. B. 1975. A field water balance study of gray squirrels *(Sciurus carolinensis)* and red squirrels *(Tamiasciurus hudsonicus)*. *Comparative Biochemistry and Physiology* 51A:759–768.

Bangs, O. 1896. A review of the squirrels of eastern North America. *Proceedings of the Biological Society of Washington* 10:145–167.

Barkalow, F. S., Jr. 1956. *Sciurus niger cinereus* Linne neotype designation. *Proceedings of the Biological Society of Washington* 69:13–20.

———. 1967. A record gray squirrel litter. *Journal of Mammalogy* 48:141.

Barkalow, F. S., Jr., R. B. Hamilton, and R. F. Soots, Jr. 1970. The vital statistics of an unexploited gray squirrel population. *Journal of Wildlife Management* 34:489–500.

Barkalow, F. S., Jr., and M. Shorten. 1973. *The world of the gray squirrel.* Philadelphia: J. B. Lippincott, 160 p.

Barkalow, F. S., Jr., and R. F. Soots, Jr. 1965a. An analysis of the effect of artificial nest boxes on a gray squirrel population. *Transactions of the North American Wildlife and Natural Resource Conference* 30:349–360.

———. 1965b. An improved squirrel nest box for ecological and management studies. *Journal of Wildlife Management* 29:679–684.

———. 1975. Life span and reproductive longevity of the gray squirrel, *Sciurus c. carolinensis* Gmelin. *Journal of Mammalogy* 56:522–524.

Barnett, R. J. 1977. Bergmann's rule and variation in structures related to feeding in the gray squirrel. *Evolution* 31:538–545.

Barr, J. P. 1974. Certain aspects of an eastern gray squirrel *(Sciurus carolinensis)* population in a multiple-use woodlot. Master's thesis, Tennessee Technological University, Cookesville, 66 p.

Barrier, M. J., and F. S. Barkalow, Jr. 1967. A rapid technique for aging gray squirrels in winter pelage. *Journal of Wildlife Management* 31:714–719.

Barry, W. J. 1972. Methoxyflurane: An anesthetic for field and laboratory use on squirrels. *Journal of Wildlife Management* 36:992–993.

Baumgartner, L. L. 1939a. Foods of the fox squirrel in Ohio. *Transactions of the North American Fish and Wildlife Conference* 4:479–484.

———. 1939b. Fox squirrel dens. *Journal of Mammalogy* 20:456–465.

———. 1940. Trapping, handling, and marking fox squirrels. *Journal of Wildlife Management* 4:444–450.

———. 1943a. Fox squirrels in Ohio. *Journal of Wildlife Management* 7:193–202.

———. 1943b. Pelage studies of fox squirrels *(Sciurus niger rufiventer)*. *American Midland Naturalist* 29:588–590.

Baumgras, P. 1944. Experimental feeding of captive fox squirrels. *Journal of Wildlife Management* 8:296–300.

Beale, D. M. 1962. Growth of the eye lens in relation to age in fox squirrels. *Journal of Wildlife Management* 26:208–211.

Bell, J. F., and J. R. Reilly. 1981. Tularemia. In *Infectious diseases of wild mammals,* ed. J. W. Davis, L. H. Karstad, and D. O. Trainer, 213–231. Ames: Iowa State University Press, 446 p.

Bendel, P. R., and G. D. Therres. 1994. Movements, site fidelity, and survival of Delmarva fox squirrels following translocation. *American Midland Naturalist* 132:227–233.

Bennett, B. 1987 Measures of relatedness. *Ethology* 74:219–236.

Benson, B. N. 1980. Dominance relationships, mating behaviour, and scent marking in fox squirrels *(Sciurus niger)*. *Mammalia* 44:143–160.

Bernard, R. J. 1972. Social organization of the western fox squirrel. Master's thesis, Michigan State University, East Lansing, 41 p.

Berry, L. A. 1975. The influence of social hierarchy on population density in eastern gray squirrels. Master's thesis, West Virginia University, Morgantown, 53 p.

Berry, L. A., E. D. Michael, and H. R. Sanderson. 1978. Effect of population density on captive gray squirrels. *Transactions of the Northeast Section of the Wildlife Society* 35:53–59.

Bertolino, S., I. Currado, and P. J. Mazzoglio. 1999. Finlayson's (variable) squirrel *Callosciurus finlaysoni* in Italy. *Mammalia* 63:522–525.

Bertram, B. C. R., and D. P. Moltu. 1986. Reintroducing red squirrels into Regent's Park. *Mammal Review* 16:81–88.

Best, T. L. 1995. *Sciurus nayaritensis. Mammalian Species* 492:1–5.

Best, T. L., and S. Riedel. 1995. *Sciurus arizonensis. Mammalian Species* 496:1–5.

Black, C. C. 1963. A review of the North American Tertiary Sciuridae. *Bulletin of the Museum of Comparative Zoology* 130:109–248.

———. 1972. Holarctic evolution and dispersal of squirrels (Rodentia: Sciuridae). *Evolutionary Biology* 6:305–322.

Blakeslee, B., G. H. Jacobs, and M. E. McCourt. 1985. Anisotropy in the preferred directions and visual field location of directionally-selective optic nerve fibers in the gray squirrel. *Vision Research* 25:615–618.

Bland, M. E. 1977. Daily and seasonal activity patterns in the eastern gray squirrel. Ph.D. diss., University of Minnesota, Minneapolis, 221 p.

Bolls, N. J., and J. R. Perfect. 1972. Summer resting metabolic rate of the gray squirrel. *Physiological Zoology* 45:54–59.

Bosc, L. A. G. 1802. Note sur l'ecureuil capistrate de la Caroline. *Annales du Museum d'Histoire Naturelle* 1:281–284.

Bouffard, S. H. 1982. Tree squirrels. In *CRC handbook of census methods for terrestrial vertebrates,* ed. D. E. Davis, 160–161. Boca Raton, Fla.: CRC Press, 397 p.

Bouffard, S. H., and D. Hein. 1978. Census methods for eastern gray squirrels. *Journal of Wildlife Management* 42:550–557.

Boulware, J. T. 1941. Eucalyptus tree utilized by fox squirrel in California. *American Midland Naturalist* 26:696–697.

Boutin, S., and K. W. Larsen. 1993. Does food availability affect growth and survival of males and females differently in a promiscuous small mammal, *Tamiasciurus hudsonicus? Journal of Animal Ecology* 62:364–370.

Boutin, S., and S. Schweiger. 1988. Manipulation of intruder pressure in red squirrels *(Tamiasciurus hudsonicus)*: Effects on territory size and acquisition. *Canadian Journal of Zoology* 66:2270–2274.

Boutin, S., Z. Tooze, and K. Price. 1993. Post-breeding dispersal by female red squirrels *(Tamiasciurus hudsonicus)*: The effect of local vacancies. *Behavioral Ecology* 4:151–155.

Bovet, J. 1984. Strategies of homing behavior in the red squirrel, *Tamiasciurus hudsonicus*. *Behavioral Ecology and Sociobiology* 16:81–88.

———. 1991. Route-based visual information has limited effect on the homing performance of red squirrels, *Tamiasciurus hudsonicus*. *Ethology* 87:59–65.

Bowers, J. R., and G. L. Kirkland, Jr. 1968. Observations on an anomalous fox squirrel. *Journal of Mammalogy* 49:345–347.

Bowers, M. A., and B. Breland. 1996. Foraging of gray squirrels on an urban-rural gradient: Use of the GUD to assess anthropogenic impact. *Ecological Applications* 6:1135–1142.

Brady, J. T. 1972. The behavior of displaced gray squirrels. Master's thesis, Virginia Polytechnic Institute and State University, Blacksburg, 69 p.

Brand, G. J., S. R. Shifley, and L. F. Ohmann. 1986. Linking wildlife and vegetation models to forecast the effects of management. In *Wildlife 2000: Modeling habitat relationships of terrestrial vertebrates*, ed. J. Verner, M. L. Morrison, and C. J. Ralph, 383–387. Madison: University of Wisconsin Press, 470 p.

Brauer, A., and A. Dusing. 1961. Seasonal cycles and breeding seasons of the gray squirrel, *Sciurus carolinensis* Gmelin. *Transactions of the Kentucky Academy of Science* 22:16–27.

Britt, D., and D. H. Molyneux. 1979. Parasites of grey squirrels in Cheshire, England. *Journal of Parasitology* 65:408.

Brown, B. W., and G. O. Batzli. 1984. Habitat selection by fox and gray squirrels: A multivariate analysis. *Journal of Wildlife Management* 48:616–621.

———. 1985a. Field manipulations of fox and gray squirrel populations: How important is interspecific competition? *Canadian Journal of Zoology* 63:2134–2140.

———. 1985b. Foraging ability, dominance relations, and competition for food by fox and gray squirrels. *Transactions of the Illinois State Academy of Science* 78:61–66.

Brown, D. E. 1984. *Arizona's tree squirrels*. Phoenix: Arizona Game and Fish Department, 114 p.

Brown, J. S. 1999. Vigilance, patch use, and habitat selection: Foraging under predation risk. *Evolutionary Ecology Research* 1:49–71.

Brown, J. S., and R. A. Morgan. 1995. Effects of foraging behavior and spatial scale on diet selectivity—a test with fox squirrels. *Oikos* 74:122–136.

Brown, L., and J. F. Downhower. 1987. *Analyses in behavioral ecology*. Sunderland, Mass.: Sinauer Associates, 194 p.

Brown, L. G., and L. E. Yeager. 1945. Fox squirrels and gray squirrels in Illinois. *Illinois Natural History Survey Bulletin* 23:449–536.

Bugbee, R. E., and A. Riegel. 1945. Seasonal food choices of the fox squirrel in western Kansas. *Transactions of the Kansas Academy of Science* 48:199–203.

Burger, G. V. 1969. Response of gray squirrels to nest boxes at Remington Farms. *Journal of Wildlife Management* 33:796–801.

Burt, W. H. 1960. Bacula of North American mammals. *Miscellaneous Publications of the Museum of Zoology, University of Michigan* 113:1–75.

Byers, C. R., R. K. Steinhorst, and P. R. Krausman. 1984. Clarification of a technique for analysis of utilization-availability data. *Journal of Wildlife Management* 48:1050–1053.

Byman, D., D. B. Hay, and G. S. Bakken. 1988. Energetic costs of the winter arboreal microclimate: The gray squirrel in a tree. *International Journal of Biometeorology* 32:112–122.

Caffara, M., and A. Scagliarini. 1999. Study of diseases of the grey squirrel *(Sciurus carolinensis)* in Italy. First isolation of the dermatophyte *Microsporum cookei*. *Medical Mycology* 37:75–77.

Cahalane, V. H. 1939. Mammals of the Chiricahua Mountains, Cochise County, Arizona. *Journal of Mammalogy* 20:418–440.

———. 1942. Caching and recovery of food by the western fox squirrel. *Journal of Wildlife Management* 6:338–352.

Cappucci, D. T., Jr., R. W. Emmons, and W. W. Sampson. 1972. Rabies in an eastern fox squirrel. *Journal of Wildlife Diseases* 8:340–342.

Carlson, B. L., D. P. Roher, and S. W. Nielsen. 1982. Notoedric mange in gray squirrels *(Sciurus carolinensis)*. *Journal of Wildlife Diseases* 18:347–348.

Carlton, R. L. 1976. Tree squirrel damage control. *Proceedings of the Great Plains Wildlife Damage Workshop* 27:31–32.

Carraway, L. N., and B. J. Verts. 1994. *Sciurus griseus*. *Mammalian Species* 474:1–7.

Carson, J. D. 1961. Epiphyseal cartilage as an age indicator in fox and gray squirrels. *Journal of Wildlife Management* 25:90–93.

Chapman, F. B. 1938. Summary of the Ohio gray squirrel investigation. *Transactions of the North American Wildlife and Natural Resources Conference* 3:677–684.

Charnov, E. L. 1976. Optimal foraging: The marginal value theorem. *Theoretical Population Biology* 9:129–136.

Christisen, D. M. 1985. Seasonal tenancy of artificial nest structures for tree squirrels. *Transactions, Missouri Academy of Science* 19:41–48.

Chung-MacCoubrey, A. L., A. E. Hagerman, and R. L. Kirkpatrick. 1997. Effects of tannins on digestion and detoxification activity in gray squirrels *(Sciurus carolinensis)*. *Physiological Zoology* 70:270–277.

Clark, W. J. 1974. Occurrence of Cuterebrid botflies and their effect on gray squirrels in Mississippi. Ph.D. diss., Mississippi State University, Mississippi State, 41 p.

Clarkson, D. P., and H. J. Ferguson. 1969. Effect of temperature upon activity in the red squirrel. *American Zoologist* 9:1110.

Clutton-Brock, T. H. 1988. *Reproductive success: Studies of individual variation in contrasting breeding systems.* Chicago: University of Chicago Press, 538 p.

———. 1989. Mammalian mating systems. *Proceedings of the Royal Society of London B* 236:339–372.

Colburn, M. L. 1986. Suspensory tuberosities for aging and sexing squirrels. *Journal of Wildlife Management* 50:456–459.

Connolly, M. S. 1979. Time-tables in home range usage by gray squirrels *(Sciurus carolinensis carolinensis). Journal of Mammalogy* 60:814–817.

Cooper, G. F., and J. G. Robson. 1966. Directionally selective movement detectors in the retina of the grey squirrel. *Journal of Physiology* 186:116–117.

———. 1969. The color of the lens of the grey squirrel. *Journal of Physiology* 203:403–410.

Copeland, J. E. 1976. Some characteristics of a gray squirrel *(Sciurus carolinensis)* population with respect to habitat at Tennessee Tech Shipley Farm, Putnam County, Tennessee. Master's thesis, Tennessee Technological University, Cookesville, 60 p.

Cordes, C. L., and F. S. Barkalow, Jr. 1972. Home range and dispersal in a North Carolina gray squirrel population. *Proceedings of the Southeastern Association of Game and Fish Commissioners* 26:124–135.

Cowles, C. J., R. L. Kirkpatrick, and J. O. Newell. 1977. Ovarian follicular changes in gray squirrels as affected by season, age, and reproductive state. *Journal of Mammalogy* 58:67–73.

Coyner D. F, J. B. Wooding, and D. J. Forrester. 1996. A comparison of parasitic helminths and arthropods from two subspecies of fox squirrels *(Sciurus niger)* in Florida. *Journal of Wildlife Disease* 32:492–497.

Craine, N. G., P. A. Nuttall, A. C. Marriott, and S. E. Randolph. 1997. Role of grey squirrels and pheasants in the transmission of *Borrelia burgdorferi* sensu lato, the Lyme disease spirochaete, in the UK. *Folia Parasitologica* 44:155–160.

Crandall, L. S. 1964. *The management of wild mammals in captivity.* Chicago: University of Chicago Press, 761 p.

Crase, F. T. 1973. New size records for the western gray squirrel. *Murrelet* 54:20–21.

Cross, S. P. 1969. Behavioral aspects of western gray squirrel ecology. Ph.D. diss., University of Arizona, Tucson, 168 p.

Currado, I. 1998. The gray squirrel *(Sciurus carolinensis* Gmelin) in Italy: A potential problem for the entire European continent. In *Ecology and evolution-*

*ary biology of tree squirrels,* ed. M. A. Steele, J. F. Merritt, and D. A. Zegers, 263–266. Martinsville: Virginia Museum of Natural History, 311 p.

Dagnall, J., J. Gurnell, and H. Pepper. 1998. Bark-stripping by gray squirrels in state forests of the United Kingdom: A review. In *Ecology and evolutionary biology of tree squirrels,* ed. M. A. Steele, J. F. Merritt, and D. A. Zegers, 249–262. Martinsville: Virginia Museum of Natural History, 311 p.

Daniel, H. J., III, and L. K. Roberson. 1987. The ossicles of the eastern gray squirrel, *Sciurus carolinensis. Journal of the Elisha Mitchell Scientific Society* 103:21–27.

David-Gray, Z. K., J. Gurnell, and D. M. Hunt. 1998a. DNA fingerprinting reveals high levels of genetic diversity within British populations of the introduced non-native grey squirrel *(Sciurus carolinensis). Journal of Zoology* (London) 246:443–445.

———. 1998b. The use of DNA fingerprinting in determining the mating system and reproductive success in a population of introduced gray squirrels, *Sciurus carolinensis,* in southern England. In *Ecology and evolutionary biology of tree squirrels,* ed. M. A. Steele, J. F. Merritt, and D. A. Zegers, 43–52. Martinsville: Virginia Museum of Natural History, 311 p.

———. 1999. Estimating the relatedness in a population of grey squirrels, *Sciurus carolinensis,* using DNA fingerprinting. *Acta Theriologica* 44:243–251.

Davidson, W. R. 1976. Endoparasites of selected populations of gray squirrels *(Sciurus carolinensis)* in the southeastern United States. *Proceedings of the Helminthological Society of Washington* 43:211–217.

Davis, D. H. S. 1950. Notes on the status of the American grey squirrel *(Sciurus carolinensis carolinensis* Gmelin) in the south-western cape (South Africa). *Proceedings of the Zoological Society of London* 120:265–268.

Davis, D. W. 1969. The behaviour and population dynamics of the red squirrel, *Tamiasciurus hudsonicus,* in Saskatchewan. *Journal of Mammalogy* 38:414–416.

Davis, D. W., and J. A. Sealander. 1971. Sex ratio and age structure in two red squirrel populations in northern Saskatchewan. *Canadian Field-Naturalist* 85:303–308.

Deanesley, R., and A. S. Parkes. 1933. The reproductive processes of certain mammals. Part 4. The oestrus cycle of the gray squirrel *(Sciurus carolinensis). Philosophical Transactions of the Royal Society of London B* 22:47–96.

Dempsey, J. A., and D. M. Keppie. 1993. Foraging patterns of eastern red squirrels. *Journal of Mammalogy* 74:1007–1013.

Dennis, W. 1930. Rejection of wormy nuts by squirrels. *Journal of Mammalogy* 11:195–201.

Derge, K. L., and R. H. Yahner. 2000. Ecology of sympatric fox squirrels *(Sciurus niger)* and gray squirrels *(S. carolinensis)* at forest-farmland interfaces of Pennsylvania. *American Midland Naturalist* 143:355–369.

Dill, L. M., and R. Houtman. 1989. The influence of distance to refuge on flight initiation distance in the gray squirrel *(Sciurus carolinensis)*. *Canadian Journal of Zoology* 67:233–235.

Dippner, R., and J. Armington. 1971. A behavioral measure of dark adaptation in the American red squirrel. *Psychonomic Science (Section on Animal Physiology and Psychology)* 24:43–45.

Doby, W. 1984. Resource base as a determinant of abundance in the flying squirrel *(Glaucomys volans)*. Ph.D. diss., Wake Forest University, Winston-Salem.

Doebel, J. H., and B. S. McGinnes. 1974. Home range and activity of a gray squirrel population. *Journal of Wildlife Management* 38:860–867.

Dolbeer, R. A. 1973. Reproduction in the red squirrel *(Tamiasciurus hudsonicus)* in Colorado. *Journal of Mammalogy* 54:536–540.

Don, B. A. C. 1983. Home range characteristics and correlates in tree squirrels. *Mammal Review* 13:123–132.

Dubinin, E. V., T. V. Sukhova, V. D. Shmid, and M. S. Vinogradova. 1995. Seasonal patterns of epithelium mitotic activity in the duodenum of two representatives of the Sciuridae with different ecological specialization. *Bulletin of Experimental Biology and Medicine* 119:619–621.

Dubock, A. C. 1979a. Male grey squirrel *(Sciurus carolinensis)* reproductive cycles in Britain. *Journal of Zoology* (London) 188:41–51.

———. 1979b. Methods of age determination in grey squirrels, *Sciurus carolinensis*, in Britain. *Journal of Zoology* (London) 188:27–40.

———. 1982. Grey squirrel (England). In *CRC handbook of census methods for terrestrial vertebrates*, ed. D. E. Davis, 166–168. Boca Raton, Fla.: CRC Press, 397 p.

Ducharme, M. B., J. Larochelle, and D. Richard. 1989. Thermogenic capacity in gray and black morphs of the gray squirrel, *Sciurus carolinensis*. *Physiological Zoology* 62:1273–1292.

Dueser, R. D., J. L. Dooley, Jr., and G. J. Taylor. 1988. Habitat structure, forest composition, and landscape dimensions as components of habitat suitability for the Delmarva fox squirrel. In *Management of amphibians, reptiles, and small mammals in North America*, ed. R. C. Szaro, K. E. Severson, and D. R. Patton, 414–421. U.S. Department of Agriculture, Forest Service, Technical Report RM, 1–166.

Dueser, R. D., and H. H. Shugart. 1978. Microhabitats in a forest-floor small mammal fauna. *Ecology* 59:89–98.

Dunaway, P. B. 1969. "Perfect" polydactylism in hind feet of a gray squirrel. *American Midland Naturalist* 81:244–247.

Dunaway, P. B., and L. L. Lewis. 1965. Taxonomic relation of erythrocyte count, mean corpuscular volume, and body-weight in mammals. *Nature* 205:481–484.

Eason, P. K. 1998. Predation of a female house finch, *Carpodacus mexicanus*, by a gray squirrel, *Sciurus carolinensis*. *Canadian Field-Naturalist* 112:713–714.

Edwards, J. W. 1986. Habitat utilization by southern fox squirrel in coastal South Carolina. Master's thesis, Clemson University, Clemson, 52 p.

Edwards, J. W., and D. C. Guynn, Jr.. 1995. Nest characteristics of sympatric populations of fox and gray squirrels. *Journal of Wildlife Management* 59:103–110.

Edwards, J. W., D. G. Heckel, and D. C. Guynn, Jr.. 1998. Niche overlap in sympatric populations of fox and gray squirrels. *Journal of Wildlife Management* 62:354–363.

Edwards, J. W., S. C. Loeb, and D. C. Guynn, Jr. 1998. Use of multiple regression and use-availability analyses in determining habitat selection by gray squirrels *(Sciurus carolinensis).* In *Ecology and evolutionary biology of tree squirrels,* ed. M. A. Steele, J. F. Merritt, and D. A. Zegers, 87–98. Martinsville: Virginia Museum of Natural History, 311 p.

Ehrlich, P. R., and P. H. Raven. 1964. Butterflies and plants: A study in coevolution. *Evolution* 18:586–608.

Elliot, P. F. 1974. Evolutionary responses of plants to seed-eaters: Pine squirrel predation on lodgepole pine. *Evolution* 28:221–231.

———. 1988. Foraging behavior of a central-place forager: Field tests of theoretical predictions. *American Naturalist* 131:159–174.

Emry, R. J., and R. W. Thorington, Jr. 1982. Descriptive and comparative osteology of the oldest fossil squirrel, *Protosciurus* (Rodentia: Sciuridae). *Smithsonian Contributions to Paleobiology* 47:1–35.

———. 1984. The tree squirrel *Sciurus carolinensis* (Sciuridae, Rodentia) as a living fossil. In *Living fossils,* ed. N. Eldredge and S. M. Stanley, 23–31. New York: Springer-Verlag, 291 p.

Erossy, P. J. 1973. Home range and social organization of a free-ranging population of gray squirrels *(Sciurus carolinensis).* Master's thesis, Bowling Green State University, Bowling Green, Ohio, 68 p.

Esteve, J. V., and G. Jeffery. 1998. Reduced retinal deficits in an albino mammal with a cone rich retina: A study of the ganglion cell layer at the area centralis of pigmented and albino grey squirrels. *Vision Research* 38:937–940.

Faccio, S. D. 1996. Predation of an eastern chipmunk, *Tamias striatus,* by a gray squirrel, *Sciurus carolinensis. Canadian Field-Naturalist* 110:538.

Fairbanks, L., and J. L. Koprowski. 1992. Piscivory in fox squirrels. *Prairie Naturalist* 24:283–284.

Fancy, S. G. 1980. Nest-tree selection by red squirrels in a boreal forest. *Canadian Field-Naturalist* 94:198.

Farentinos, R. C. 1972a. Nests of the tassel-eared squirrel. *Journal of Mammalogy* 53:900–903.

———. 1972b. Observations on the ecology of the tassel-eared squirrel. *Journal of Wildlife Management* 36:1234–1239.

———. 1972c. Social dominance and mating activity in the tassel-eared squirrel *(Sciurus aberti fremonti). Animal Behaviour* 20:316–326.

———. 1974. Social communication of the tassel-eared squirrel *(Sciurus aberti)*: A descriptive analysis. *Zeitschrift für Tierpsychologie* 34:441–458.

———. 1980. Sexual solicitation of subordinate males by female tassel-eared squirrels *(Sciurus aberti)*. *Journal of Mammalogy* 61:337–341.

Fenske-Crawford, T. J., and G. J. Niemi. 1997. Predation of artificial ground nests at two types of edges in a forest-dominated landscape. *Condor* 99:14–24.

Ferner, J. W. 1974. Habitat relationship of *Tamiasciurus hudsonicus* and *Sciurus aberti* in the Rocky Mountains. *Southwestern Naturalist* 18:470–473.

Ferron, J. 1975. Solitary play of the red squirrel *(Tamiasciurus hudsonicus)*. *Canadian Journal of Zoology* 53:1495–1499.

———. 1981. Comparative ontogeny of behaviour in four species of squirrels (Sciuridae). *Zeitschrift für Tierpsychologie* 55:193–216.

Ferron, J., J. P. Ouellet, and Y. Lemay. 1986. Spring and summer time budgets and feeding behaviour of the red squirrel *(Tamiasciurus hudsonicus)*. *Canadian Journal of Zoology* 64:385–391.

Ferron, J., and J. Prescott. 1977. Gestation, litter size, and number of litters of the red squirrel *(Tamiasciurus hudsonicus)* in Quebec. *Canadian Field-Naturalist* 91:83–84.

Fisher, E. W., and A. E. Perry. 1970. Estimating ages of gray squirrels by lens-weight. *Journal of Wildlife Management* 34:825–828.

Fisher, J. T., and G. Merriam. 2000. Resource patch array use by two squirrel species in an agricultural landscape. *Landscape Ecology* 15:333–338.

Fitzgibbon, C. D. 1993. The distribution of gray squirrel dreys in farm woodland—the influence of wood area, isolation, and management. *Journal of Applied Ecology* 30:736–742.

Fitzwater, W. D., Jr. 1943. Color marking of mammals with special reference to squirrels. *Journal of Wildlife Management* 7:190–192.

Fitzwater, W. D., Jr., and W. J. Frank. 1944. Leaf nests of gray squirrels in Connecticut. *Journal of Mammalogy* 25:160–170.

Flyger, V. 1955. Implications of social behavior in gray squirrel management. *Transactions of the North American Wildlife and Natural Resources Conference* 20:381–389.

Flyger, V., and H. R. Cooper. 1967. The utilization of nesting boxes by gray squirrels. *Proceedings of the Southeastern Association of Game and Fish Commissioners* 21:113–117.

Flyger, V., and J. E. Gates. 1982a. Fox and gray squirrels. In *Wild Mammals of North America,* ed. J. A. Chapman and G. A. Feldhamer, 209–229. Baltimore: Johns Hopkins University Press, 1147 p.

———. 1982b. Pine squirrels: *Tamiasciurus hudsonicus, T. douglasii.* In *Wild Mammals of North America,* ed. J. A. Chapman and G. A. Feldhamer, 230–237. Baltimore: Johns Hopkins University Press, 1147 p.

Flyger, V. and E. Y. Levin. 1969. The 1968 squirrel "migration" in the eastern

United States. *Transactions of the Northeast Section of the Wildlife Society* 26:69–79.

———. 1977. Animal model of human disease: Congenital erythopoietic porphyria. *American Journal of Pathology* 87:269–272.

Flyger, V., and D. A. Smith. 1980. A comparison of Delmarva fox squirrel and gray squirrel habitats and home range. *Transactions of the Northeast Section of the Wildlife Society* 37:19–22.

Fogl, J. G., and H. S. Mosby. 1978. Aging gray squirrels by cementum annuli in razor-sectioned teeth. *Journal of Wildlife Management* 42:444–448.

Fox, J. F. 1982. Adaptation of gray squirrel behavior to autumn germination by white oak acorns. *Evolution* 36:800–809.

Frey, J. K., and M. L. Campbell. 1997. Introduced populations of fox squirrel *(Sciurus niger)* in the Trans-Pecos and Llano Estacado regions of New Mexico and Texas. *Southwestern Naturalist* 42:356–358.

Fryxell, F. M. 1926. Squirrels migrate from Wisconsin to Iowa. *Journal of Mammalogy* 7:60.

Geeslin, H. G., Jr. 1970. A radio-tracking study of home range, movements, and habitat uses of the fox squirrel *(Sciurus niger)* in east Texas. Master's thesis, Texas A&M University, College Station, 118 p.

Glass, G. E., and N. A. Slade. 1980. The effect of *Sigmodon hispidus* on spatial and temporal activity of *Microtus ochrogaster:* Evidence for competition. *Ecology* 6:358–370.

Gmelin, J. F. 1788. *Caroli a Linne Systema naturae.* 13th edition. Leipzig: George Emanuel Beer, 4120 p.

Goetz, J. W., R. M. Dawson, and E. E. Mowbray. 1975. Response to nest boxes and reproduction by *Glaucomys volans* in northern Louisiana. *Journal of Mammalogy* 56:933–939.

Goodrum, P. D. 1937. Notes on the gray and fox squirrels of eastern Texas. *Transactions of the North American Fish and Wildlife Conference* 2:499–504.

———. 1940. A population study of the gray squirrel in eastern Texas. *Texas Agricultural Experiment Station Bulletin* 591:1–43.

———. 1961. The gray squirrel in Texas. *Texas Parks and Wildlife Department Bulletin* 42:1–43.

———. 1972. Adult fox squirrel weights in eastern Texas. *Transactions of the North American Wildlife Conference* 37:670–676.

Gorman, O. T., and R. R. Roth. 1989. Consequences of a temporally and spatially variable food supply for an unexploited gray squirrel *(Sciurus carolinensis)* population. *American Midland Naturalist* 121:41–60.

Gould, H. J., III. 1984. Interhemispheric connections of the visual cortex in the grey squirrel *(Sciurus carolinensis)*. *Journal of Comparative Neurology* 223:259–301.

Gouras, P. 1964. Duplex function in the grey squirrel's electroretinogram. *Nature* 203:767–768.

Gray, J. E. 1867. Synopsis of the species of American squirrels in the collection of the British Museum. *Annals and Magazine of Natural History* 20:415–434.

Green, D. G., and J. E. Dowling. 1975. Electrophysiological evidence for rod-like receptors in the grey squirrel, ground squirrel, and prairie dog retinas. *Journal of Comparative Neurology* 159:461–472.

Gronwall, O. 1982. Aspects of the food of the red squirrel (*Sciurus vulgaris* L.) Ph.D. diss., University of Stockholm, Sweden, 139 p.

Guerrero, R. 1994. *Sciurodendrium gardneri,* new species (Nematoda, Trichostrongyloidea, Heligmonellidae), a parasite of *Sciurus carolinensis* Gmelin, 1788 (Mammalia, Sciuridae), with comments on the biogeography of *Sciurodendrium* Durette-Desset, 1971. *Proceedings of the Biological Society of Washington* 107:179–184.

Guiguet, C. J. 1975. An introduction of the grey squirrel, *Sciurus carolinensis* (Gmelin), to Vancouver Island, British Columbia. *Syesis* 8:399.

Gull, J. 1977. Movement and dispersal patterns of immature gray squirrels *(Sciurus carolinensis carolinensis)* in east-central Minnesota. Master's thesis, University of Minnesota, Minneapolis, 117 p.

Gurnell, J. C. 1983. Squirrel numbers and the abundance of tree seeds. *Mammal Review* 13:133–148.

———. 1984. Home range, territoriality, caching behaviour and food supply of the red squirrel *(Tamiasciurus hudsonicus fremonti)* in a subalpine forest. *Animal Behaviour* 32:1119–1131.

———. 1987. *The natural history of squirrels.* New York: Facts on File, 201 p.

———. 1996. The effects of food availability and winter weather on the dynamics of a grey squirrel population in southern England. *Journal of Applied Ecology* 33:325–338.

Gustafson, E. J., and L. W. VanDruff. 1990. Behavior of black and gray morphs of *Sciurus carolinensis* in an urban environment. *American Midland Naturalist* 123:186–192.

Guthrie, D. R., H. S. Mosby, and J. C. Osborne. 1966. Hematological values for the eastern gray squirrel *(Sciurus carolinensis). Canadian Journal of Zoology* 44:323–327.

Guthrie, D. R., J. C. Osborne, and H. S. Mosby. 1967. Physiological changes associated with shock in confined gray squirrels. *Journal of Wildlife Management* 31:102–108.

Ha, J. C. 1983. Food supply and home range in the fox squirrel *(Sciurus niger).* Master's thesis, Wake Forest University, Winston-Salem.

Hadj-Chikh, L. Z., M. A. Steele, and P. D. Smallwood. 1996. Caching decisions by grey squirrels: A test of the handling time and perishability hypotheses. *Animal Behaviour* 52:941–948.

Hadow, H. H. 1972. Freeze-branding: A permanent marking technique for pigmented animals. *Journal of Wildlife Management* 36:645–649.

Hafner, D. J. 1984. Evolutionary relationships of the Nearctic Sciuridae. In *Biology of ground-dwelling squirrels,* ed. J. O. Murie and G. R. Michener, 3–23. Lincoln: University of Nebraska Press, 459 p.

Hall, E. R. 1981. *The mammals of North America.* Vol. 1. New York: Wiley.

Hall, F. G. 1965. Hemoglobin and oxygen: Affinities in seven species of Sciuridae. *Science* 148:1350–1351.

Hall, J. G. 1981. A field study of the Kaibab squirrel in Grand Canyon National Park. *Wildlife Monographs* 75:1–54.

Halloran, M. E., and M. Bekoff. 1994. Nesting-behavior of Abert's squirrels *(Sciurus aberti). Ethology* 97:236–248.

———. 1995. Cheek rubbing as grooming by Abert's squirrels. *Animal Behaviour* 50:987–993.

Halvorson, C. H., and R. M. Engeman. 1983. Survival analysis for a red squirrel population. *Journal of Mammalogy* 64:332–333.

Hamilton, J. C., R. J. Johnson, R. M. Case, and M. W. Riley. 1989. Assessment of squirrel-caused power outages. *Vertebrate pest control and management materials,* 6:34–40. Vol. 6, ed. K. A. Fagerstone and R. D. Curnow. Philadelphia: American Society for Testing Materials, 75 p.

Hamilton, W. D. 1964. The genetical evolution of social behavior 1, 2. *Journal of Theoretical Biology* 7:1–52.

Hamilton, W. J., Jr. 1933. The weasels of New York. *American Midland Naturalist* 14:289–337.

———. 1934. Red squirrel killing young cottontail and young gray squirrel. *Journal of Mammalogy* 15:322.

Hampshire, R. J. 1985. A study on the social and reproductive behaviour of captive grey squirrels *(Sciurus carolinensis).* Ph.D. diss., University of Reading, Reading, England, 246 p.

Hansen, L. P., and C. M. Nixon. 1986. Effects of adults on the demography of fox squirrels *(Sciurus niger). Canadian Journal of Zoology* 63:861–867.

Hansen, L. P., C. M. Nixon, and S. P. Havera. 1986. Recapture rates and length of residence in an unexploited fox squirrel population. *American Midland Naturalist* 115:209–215.

Harnishfeger, R. L., J. L. Roseberry, and W. D. Klimstra. 1978. Reproductive levels in unexploited woodlot fox squirrels. *Transactions of the Illinois State Academy of Science* 71:342–355.

Hauser, D.C. 1964. Anting by gray squirrels. *Journal of Mammalogy* 45:358–359.

Havera, S. P. 1979. Temperature variation in a fox squirrel nest box. *Journal of Wildlife Management* 43:251–253.

Havera, S. P., and R. E. Duzan. 1977. Residues of organochloride insecticides in fox squirrels from south-central Illinois. *Transactions of the Illinois State Academy of Science* 70:375–379.

Havera, S. P., and C. M. Nixon. 1978a. Geographic variation of Illinois gray squirrels. *American Midland Naturalist* 100:396–407.

———. 1978b. Interaction among adult female fox squirrels during their winter breeding season. *Transactions of the Illinois State Academy of Science* 71:24–38.

———. 1979a. Energy and nutrient cost of lactation in fox squirrels. *Journal of Wildlife Management* 43:958–965.

———. 1979b. Temperature variation in a fox squirrel nest box. *Journal of Wildlife Management* 43:251–253.

———. 1980. Winter feeding of fox and gray squirrel populations. *Journal of Wildlife Management* 44:41–55.

Havera, S. P., C. M. Nixon, and H. K. Belcher. 1985. Ovarian characteristics of fox squirrels. *American Midland Naturalist* 114:396–399.

Havera, S. P., C. M. Nixon, and F. I. Collins. 1976. Fox squirrels feeding on buckeye pith. *American Midland Naturalist* 95:462–464.

Havera, S. P., and K. E. Smith. 1979. A nutritional comparison of selected fox squirrel foods. *Journal of Wildlife Management* 43:691–704.

———. 1980. Winter feeding of fox and gray squirrel populations. *Journal of Wildlife Management* 44:41–55.

Heaney, L. R. 1984. Climatic influences on the life-history tactics and behavior of the North American tree squirrels. In *The biology of ground-dwelling squirrels,* ed. J. O. Murie and G. R. Michener, 43–78. Lincoln: University of Nebraska Press, 459 p.

Hedrick, L. D. 1973. Silvicultural practices and tree squirrels (*Sciurus carolinensis* L.) in east Texas. Master's thesis, Texas A&M University, College Station, 97 p.

Hefner, J. M. 1971. Age determination of the gray squirrel. Master's thesis, Ohio State University, Columbus, 51 p.

Hein, E. W. 1997. Demonstration of line transect methodologies to estimate urban gray squirrel density. *Environmental Management* 21:943–947.

Heinrich, B. 1992. Maple sugaring by red squirrels. *Journal of Mammalogy* 73:51–54.

Heller, D. M. 1978. The effect of supplemental food on gray squirrel movements and reproduction. Master's thesis, Texas A&M University, College Station, 97 p.

Hench, J. E., G. L. Kirkland, Jr., H. W. Setzer, and L. W. Douglass. 1984. Age classification for the gray squirrel based on eruption, replacement, and wear of molariform teeth. *Journal of Wildlife Management* 48:1409–1414.

Hibbard, C. W. 1935. Breeding seasons of gray squirrels and flying squirrels. *Journal of Mammalogy* 16:325–326.

Hicks, E. A. 1949. Ecological factors affecting the activity of the western fox squirrel, *Sciurus niger rufiventer* (Geoffroy). *Ecological Monographs* 19:287–302.

Hilliard, T. H. 1979. Radio-telemetry of fox squirrels in the Georgia coastal plain. Master's thesis, University of Georgia, Athens, 121 p.

Himelick, E. B., and E. A. Curl. 1955. Experimental transmission of oak wilt fungus by caged squirrels. *Phytopathology* 45:581–584.

Hirth, R. S., D. S. Wyand, A. D. Osborne, and C. N. Burke. 1969. Epidermal changes caused by squirrel poxviruses. *Journal of the American Veterinary Medical Association* 155:1120–1125.

Hobbs, D. E. 1980. The effect of habitat sound properties on alarm calling behavior in two species of tree squirrels *(Sciurus nayaritensis* and *Sciurus arizonensis)*. Ph.D. diss., University of Arizona, Tucson, 66 p.

Hodder, K. K., and R. E. Kenward. 1998. An experimental release of red squirrels into conifer woodland occupied by gray squirrels in southern Britain: Implications for conservation of red squirrels. In *Ecology and evolutionary biology of tree squirrels,* ed. M. A. Steele, J. F. Merritt, and D. A. Zegers, 267–274. Martinsville: Virginia Museum of Natural History, 311 p.

Hoff, G. L., W. J. Bigler, F. M. Wellings, and A. L. Lewis. 1980. Human enteroviruses and wildlife: Isolation from gray squirrels. *Journal of Wildlife Diseases* 16:131–133.

Hoff, G. L., E. B. Lassing, M. S. Chan, W. J. Bigler, and T. J. Doyle. 1976. Hematologic values for free-ranging urban gray squirrels *(Sciurus carolinensis carolinensis)*. *American Journal of Veterinary Research* 37:99–101.

Hoff, G. L., L. E. McEldowning, W. J. Bigler, L. J. Kuhns, and J. A. Tomas. 1976. Blood and urinary values in the gray squirrel. *Journal of Wildlife Diseases* 12:349–352.

Hoffman, R. A., and C. M. Kirkpatrick. 1956. An analysis of techniques for determining male squirrel reproductive development. *Transactions of the North American Wildlife and Natural Resources Conference* 21:346–355.

———. 1959. Current knowledge of tree squirrel reproductive cycles and development. *Proceedings of the Southeastern Association of Game and Fish Commissioners* 13:363–367.

———. 1960. Seasonal changes in thyroid gland morphology of male gray squirrels. *Journal of Wildlife Management* 24:421–425.

Hoffman, R. S., C. G. Anderson, R. W. Thorington, and L. R. Heaney. 1993. Family Sciuridae. In *Mammal species of the world: A taxonomic and geographic reference,* ed. D. E. Wilson and D. M. Reeder, 419–465. Washington, D.C.: Smithsonian Institution Press, 1206 p.

Hoffmeister, D. F. 1986. *Mammals of Arizona.* Tucson: University of Arizona Press and Arizona Game and Fish Department, 602 p.

Holm, R. F. 1976. Observations on a cannibalistic gray squirrel. *Natural History Miscellanea* 197:1–2.

Honacki, J. H., K. E. Kinman, and J. W. Koeppl. 1982. *Mammal species of the world: A taxonomic and geographic reference.* Lawrence, Kans.: Allen Press and Association of Systematics Collections, 694 p.

Hoover, R. L. 1954. Seven fetuses in western fox squirrel *(Sciurus niger rufiventer)*. *Journal of Mammalogy* 35:447–448.

Horwich, R. H. 1972. The ontogeny of social behavior in the gray squirrel *(Sciurus carolinensis carolinensis)*. *Advances in Ethology* 8:1–103.

Hougart, B., and V. Flyger. 1981. Activity patterns of radio-tracked squirrels. *Transactions of the Northeast Section of the Wildlife Society* 38:11–16.

Howe, H. F. 1989. Scatter- and clump-dispersal and seedling demography: Hypothesis and implications. *Oecologia* 79:417–426.

Howe, H. F., and L. C. Westley. 1988. *Ecological relationships between plants and animals*. Oxford: Oxford University Press, 273 p.

Howell, A. H. 1919. Notes on the fox squirrels of the southeastern United States, with description of a new form from Florida. *Journal of Mammalogy* 1:36–38.

Howell, D. J., and D. L. Hartl. 1980. Optimal foraging in glossophagine bats: When to give up. *American Naturalist* 115:696–704.

Huggins, J. G. 1995. Blue jay and fox squirrel damage preference among pecan trees. *Crop Protection* 14:585–587.

Huggins, J. G., and K. L. Gee. 1995. Efficiency and selectivity of cage trap sets for gray and fox squirrels. *Wildlife Society Bulletin* 23:204–207.

Hungerford, K. E., and N. G. Wilder. 1941. Observations on the homing behavior of the gray squirrel *(Sciurus carolinensis)*. *Journal of Wildlife Management* 5:458–460.

Huntley, J. C. 1983. Squirrel den tree management: Reducing incompatibility with timber production in upland hardwoods. In *Proceedings of the Second Biennial Southern Silvicultural Conference*, ed. E. P. Jones, Jr., 488–495. U.S. Department of Agriculture, Forest Service, General Technical Report SE-24, 514 p.

Hurly, T. A. 1987. Male biased adult sex ratios in a red squirrel population. *Canadian Journal of Zoology* 65:1284–1286.

Hurly, T. A., and R. J. Robertson. 1986. Scatter-hoarding by territorial red squirrels: A test of the optimal density model. *Canadian Journal of Zoology* 65:1247–1252.

Husband, T. P. 1976. Energy metabolism and body composition of the fox squirrel. *Journal of Wildlife Management* 40:255–263.

Ingles, L. G. 1947. Ecology and life history of the California gray squirrel. *California Fish and Game* 33:139–158.

Innes, S., and D. M. Lavigne. 1979. Comparative energetics of coat colour polymorphs in the eastern gray squirrel, *Sciurus carolinensis*. *Canadian Journal of Zoology* 57:585–592.

Ivan, J. S., and R. K. Swihart. 2000. Selection of mast by granivorous rodents of the central hardwood forest region. *Journal of Mammalogy* 81:549–562.

Iverson, L. R. 1988. Land-use changes in Illinois, U.S.A.: The influence of landscape attributes on current and historic land use. *Landscape Ecology* 2:45–61.

Jackson, H. H. T. 1921. A recent migration of the gray squirrel in Wisconsin. *Journal of Mammalogy* 2:113–114.

Jackson, J. J. 1983. Tree squirrels. In *Prevention and control of wildlife damage*, ed. R. M. Timm, B141-B146. Lincoln: Great Plains Agricultural Council, unpaged.

Jackson, L. L., H. E. Heffner, and R. S. Heffner. 1997. Audiogram of the fox squirrel *(Sciurus niger)*. *Journal of Comparative Psychology* 111:100–104.

Jacobs, G. H. 1974. Scotopic and photopic visual capacities of an arboreal squirrel *(Sciurus niger)*. *Brain, Behavior, and Evolution* 10:307–321.

———. 1981. *Comparative color vision*. New York: Academic Press, 209 p.

Jacobs, G. H., D. G. Birch, and B. Blakeslee. 1982. Visual acuity and spatial contrast sensitivity in tree squirrels. *Behavioural Processes* 7:367–375.

Jacobs, L. 1989. Cache economy of the gray squirrel. *Natural History* 98:40–47.

Jacobs, L. F. 1992. The effects of handling time on the decision to cache by grey squirrels. *Animal Behaviour* 43:522–524.

Jacobs, L. F., and E. R. Liman. 1991. Grey squirrels remember the locations of buried nuts. *Animal Behaviour* 41:103–110.

Jacobs, L. F., and M. W. Shiflett. 1999. Spatial orientation on a vertical maze in free-ranging fox squirrels *(Sciurus niger)*. *Journal of Comparative Psychology* 113:116–127.

Jacobson, H. A., D. C. Guynn, Jr., and E. J. Hackett. 1979. Impact of the botfly on squirrel hunting in Mississippi. *Wildlife Society Bulletin* 7:46–48.

Jacobson, H. A., M. S. Hetrick, and D. C. Guynn, Jr. 1981. Prevalence of *Cuterebra emasculator* in squirrels in Mississippi. *Journal of Wildlife Diseases* 17:79–87.

Janzen, D. H. 1971. Seed predation by animals. *Annual Review of Ecology and Systematics* 2:465–492.

———. 1980. When is it coevolution? *Evolution* 34:611–612.

Jenkins, F. A., Jr., and D. McClearn. 1984. Mechanisms of hind foot reversal in climbing mammals. *Journal of Morphology* 182:197–219.

Jenness, R., and R. Sloan. 1970. The composition of milks of various species: A review. *Dairy Abstracts* 32:599–612.

Jodice, P. G. R., and S. R. Humphrey. 1992. Activity and diet of an urban population of Big Cypress fox squirrels. *Journal of Wildlife Management* 56:685–692.

Johnson, W. C., L. Thomas, and C. S. Adkisson. 1993. Dietary circumvention of acorn tannins by blue jays: Implications for oak demography. *Oecologia* 94:159–164.

Jones, C. B., R. S. Ostfeld, and J. O. Wolff. 1998. Chain reactions linking acorns to gypsy moth outbreak and Lyme disease risk. *Science* 279:1023–1025.

Joseph, T. 1975. Experimental transmission of *Eimeria confusa* Joseph 1969 to the fox squirrel. *Journal of Wildlife Diseases* 11:402–403.

Judd, W. W. 1955. Gray squirrels feeding on samaras of elm. *Journal of Mammalogy* 36:296.

Kaas, J. H., W. C. Hall, and I. T. Diamond. 1972. Visual cortex of the grey squirrel *(Sciurus carolinensis):* Architectonic subdivision and connections from the visual thalmus. *Journal of Comparative Neurology* 145:273–306.

Kantola, A. T., and S. R. Humphrey. 1990. Habitat use by Sherman's fox squirrel *(Sciurus niger shermani)* in Florida. *Journal of Mammalogy* 71:411–419.

Kazacos, E. A., K. R. Kazacos, and H. A. Demaree, Jr. 1983. Notoedric mange in two fox squirrels. *Journal of the American Veterinary Medical Association* 183:1281–1282.

Keator, G. 1998. *The life of an oak.* Berkeley and Oakland: Heyday Books and California Oak Foundation, 256 p.

Keith, J. G. 1965. The Abert's squirrel and its dependence on Ponderosa pine. *Ecology* 46:150–163.

Kemp, G. A., and L. B. Keith. 1970. Dynamics and regulation of red squirrel *(Tamiasciurus hudsonicus)* populations. *Ecology* 51:763–779.

Kenward, R. E. 1983. The causes of damage by red and grey squirrels. *Mammal Review* 13:159–166.

———. 1985. Ranging behaviour and population dynamics in grey squirrels. *Symposia of the British Ecological Society* 25:319–330.

Kenward, R. E., and K. H. Hodder. 1998. Red squirrels *(Sciurus vulgaris)* released in conifer woodland: The effects of source habitat, predation, and interactions with gray squirrels *(Sciurus carolinensis). Journal of Zoology* (London) 244:23–32.

Kenward, R. E., K. H. Hodder, R. J. Rose, C. A. Walls, T. Parish, J. L. Holm, P. A. Morris, S. S. Walls, and F. I. Doyle. 1998. Comparative demography of red squirrels *(Sciurus vulgaris)* and grey squirrels *(Sciurus carolinensis)* in deciduous and conifer woodland. *Journal of Zoology* (London) 244:7–21.

Kenward, R. E., and T. Parish. 1986. Bark-stripping by grey squirrels *(Sciurus carolinensis). Journal of Zoology* (London) 210:473–481.

Kenward, R. E., and J. M. Tonkin. 1986. Red and grey squirrels: Some behavioural and biometric differences. *Journal of Zoology* (London) 209:279–304.

Kerr, G., and J. Niles. 1998. Growth and provenance of Norway maple *(Acer platanoides)* in lowland Britain. *Forestry* 71 (3):219–224.

Keymer, I. F. 1983. Diseases of squirrels in Britain. *Mammal Review* 13:155–158.

Kilham, L. 1954. Territorial behavior of red squirrel. *Journal of Mammalogy* 35:252–253.

Kiltie, R. A. 1989. Wildfire and the evolution of dorsal melanism in fox squirrels, *Sciurus niger. Journal of Mammalogy* 70:726–739.

———. 1992. Camouflage comparisons among fox squirrels from the Mississippi River delta. *Journal of Mammalogy* 73:906–913.

Kiltie, R. A., and R. Edwards. 1998. Interspecific correlates of squirrel coat patterns: Ecology, taxonomy, and body size. In *Ecology and evolutionary biology of tree squirrels,* ed. M. A. Steele, J. F. Merritt, and D. A. Zegers, 161–170. Martinsville: Virginia Museum of Natural History, 311 p.

Kirkpatrick, C. M. 1955. The testis of the fox squirrel in relation to age and seasons. *American Journal of Anatomy* 97:229–256.

Kirkpatrick, C. M., and E. M. Barnett. 1957. Age criteria in male gray squirrels. *Journal of Wildlife Management* 21:341–347.

Kirkpatrick, C. M., and R. A. Hoffman. 1960. Ages and reproductive cycles in a male gray squirrel population. *Journal of Wildlife Management* 24:218–221.

Klugh, A. B. 1927. Ecology of the red squirrel. *Journal of Mammalogy* 8:1–32.

Knapp, S. J., and J. E. Swenson. 1986. New range records for the fox squirrel in the Yellowstone River Drainage, Montana. *Prairie Naturalist* 18:128.

Knee, C. 1983. Squirrel energetics. *Mammal Review* 13:113–122.

Kneeland, M. C., J. L. Koprowski, and M. C. Corse. 1995. Potential predators of Chiricahua fox squirrels *(Sciurus nayaritensis chiricahuae). Southwestern Naturalist* 40:340–342.

Koenig, W. D. 1991. The effects of tannins and lipids on digestion of acorns by acorn woodpeckers. *Auk* 108:79–88.

Koford, R. R. 1992. Does supplemental feeding of red squirrels change population density, movements, or both? *Journal of Mammalogy* 73:930–932.

Koprowski, J. L. 1985. Fox squirrel population trends and regulation in a southern Illinois woodlot, 1968–1984. Master's thesis, Southern Illinois University, Carbondale, 85 p.

———. 1991a. Damage due to scent marking by eastern gray and fox squirrels. *Proceedings of the Great Plains Wildlife Damage Conference* 10:101–105.

———. 1991b. The evolution of sociality in tree squirrels: The comparative behavioral ecology of fox squirrels and eastern gray squirrels. Ph.D. diss., University of Kansas, Lawrence, 117 p.

———. 1991c. Mixed-species mating chases of fox squirrels and gray squirrels. *Canadian Field-Naturalist* 105:117–118.

———. 1991d. Response of fox squirrels and gray squirrels to a late spring–early summer food shortage. *Journal of Mammalogy* 72:367–372.

———. 1992. Removal of copulatory plugs by female tree squirrels. *Journal of Mammalogy* 73:572–576.

———. 1993a. Alternative reproductive tactics in male eastern gray squirrels: "Making the best of a bad job." *Behavioral Ecology* 4:165–171.

———. 1993b. Behavioral tactics, dominance, and copulatory success among male fox squirrels. *Ethology, Ecology, and Evolution* 5:169–176.

———. 1993c. The role of kinship in field interactions among juvenile gray squirrels *(Sciurus carolinensis). Canadian Journal of Zoology* 71:224–226.

———. 1993d. Sex and species biases in scent marking by fox squirrels and eastern gray squirrels. *Journal of Zoology* (London) 230:319–323.

————. 1994a. *Sciurus carolinensis. Mammalian Species* 480:1–9.

————. 1994b. *Sciurus niger. Mammalian Species* 479:1–9.

————. 1996. Natal philopatry, communal nesting, and kinship in fox squirrels and gray squirrels. *Journal of Mammalogy* 77:1006–1016.

————. 1998. Conflict between the sexes: A review of social and mating systems of the tree squirrels. In *Ecology and evolutionary biology of tree squirrels,* ed. M. A. Steele, J. F. Merritt, and D. A. Zegers, 33–42. Martinsville: Virginia Museum of Natural History, 311 p.

Koprowski, J. L., J. L. Roseberry, and W. D. Klimstra. 1988. Longevity records for the fox squirrel. *Journal of Mammalogy* 69:383–384.

Korschgen, L. J. 1981. Foods of fox and gray squirrels in Missouri. *Journal of Wildlife Management* 45:260–266.

Kotler, B. P., J. S. Brown, and M. Hickey. 1999. Food storability and the foraging behavior of fox squirrels *(Sciurus niger). American Midland Naturalist* 142:77–86.

Kramm, K. R., D. E. Maki, and J. M. Glime. 1975. Variation within and among populations of red squirrel in the Lake Superior region. *Journal of Mammalogy* 56:258–262.

————. 1985. Length of gestation in the red squirrel, *Tamiasciurus hudsonicus. Journal of Mammalogy* 66:809–810.

————. 1990. The calls of the red squirrel: a contextual analysis of function. *Behaviour* 115:254–282.

Krebs, J. R., and N. B. Davies. 1991. *Behavioural ecology.* Oxford: Blackwell Scientific Publications, 482 p.

————. 1993. *An introduction to behavioural ecology.* 3d ed. London: Blackwell Scientific Publications, 420 p.

Kurten, B., and E. Anderson. 1980. *Pleistocene mammals of North America.* New York: Columbia University Press, 442 p.

Lair, H. 1985. Length of gestation in the red squirrel, *Tamiasciurus hudsonicus. Journal of Mammalogy* 66:809–810.

Lalonde, R. G., and B. D. Roitberg. 1992. On the evolution of masting behavior in trees: Predation or weather? *American Naturalist* 139:1293–1304.

Lamb, T., T. R. Jones, and P. J. Wettstein. 1997. Evolutionary genetics and phylogeography of tassel-eared squirrels *(Sciurus aberti). Journal of Mammalogy* 78:117–133.

Landry, S. O., Jr. 1957. Factors affecting the precumbency of rodent upper incisors. *Journal of Mammalogy* 38:223–234.

Lang, H. 1925. How squirrels and other rodents carry their young. *Journal of Mammalogy* 6:18–24.

Lange, K. I. 1960. Mammals of the Santa Catalina Mountains, Arizona. *American Midland Naturalist* 64:436–458.

Langham, R. F., R. L. Rausch, and J. F. Williams. 1990. Cysticerci of *Taenia mustelae* in the fox squirrel. *Journal of Wildlife Disease* 26:295–296.

Larsen, K. W., and S. Boutin. 1994. Movements, survival, and settlement of red squirrel *(Tamiasciurus hudsonicus)* offspring. *Ecology* 75:214–223.

Larson, J. S., and R. D. Taber. 1980. Criteria of sex and age. In *Wildlife management techniques manual,* ed. S. D. Schemnitz, 143–202. 4th ed. Washington, D.C.: Wildlife Society, 686 p.

Lavenex, P., M. W. Shiflett, R. K. Lee, and L. F. Jacobs. 1998. Spatial versus nonspatial relational learning in free-ranging fox squirrels *(Sciurus niger)*. *Journal of Comparative Psychology* 112:127–136.

Lavenex, P., M. A. Steele, and L. F. Jacobs. 2000a. The seasonal pattern of cell proliferation and neuron number in the dentate gyrus of wild adult eastern grey squirrels. *European Journal of Neuroscience* 12:643–648.

———. 2000b. Sex differences, but no seasonal variations in the hippocampus of food-caching squirrels: A stereological study. *Journal of Comparative Neurology* 425:152–166.

Layne, J. N. 1954a. The biology of the red squirrel *Tamiasciurus hudsonicus loquax* in central New York. *Ecological Monographs* 24:227–267.

———. 1954b. The os clitoridis of some North American Sciuridae. *Journal of Mammalogy* 35:357–366.

———. 1998. Use of nest boxes and reproduction in gray squirrels *(Sciurus carolinensis)* in Florida. In *Ecology and evolutionary biology of tree squirrels,* ed. M. A. Steele, J. F. Merritt, and D. A. Zegers, 61–70. Martinsville: Virginia Museum of Natural History, 311 p.

Layne, J. N., and A. H. Benton. 1954. Some speeds of small mammals. *Journal of Mammalogy* 35:103–104.

Layne, J. N., and G. E. Woolfenden. 1958. Gray squirrels feeding on insects in car radiators. *Journal of Mammalogy* 39:595–596.

Lee, M. R., and D. F. Hoffmeister. 1963. Status of certain fox squirrels in Mexico and Arizona. *Proceedings of the Biological Society of Washington* 76:181–189.

Lewis, A. R. 1980. Patch use by gray squirrels and optimal foraging. *Ecology* 61:1371–1379.

———. 1982. Selection of nuts by gray squirrels and optimal foraging theory. *American Midland Naturalist* 107:250–257.

Lewis, E., G. L. Hoff, W. J. Bigler, and M. B. Jeffries. 1975. Public health and the urban gray squirrel: Mycology. *Journal of Wildlife Diseases* 11:502–504.

Lima, S. L., and L. M. Dill. 1989. Behavioral decisions under risk of predation: A review and prospectus. *Canadian Journal of Zoology* 34:536–544.

Lima, S. L., and T. J. Valone. 1986. Influence of predation risk on diet selection: A simple example in the grey squirrel. *Animal Behaviour* 34:536–544.

Lima, S. L., T. J. Valone, and T. Caraco. 1985. Foraging efficiency–predation risk trade-off in grey squirrels. *Animal Behaviour* 33:155–165.

Lindsay, S. L. 1981. Taxonomic and biogeographic relationships of the Baja California chickarees *(Tamiasciurus)*. *Journal of Mammalogy* 63:446–452.

————. 1982. Systematic relationship of parapatric tree squirrel species *(Tamiasciurus)* in the Pacific Northwest. *Canadian Journal of Zoology* 60:2149–2156.

Linnaeus, C. 1758. *Systema naturae.* 10th ed. Vol. 1. Stockholm: Laurentii Salvii.

Lishak, R. S. 1982a. Gray squirrel mating calls: Spectrographic and ontogenic analysis. *Journal of Mammalogy* 63:661–663.

————. 1982b. Vocalizations of nestling gray squirrels. *Journal of Mammalogy* 63:446–452.

————. 1984. Alarm vocalizations of adult gray squirrels. *Journal of Mammalogy* 65:681–684.

Littlefield, V. M. 1984. Habitat interrelationships of Abert's squirrels *(Sciurus aberti)* and fox squirrels *(Sciurus niger)* in Boulder County, Colorado. Ph. D. diss., Miami University, Oxford, Ohio, 93 p.

Lloyd, H. G. 1968. Observations on nut selection by a hand-reared grey squirrel *(Sciurus carolinensis)*. *Journal of Zoology* (London) 156:240–244.

————. 1983. Past and present distribution of red and grey squirrels. *Mammal Review* 13:69–80.

Loeb, S. C. 1999. Responses of small mammals to coarse woody debris in a southeastern pine forest. *Journal of Mammalogy* 80:460–471.

Long, C. A., and J. Captain. 1977. Investigations on the sciurid manus. II. Analysis of functional complexes by morphological integration and by coefficients of belonging. *Zeitschrift für Saugetierkunde* 42:214–221.

Long, C. A., and J. E. Long. 1986. Mass drowning of gray squirrels off Washington Island, Lake Michigan. *Jack-Pine Warbler* 64:21–22.

Lowe, V. P. W. 1993. The spread of the gray squirrel *(Sciurus carolinensis)* into Cumbria since 1960 and its present distribution. *Journal of Zoology* (London) 231:663–667.

Lowery, G. H., and W. B. Davis. 1942. A revision of the fox squirrels of the lower Mississippi Valley and Texas. *Occasional Papers of the Museum of Zoology, Louisiana State University* 9:153–172.

Ludwick, R. L., J. P. Fontenot, and H. S. Mosby. 1969. Energy metabolism of the eastern gray squirrel. *Journal of Wildlife Management* 33:569–575.

Lurz, P. W .W., P. J. Garson, and S. P. Rushton. 1995. The ecology of squirrels in spruce-dominated plantations: Implications for forest management. *Forest Ecology and Management* 79:79–90.

MacArthur, R. H., and E. R. Pianka. 1966. On optimal use of a patchy environment. *American Naturalist* 100:603–609.

MacDonald, I. M. V. 1992. Grey squirrels discriminate red from green in a foraging situation. *Animal Behaviour* 43:694–695.

————. 1997. Field experiments on duration and precision of grey and red squirrel spatial memory. *Animal Behaviour* 54:879–891.

Mace, G. W., P. H. Harvey, and T. H. Clutton-Brock. 1981. Brain size and ecology in small mammals. *Journal of Zoology* (London) 193:333–354.

Maddox, R. S. 1929. Are gray squirrels carnivorous? *American Forests* 35:427–428.

Madson, J. 1964. *Gray and fox squirrels.* East Alton, Ill.: Conservation Department, Olin Mathieson Chemical Corp., 112 p.

Mahan, C. G., and R. H. Yahner. 1992. Microhabitat use by red squirrels in central Pennsylvania. *Northeast Wildlife* 49:49–56.

Mahan, C. G., R. H. Yahner, and L. R. Stover. 1994. Development of remote-collaring techniques for red squirrels. *Wildlife Society Bulletin* 22:270–273.

Manski, D. A., L. W. VanDruff, and V. Flyger. 1981. Activities of gray squirrels and people in a downtown Washington, D.C., park: Management implications. *Transactions of the North American Wildlife and Natural Resources Conference* 46:439–454.

Marsh, R. E., and W. E. Howard. 1977. Vertebrate control manual: Tree squirrels. *Pest Control Manual* 45:36–48.

Martan, J., C. S. Adams, and B. L. Perkins. 1970. Epididymal spermatozoa of two species of squirrel. *Journal of Mammalogy* 51:376–378.

Maser, C., B. R. Mate , and J. F. Franklin. 1981. *Natural history of Oregon coast mammals.* U.S. Department of Agriculture, Forest Service, General Technical Report, PNW-133:1–496.

McAdam, A. G., and D. L. Kramer. 1998. Vigilance as a benefit of intermittent locomotion in small mammals. *Animal Behaviour* 55:109–117.

McCarthy, B. C. 1994. Experimental studies of hickory recruitment in a wooded hedgerow and forest. *Bulletin of the Torrey Botanical Club* 121:240–250.

McCloskey, R. J. 1975. Description and analysis of the behavior of the fox squirrel in Iowa. Ph.D. diss., Iowa State University, Ames, 230 p.

———.1977. Accuracy of criteria used to determine age of fox squirrels. *Proceedings of the Iowa Academy of Science* 84:32–34.

McCloskey, R. J., and K. C. Shaw. 1977. Copulatory behavior of the fox squirrel. *Journal of Mammalogy* 58:663–665.

McCloskey, R. J., and P. A. Vohs, Jr. 1971. Chronology of reproduction of the fox squirrel in Iowa. *Proceedings of the Iowa Academy of Science* 78:12–15.

McComb, W. C. 1984. Managing urban forests to increase or decrease gray squirrel populations. *Southern Journal of Applied Forestry* 8:31–34.

McComb, W. C., and R. E. Noble. 1981a. Microclimates of nest boxes and natural cavities in bottomland hardwoods. *Journal of Wildlife Management* 45:284–289.

———. 1981b. Nest-box and natural-cavity use in three mid-south forest habitats. *Journal of Wildlife Management* 45:93–101.

McGrath, G. 1987. Relationships of Nearctic tree squirrels of the genus *Sciurus carolinensis.* Ph.D. diss., University of Kansas, Lawrence, 101 p.

McKinnon, J. L., G. L. Hoff, W. J. Bigler, and E. C. Prather. 1976. Heavy metal concentrations in kidneys of urban gray squirrels. *Journal of Wildlife Diseases* 12:367–371.

McPherson, E. G., and C. Nilon. 1987. A habitat suitability index model for gray squirrel in an urban cemetery. *Landscape Journal* 6:21–30.

McShea, W. J. 2000. The influence of acorn crops on annual variation in rodent and bird populations. *Ecology* 81:228–238.

Mearns, E. A. 1907. Mammals of the Mexican boundary of the United States. Part 1. *United States National Museum Bulletin* 56:1–530.

Meier, P. T. 1983. Relative brain size within the North American Sciuridae. *Journal of Mammalogy* 64:642–647.

Merriam, C. H. 1886. Preliminary description of a new squirrel from Minnesota *(Sciurus carolinensis hypophaeus,* sp. nov.). *Science* 7:351.

Merritt, J. F. 1987. *Guide to the mammals of Pennsylvania.* Pittsburgh: University of Pittsburgh Press, 401 p.

Merson, M. H., C. J. Cowles, and R. L. Kirkpatrick. 1978. Characteristics of captive gray squirrels exposed to cold and food deprivation. *Journal of Wildlife Management* 42:202–205.

Merzenich, M. M., J. H. Kaas, and G. Linn Roth. 1976. Auditory cortex in the grey squirrel: Tonotopic organization and architectonic fields. *Journal of Comparative Neurology* 166:387–401.

Middleton, A. D. 1930. The ecology of the American gray squirrel in the British Isles. *Proceedings of the Zoological Society of London* 130:809–843.

Millar, J. C. G. 1980. Aspects of the ecology of the American grey squirrel *Sciurus carolinensis carolinensis* Gmelin in South Africa. Master's thesis, University of Stellenbosch, South Africa, 313 p.

Mollar, H. 1986. Red squirrels *(Sciurus vulgaris)* feeding in a Scots pine plantation in Scotland. *Journal of Zoology* (London) 209:61–84.

Moncrief, N. D. 1987. Geographic variation in morphology and allozymes within tree squirrels, *Sciurus niger* and *S. carolinensis,* of the lower Mississippi Valley. Ph.D. diss., Louisiana State University, Baton Rouge, 154 p.

———.1993. Geographic variation in fox squirrels *(Sciurus niger)* and gray squirrels *(S. carolinensis)* of the lower Mississippi River Valley. *Journal of Mammalogy* 74:547–576.

———. 1998. Allozymic variation in populations of fox squirrels *(Sciurus niger)* and gray squirrels *(S. carolinensis)* from the eastern United States. In *Ecology and evolutionary biology of tree squirrels,* ed. M. A. Steele, J. F. Merritt, and D. A. Zegers, 145–160. Martinsville: Virginia Museum of Natural History, 311 p.

Montgomery, S. D., J. B. Whelan, and H. S. Mosby. 1975. Bioenergetics of a woodlot gray squirrel population. *Journal of Wildlife Management* 39:709–717.

Moore, G. C. 1941. Prey chases predator. *Journal of Mammalogy* 22:198.

Moore, H. D. M., N. M. Jenkins, and C. Wong. 1997. Immunocontraception in rodents: A review of the development of a sperm-based immunocontraceptive vaccine for the grey squirrel *(Sciurus carolinensis)*. *Reproduction Fertility and Development* 9:125–129.

Moore, J. C. 1956. Variation in the fox squirrel in Florida. *American Midland Naturalist* 55:41–65.

———. 1957. The natural history of the fox squirrel, *Sciurus niger shermani*. *Bulletin of the American Museum of Natural History* 113:1–71.

———. 1959. Relationships among living squirrels of the Sciurinae. *Bulletin of the American Museum of Natural History* 118:153–248.

———. 1968. Sympatric species of tree squirrel mix in mating chase. *Journal of Mammalogy* 49:531–533.

Morgan, R. A., J. S. Brown, and J. M. Thorson. 1997. The effect of spatial scale on the functional response of fox squirrels. *Ecology* 78:1087–1097.

Mosby, H. S. 1969. The influence of hunting on the population dynamics of a woodlot gray squirrel population. *Journal of Wildlife Management* 33:59–73.

Mossman, H. W. 1933. The fetal membranes of the Sciuridae and their significance. *Anatomical Record* 55 (supp. 4):30.

———. 1934. Mammalian implantation with particular reference to that of rodents. *Anatomical Record* 58 (supp. 4):29.

———. 1940. What is the red squirrel? *Transactions of the Wisconsin Academy of Science, Arts, and Letters* 32:123–134.

Mossman, H. W., R. A. Hoffman, and C. M. Kirkpatrick. 1955. The accessory genital glands of male gray and fox squirrels correlated with age and reproductive cycles. *American Journal of Anatomy* 97:257–302.

Mountford, E. P. 1997. A decade of grey squirrel bark-stripping damage to beech in Lady Park Wood, UK. *Forestry* 70:17–29.

Muchlinski, A. E., and K. A. Shump, Jr. 1979. The Sciurid tail: A possible thermoregulatory mechanism. *Journal of Mammalogy* 60:652–654.

Munger, J. C. 1984. Optimal foraging patch use by horned lizards (Iguanidae: *Phrynosoma*). *American Naturalist* 123:654–680.

Nadler, C. F., and D. A. Sutton. 1967. Chromosomes of some squirrels (Mammalia-Sciuridae) from the genera *Sciurus* and *Glaucomys*. *Experientia* 24:249–251.

Nash, D. J., and R. N. Seaman. 1977. *Sciurus aberti. Mammalian Species* 80:1–5.

Nelson, B. A. 1945. The spring molt of the northern red squirrel in Minnesota. *Journal of Mammalogy* 26:397–400.

Nelson, R. J., M. Sur, and J. H. Kaas. 1979. The organization of the second somatosensory area (SmII) of the grey squirrel. *Journal of Comparative Neurology* 184:473–490.

Nero, R. W. 1958. Additional gray squirrel information. *Blue Jay* 16:80.

Neu, C. W., C. R. Byers, and J. M. Peek. 1974. A technique for analysis of utilization-availability data. *Journal of Wildlife Management* 38:541–545.

Newman, J. A., G. M. Recer, S. M. Zwicker, and T. Caraco. 1988. Effects of predation hazard on foraging "constraints": Patch-use strategies in grey squirrels. *Oikos* 53:93–97.

Nicholas, J. T. 1927. Notes on the food habits of the gray squirrel. *Journal of Mammalogy* 8:55–57.

Nielsen, R. R. 1973. Dehusking black walnuts controls rodent pilferage. *Tree Planter's Notes* 24:33.

Nixon, C. M. 1970. Insects as food for juvenile gray squirrels. *American Midland Naturalist* 84:283.

Nixon, C. M., and R. W. Donohoe. 1979. Squirrel nest boxes—are they effective in young hardwood stands? *Wildlife Society Bulletin* 7:283–284.

Nixon, C. M., R. W. Donohoe, and T. Nash. 1974. Overharvest of fox squirrels from two woodlots in western Ohio. *Journal of Wildlife Management* 38:67–80.

Nixon, C. M., W. R. Edwards, and L. Eberhardt. 1967. Estimating squirrel abundance from live-trapping data. *Journal of Wildlife Management* 31:96–101.

Nixon, C. M., and L. P. Hansen. 1987. Managing forests to maintain populations of gray and fox squirrels. *Illinois Department of Conservation Technical Bulletin* 5:1–35.

Nixon, C. M., L. P. Hansen, and S. P. Havera. 1991. Growth patterns of fox squirrels in east-central Illinois. *American Midland Naturalist* 125:168–172.

Nixon, C. M., and W. J. Harper. 1972. Composition of gray squirrel milk. *Ohio Journal of Science* 72:3–6.

Nixon, C. M., S. P. Havera, and J. A. Ellis. 1978. *Squirrel hunting in Illinois.* Springfield: Illinois Department of Conservation, 37 p.

Nixon, C. M., S. P. Havera, and R. E. Greenberg. 1978. Distribution and abundance of the gray squirrel in Illinois. *Biological Notes, Illinois Natural History Survey* 105:1–55.

Nixon, C. M., S. P. Havera, and L. P. Hansen. 1980. Initial response of squirrels to forest changes associated with selection cutting. *Wildlife Society Bulletin* 8:298–306.

———. 1984. Effects of nest boxes on fox squirrel demography, condition, and shelter use. *American Midland Naturalist* 112:157–171.

Nixon, C. M., and M. W. McClain. 1969. Squirrel population decline following a late spring frost. *Journal of Wildlife Management* 33:353–357.

———. 1975. Breeding seasons and fecundity of female gray squirrels in Ohio. *Journal of Wildlife Management* 39:426–438.

Nixon, C. M., M. W. McClain, and R. W. Donohoe. 1975. Effects of hunting and mast crops on a squirrel population. *Journal of Wildlife Management* 39:1–25.

———. 1980. Effects of clear-cutting on gray squirrels. *Journal of Wildlife Management* 44:403–412.

Nixon, C. M., D. M. Worley, and M. W. McClain. 1968. Food habits of squirrels in southeast Ohio. *Journal of Wildlife Management* 32:294–305.

Novilla, M. N., V. Flyger, E. R. Jacobson, S. K. Dutta, and E. M. Sacchi. 1981. Systemic phycomycosis and multiple fibromas in a gray squirrel *(Sciurus carolinensis carolinensis)*. *Journal of Wildlife Diseases* 17:89–95.

Nupp T. E., and R. K. Swihart. 2000. Landscape-level correlates of small-mammal assemblages in forest fragments of farmland. *Journal of Mammalogy* 81:512–526.

Obbard, M. E. 1987. Red squirrel. In *Wild Furbearer Management and Conservation in North America,* ed. M. Novack, M. E. Obbard, and B. Malloch, pp. 265–281. Toronto: Ontario Ministry of Natural Resources, 1150 p.

O'Connor, D. J., R. W. Ditters, and S. W. Nielsen. 1980. Poxvirus and multiple tumors in an eastern grey squirrel. *Journal of the American Veterinary Medical Association* 177:792–795.

Odum, E. P. 1983. *Basic ecology.* Philadelphia: Saunders College Publishing, 613 p.

Ofcarcik, R. P., E. E. Burns, and J. G. Teer. 1973. Acceptance of selected acorns by captive fox squirrels. *Southwestern Naturalist* 17:349–355.

Osgood, W. H. 1907. Some unrecognized and misapplied names of American mammals. *Proceedings of the Biological Society of Washington* 20:43–52.

Ostfeld, R. S., C. G. Jones, and J. O. Wolff. 1996. Of mice and mast: Ecological connections in eastern deciduous forests. *Bioscience* 46:323–330.

Pack, J. C., H. S. Mosby, and P. B. Siegel. 1967. Influence of social hierarchy on gray squirrel behavior. *Journal of Wildlife Management* 31:720–728.

Packard, R. L. 1956. The tree squirrels of Kansas: Ecology and economic importance. *Miscellaneous Publications, Museum of Natural History, University of Kansas* 11:1–67.

Page, L. K., R. K. Swihart, and K. R. Kazacos. 1999. Implications of raccoon latrines in the epizootiology of *Baylisascariasis. Journal of Wildlife Disease* 35:474–480.

Parker, J. C. 1968. Parasites of the gray squirrel in Virginia. *Journal of Parasitology* 54:633–634.

Parker, J. C., E. J. Riggs, and R. B. Holliman. 1972. Notes on parasites of gray squirrels from Florida. *Quarterly Journal of the Florida Academy of Sciences* 35:161–162.

Pasitschniak-Arts, M., and J. F. Bendell. 1990. Behavioural differences between locally recruiting and dispersing gray squirrels, *Sciurus carolinensis. Canadian Journal of Zoology* 68:935–941.

Pauls, R. W. 1978. Behavioural strategies relevant to the energy economy of the red squirrel *(Tamiasciurus hudsonicus). Canadian Journal of Zoology* 56:1519–1525.

———. 1979. Body temperature dynamics of the red squirrel *(Tamiasciurus hudsonicus):* Adaptations for energy conservation. *Canadian Journal of Zoology* 57:1349–1354.

Penner, R., G. E. E. Moodie, and R. J. Staniforth. 1999. The dispersal of fruits and seeds of poison ivy, *Toxicodendron radicans,* by ruffed grouse, *Bonasa umbellus,* and squirrels, *Tamiasciurus hudsonicus* and *Sciurus carolinensis. Canadian Field-Naturalist* 113:616–620.

Perry, H. R., Jr. 1982. Gray squirrel (Sough). In *CRC handbook of census methods for terrestrial vertebrates,* ed. D. E. Davis, 162–163. Boca Raton, Fla.: CRC Press, 397 p.

Perry, H. R., Jr., G. B. Pardue, F. S. Barkalow, Jr., and R. J. Monroe. 1977. Factors affecting trap responses of the gray squirrel. *Journal of Wildlife Management* 41:135–143.

Peterka, H. E. 1936. A study of the myology and osteology of tree sciurids with regard to adaptation to arboreal, glissant, and fossorial habits. *Transactions of Kansas Academy of Science* 39:313–332.

Petrides, G. A. 1944. A gall insect food of the gray squirrel. *Journal of Mammalogy* 25:410.

Phares, R. E., D. T. Funk, and C. M. Nixon. 1974. Removing black walnut hulls before direct seeding not always protection against rodent pilferage. *Tree Planter's Notes* 25:23–24.

Phillips, J., and R. R. Dubielzig. 1980. Congenital aortic stenosis in an eastern gray squirrel. *Journal of the American Veterinary Medical Association* 177:939.

Pijl, L. van der. 1972. *Principles of dispersal in higher plants.* New York: Springer-Verlag, 162 p.

Pocock, R. I. 1923. The classification of the Sciuridae. *Proceedings of the Zoological Society of London* 1923:209–246.

Post, D. M., and O. J. Reichman. 1991. Effects of food perishability, distance, and competitors on caching behavior by eastern wood rats. *Journal of Mammalogy* 72:513–517.

Potter, B. 1903. *The tale of squirrel nutkin.* New York: F. Warne, 58 p.

Powers, M. E., D. Tilman, J. A. Estes, B. A. Menge, W. J. Bond, L. S. Mills, G. Daily, J. C. Castilla, J. Lubchenco, and R. T. Paine. 1996. Challenges in the quest for keystones. *Bioscience* 46:609–620.

Pratt, C. R. 1987. Gray squirrels as subjects in independent study. *American Biology Teacher* 49:434–437.

Preno, W. L., and R. F. Labisky. 1971. Abundance and harvest of doves, pheasants, bobwhites, squirrels, and cottontails in Illinois. *Illinois Department of Conservation Technical Bulletin* 4:1–76.

Price, K. 1992. Territorial bequeathal by red squirrel mothers: A dynamic model. *Bulletin of Mathematical Biology* 54:335–354.

Price, K., and S. Boutin. 1993. Territorial bequeathal by red squirrel mothers. *Behavioral Ecology* 4:144–150.

Price, K., K. Broughton, S. Boutin, and A. R. E. Sinclair. 1986. Territory size and ownership in red squirrels: Response to removals. *Canadian Journal of Zoology* 64:1144–1147.

Price, M. V., and S. H. Jenkins. 1986. Rodents as seed consumers and dispersers. In *Seed dispersal*, ed. D. R. Murray, 191–235. Sydney, Australia: Academic Press.

Pritchett, H. D. 1938. Rabies in two gray squirrels. *Journal of the American Veterinary Medical Association* 45:563–564.

Pruitt, W. O., and C. V. Lucier. 1958. Winter activity of red squirrels in interior Alaska. *Journal of Mammalogy* 39:443–444.

Pudney, J. 1976. Season changes in the testis and epididymis of the American grey squirrel, *Sciurus carolinensis*. *Journal of Zoology* (London) 179:107–120.

Pudney, J., and D. Lacy. 1977. Correlation between ultrastructure and biochemical changes in the testis growth of the American grey squirrel, *Sciurus carolinensis*, during the reproductive cycle. *Journal of Reproduction and Fertility* 49:5–16.

Purdue, J. R. 1980. Clinal variation of some mammals during the Holocene in Missouri. *Quaternary Research* 13:242–258.

Ramey, C. A., and D. J. Nash. 1971. Abert's squirrel in Colorado. *Southwestern Naturalist* 16:125–126.

———. 1976. Coat color polymorphism of Abert's squirrel, *Sciurus aberti*, in Colorado. *Southwestern Naturalist* 21:209–217.

Rausch, R., and J. D. Tiner. 1948. Studies on the parasitic helminths of the north central states. Part 1, Helminths of Sciuridae. *American Midland Naturalist* 39:728–747.

Reichard, T. A. 1976. Spring food habits and feeding behavior of fox squirrels and red squirrels. *American Midland Naturalist* 96:443–450.

Reichman, O. J. 1988. Caching behavior by eastern wood rats, *Neotoma floridana*, in relation to food perishability. *Animal Behaviour* 36:1525–1532.

Reichman, O. J., A. Fattaey, and K. Fattaey. 1986. Management of sterile and mouldy seeds by a desert rodent. *Animal Behaviour* 34:221–225.

Reitsma, L. R., R. T. Holmes, and T. W. Sherry. 1990. Effects of removal of red squirrels, *Tamiasciurus hudsonicus*, and eastern chipmunks, *Tamias striatus*, on nest predation in northern hardwood forests: An artificial nest experiment. *Oikos* 57:375–380.

Reynolds, J. C. 1985a. Autumn-winter energetics of holarctic tree squirrels: A review. *Mammal Review* 15:137–150.

———. 1985b. Details of the geographic replacement of the red squirrel *(Sciurus vulgaris)* by the grey squirrel *(Sciurus carolinensis)*. *Journal of Animal Ecology* 54:149–162.

Ribbens, E., J. A. Silander, and S. W. Pacala. 1994. Seedling recruitment in forests: Calibration models to predict patterns of tree seedling dispersion. *Ecology* 75:1794–1806.

Riege, D. A. 1991. Habitat specialization and social factors in distribution of red and gray squirrels. *Journal of Mammalogy* 72:152–162.

Robb, J. R., and T. A. Bookhout. 1995. Factors influencing wood duck use of natural cavities. *Journal of Wildlife Management* 59:372–383.

Robb, J. R., M. S. Cramer, A. R. Parker, and R. P. Urbanek. 1996. Use of tree cavities by fox squirrels and raccoons in Indiana. *Journal of Mammalogy* 77:1017–1027.

Robbins, C. T., S. Mole, A. E. Hagerman, and T. A. Hanley. 1987. Role of tannins in defending plants against ruminants: Reduction in protein availability. *Ecology* 68:98–107.

Robinson, D. J., and I. M. Cowan. 1954. An introduced population of the gray squirrel (*Sciurus carolinensis* Gmelin) in British Columbia. *Canadian Journal of Zoology* 32:261–282.

Roher, D. P., M. J. Ryan, S. W. Nielsen, and D. E. Roscoe. 1981. Acute fatal toxoplasmosis in squirrels. *Journal of American Veterinary Medical Association* 179:1099–1101.

Rood, J. P., and D. W. Nellis. 1980. Freeze marking mongooses. *Journal of Wildlife Management* 44:500–502.

Ross, R. C. 1930. California Sciuridae in captivity. *Journal of Mammalogy* 11:76–78.

Rothwell, R. H. 1979. Nest sites of squirrels *(Tamiasciurus hudsonicus)* in the Laramie range of southeastern Wyoming. *Journal of Mammalogy* 60:404–405.

Rusch, D. A., and W. G. Reeder. 1978. Population ecology of Alberta red squirrels. *Ecology* 59:400–420.

Ryan, L. A., and A. B. Carey. 1995. Distribution and habitat of the western gray squirrel *(Sciurus griseus)* on Ft. Lewis, Washington. *Northwest Science* 69:204–216.

Saenz, D., R. N. Conner, C. E. Shackelford, and D. C. Rudolph. 1998. Pileated woodpecker damage to red-cockaded woodpecker cavity trees in eastern Texas. *Wilson Bulletin* 110:362–367.

Sanderson, H. R. 1975. Den-tree management for gray squirrels. *Wildlife Society Bulletin* 3:125–131.

Sanderson, H. R., C. M. Nixon, R. W. Donohoe, and L. P. Hansen. 1980. Grapevine: An important component of gray and fox squirrel habitat. *Wildlife Society Bulletin* 8:307–310.

Sauer, R. M. 1966. Cutaneous mucomycosis (phycomycosis) in a squirrel *(Sciurus carolinensis)*. *American Journal of Veterinary Research* 27:380–383.

Say, T. 1823. *Account of an expedition from Pittsburgh to the Rocky Mountains, performed in the years 1819 and '20, by order of the Hon. J. C. Calhoun, Sec'y of War: Under the command of Major Stephen H. Long from the notes of Major Long, Mr. T. Say, and other gentlemen of the exploring party.* Compiled by E. James. Vol. 1. Philadelphia: Carey and Lea, 503 p.

Schmidt, K. A. 2000. Interactions between food chemistry and predation risks in fox squirrels. *Ecology* 81(8):2077–2085.

Schmidt, K. A., and J. S. Brown. 1996. Patch assessment in fox squirrels: The role of resource density, patch size, and patch boundaries. *American Naturalist* 147:360–380.

Schmidt, K. A., J. S. Brown, and R. A. Morgan. 1998. Plant defenses as complementary resources: A test with squirrels. *Oikos* 81:130–142.

Schorger, A. W. 1949. Squirrels in early Wisconsin. *Transactions of the Wisconsin Academy of Science, Arts, and Letters* 39:195–247.

Seebeck, J. H. 1984. The eastern grey squirrel, *Sciurus carolinensis,* in Victoria. *Victorian Naturalist* 101:61–66.

Seton, E. T. 1920. Migrations of the gray squirrel *(Sciurus carolinensis). Journal of Mammalogy* 1:53–58.

Sexton, O. J. 1990. Replacement of fox squirrels by gray squirrels in suburban habitat. *American Midland Naturalist* 124:198–205.

Seymour, C., and T. M. Yuill. 1981. Arboviruses. In *Infectious diseases of wild mammals,* ed. J. W. Davis, L. H. Karstad, and D. O. Trainer, 54–86. Ames: Iowa State University Press, 446 p.

Shaffer, B. S., and B. W. Baker. 1991. Observations of predation on a juvenile blue jay, *Cyanocitta cristata,* by a fox squirrel, *Sciurus niger. Texas Journal of Science* 43:105–106.

Sharp, W. M. 1958. Aging gray squirrels by use of tail pelage characteristics. *Journal of Wildlife Management* 22:29–34.

———. 1959. A commentary on the behavior of free-running gray squirrels. *Proceedings of the Southeastern Association Game and Fish Commissioners* 13:382–387.

Shaw, W. W., and W. R. Mangun. 1984. *Nonconsumptive use of wildlife in the United States.* Washington, D.C.: U.S. Fish and Wildlife Service Resource Publication 154, 20 p.

Sheail, J. 1999. The grey squirrel *(Sciurus carolinensis):* A UK historical perspective on a vertebrate pest species. *Journal of Environmental Management* 55:145–156.

Shealer, D. A., J. P. Snyder, V. C. Dreisbach, D. F. Sunderlin, and J. A. Novak. 1999. Foraging patterns of eastern gray squirrels *(Sciurus carolinensis)* on goldenrod gall insects, a potentially important winter food resource. *American Midland Naturalist* 142:102–109.

Sheperd, B. F., and R. K. Swihart. 1995. Spatial dynamics of fox squirrels *(Sciurus niger)* in fragmented landscapes. *Canadian Journal of Zoology* 73:2098–2105.

Sherburne, S. S., and J. A. Bissonette. 1993. Squirrel middens influence marten *(Martes americana)* use of subnivean access points. *American Midland Naturalist* 129:204–207.

Shipley, D. D. 1941. A study of the habits and management of the gray squirrel in southwest Virginia. Master's thesis, Virginia Polytechnic Institute and State University, Blacksburg, 166 p.

Shivaprasad, H. L., J. P. Sundberg, and R. Ely. 1984. Malignant mixed (carcinosarcoma) mammary tumor in a gray squirrel. *Veterinary Pathology* 21:115–117.

Short, H. L. 1976. Composition and squirrel use of acorns of black and white oak groups. *Journal of Wildlife Management* 40:479–480.

Short, H. L., and W. B. Duke. 1971. Seasonal food consumption and body weights of captive tree squirrels. *Journal of Wildlife Management* 35:435–439.

Shorten, M. 1945. Inheritance of melanism in grey squirrels. *Nature* 156:46–47.

———. 1951. Some aspects of the biology of the grey squirrel *(Sciurus carolinensis carolinensis)* in Great Britain. *Proceedings of the Zoological Society of London* 121:427–459.

———. 1954. *Squirrels.* Cleveland, Ohio: Collins, 212 p.

Shorten, M., and F. A. Courtier. 1955. A population study of the gray squirrel *(Sciurus carolinensis carolinensis)* in May 1954. *Annals of Applied Biology* 43:494–510.

Shotts, E. B., Jr., C. L. Andrews, and T. W. Harvey. 1975. Leptospirosis in selected wild mammals of the Florida panhandle and southwestern Georgia, U.S.A. *Journal of the American Veterinary Medical Association* 167:587–589.

Singleton, W. R. 1967. *Elementary genetics.* Princeton, N.J.: Van Nostrand, 576 p.

Siwela, A. A., and W. H. Tam. 1981. Metabolism of androgens by the active and inactive prostate gland and seasonal changes in systemic androgen levels in the grey squirrel *(Sciurus carolinensis* Gmelin). *Journal of Endocrinology* 88:381–392.

———. 1984. Ultrastructural changes in the prostate gland of a seasonally breeding mammal, the grey squirrel *(Sciurus carolinensis* Gmelin). *Journal of Anatomy* 138:153–162.

Smallwood, P. D., and W. D. Peters. 1986. Grey squirrel food preferences: The effects of tannin and fat concentration. *Ecology* 67:168–174.

Smallwood, P. D., M. A. Steele, E. Ribbens, and W. J. McShea. 1998. Detecting the effects of seed hoarders on the distribution of tree species: Gray squirrels *(Sciurus carolinensis)* and oaks *(Quercus)* as a model system. In *Ecology and evolutionary biology of tree squirrels,* ed. M. A. Steele, J. F. Merritt, and D. A. Zegers, 211–222. Martinsville: Virginia Museum of Natural History, 311 p.

Smith, A. A., and R. W. Mannan. 1994. Distinguishing characteristics of Mount Graham red squirrel midden sites. *Journal of Wildlife Management* 58:437–445.

Smith, C. C. 1965. Interspecific competition in the genus of tree squirrels, *Tamiasciurus.* Ph.D. diss., University of Washington, Seattle, 269 p.

———. 1968. The adaptive nature of social organization in the genus of tree squirrel *Tamiasciurus. Ecological Monographs* 38:30–63.

————. 1970. The coevolution of pine squirrels *(Tamiasciurus)* and conifers. *Ecological Monographs* 40:349–371.

————. 1978. Structure and function of the vocalizations of tree squirrels *(Tamiasciurus)*. *Journal of Mammalogy* 59:793–808.

————. 1981. The indivisible niche of *Tamiasciurus*: An example of nonpartitioning of resources. *Ecological Monographs* 51:343–363.

————. 1998. The evolution of reproduction in trees: Its effects on ecology and behavior of squirrels. In *Ecology and evolutionary biology of tree squirrels,* ed. M. A. Steele, J. F. Merritt, and D. A. Zegers, 203–210. Martinsville: Virginia Museum of Natural History, 311 p.

Smith, C. C., and D. Follmer. 1972. Food preferences of squirrels. *Ecology* 53:82–91.

Smith, C. C., and O. J. Reichman. 1984. The evolution of food caching by birds and mammals. *Annual Review of Ecology and Systematics* 15:329–351.

Smith, D. D., and J. K. Frenkel. 1995. Prevalence of antibodies to *Toxoplasma gondii* in wild mammals of Missouri and east central Kansas—biologic and ecologic considerations of transmission. *Journal of Wildlife Disease* 31:15–21.

Smith, E. N., and C. Johnson. 1984. Fear bradycardia in the eastern fox squirrel, *Sciurus carolinensis niger,* and eastern grey squirrel, *S. carolinensis*. *Comparative Biochemistry and Physiology, A Comparative Physiology* 78:409–411.

Smith, M. C. 1968. Red squirrel responses to spruce cone failure. *Journal of Wildlife Management* 32:305–316.

Smith, N. B. 1967. Some aspects of reproduction in the female gray squirrel, *Sciurus carolinensis carolinensis* Gmelin, in Wake County, North Carolina. Master's thesis, North Carolina State University, Raleigh, 92 p.

Smith, N. B., and F. S. Barkalow, Jr. 1967. Precocious breeding in the gray squirrel. *Journal of Mammalogy* 48:328–329.

Snyder, L. L. 1923. A method employed by a black squirrel in carrying its young. *Journal of Mammalogy* 4:59.

Snyder, M. A. 1992. Selective herbivory by Abert's squirrel mediated by chemical variability in ponderosa pine. *Ecology* 73:1730–1741.

————. 1993. Interactions between Abert's squirrel and ponderosa pine: The relationship between selective herbivory and host plant fitness. *American Naturalist* 141:866–879.

————. 1998. Abert's squirrels *(Sciurus aberti)* in ponderosa pine *(Pinus ponderosa)* forests: Directional selection, diversifying selection. In *Ecology and evolutionary biology of tree squirrels,* ed. M. A. Steele, J. F. Merritt, and D. A. Zegers, 195–201. Martinsville: Virginia Museum of Natural History, 311 p.

Snyder, M. A., and Y. B. Linhart. 1993. Barking up the right tree. *Natural History* 102:44–49.

————. 1994. Nest-site selection by Abert's squirrel—chemical characteristics of nest trees. *Journal of Mammalogy* 75:136–141.

———. 1998. Subspecific selectivity by a mammalian herbivore: geographic differentiation of interactions between two taxa of *Sciurus aberti* and *Pinus ponderosa*. *Evolutionary Ecology* 12:755–765.

Sork, V. L., J. Bramble, and O. Sexton. 1993. Ecology of mast-fruiting in three species of North American deciduous oaks. *Ecology* 74:528–541.

Staines, B. W. 1986. The spread of grey squirrels (*Sciurus carolinensis* Gm). *Scottish Forestry* 40:190–196.

Stapanian, M. A., and C. C. Smith. 1978. A model for seed scatterhoarding: Coevolution of fox squirrels and black walnuts. *Ecology* 59:884–896.

———. 1984. Density-dependent survival of scatterhoarded nuts: An experimental approach. *Ecology* 65:1387–1396.

———. 1986. How fox squirrels influence the invasion of prairies by nut-bearing trees. *Journal of Mammalogy* 67:326–332.

Steele, M. A. 1988. Patch use and foraging behavior by the fox squirrel *(Sciurus niger)*: Tests of theoretical predictions. Ph.D. diss., Wake Forest University, Winston-Salem, 220 p.

———. 1998. *Tamiasciurus hudsonicus*. *Mammalian Species* 586:1–9.

———. 1999. *Tamiasciurus douglasii*. *Mammalian Species* 630:1–8.

Steele, M. A., K. Gavel, and W. Bachman. 1998. Dispersal of half-eaten acorns by gray squirrels: Effects of physical and chemical seed characteristics. In *Ecology and evolutionary biology of tree squirrels,* ed. M. A. Steele, J. F. Merritt, and D. A. Zegers, 223–232. Martinsville: Virginia Museum of Natural History, 311 p.

Steele, M. A., L. Z. Hadj-Chikh, and J. Hazeltine. 1996. Caching and feeding decisions by *Sciurus carolinensis*: Responses to weevil-infested acorns. *Journal of Mammalogy* 77:305–314.

Steele, M. A., T. Knowles, K. Bridle, and E. Simms. 1993. Tannins and partial consumption of acorns: Implications for dispersal of oaks by seed predators. *American Midland Naturalist* 130:229–238.

Steele, M. A., J. F. Merritt, and D. A. Zegers, eds. 1998. *Ecology and evolutionary biology of tree squirrels*. Martinsville: Virginia Museum of Natural History, 311 p.

Steele, M. A., and P. D. Smallwood. 1994. What are squirrels hiding? *Natural History* 103:4045.

———. In press. Acorn dispersal by birds and mammals. In *Oak Forest Ecosystems: The Ecology and Management of Oaks for Wildlife*, ed. W. McShea and W. Healey. Baltimore: Johns Hopkins University Press.

Steele, M. A., P. D. Smallwood, A. Spunar, and E. Nelsen. In press. The proximate basis of food-hoarding decisions and the oak dispersal syndrome: A case study of plant-animal mutualism. *American Zoologist*.

Steele, M. A., G. Turner, P. D. Smallwood, J. O. Wolff, and J. Radillo. 2001. Cache management by small mammals: Experimental evidence for the significance of acorn embryo excision. *Journal of Mammalogy* 82:35–42.

Steele, M. A., and P. D. Weigl. 1992. Energetics and patch use in the fox squirrel *Sciurus niger:* Responses to variation in prey profitability and patch density. *American Midland Naturalist* 128:156–167.

———. 1993. The ecological significance of body size in fox squirrels *(Sciurus niger)* and gray squirrels *(S. carolinensis).* In *Proceedings of the Second Symposium on Southeastern Fox Squirrels, Sciurus niger,* ed. N. D. Moncrief, J. W. Edwards, and P. A. Tappe. Martinsville: Virginia Museum of Natural History.

Stencel, J. E., and A. W. Ghent. 1987. Analyses of annual surveys of white and gray squirrels *(Sciurus carolinensis)* in Olney, Illinois, 1977–1986. *American Midland Naturalist* 118:251–257.

Stephens, D. W., and J. R. Krebs. 1986. *Foraging theory.* Princeton, N.J.: Princeton University Press, 247 p.

Stienecker, W. E. 1977. Supplemental data on the food habits of the western gray squirrel. *California Fish and Game* 63:11–21.

Stienecker, W. E., and B. M. Browning. 1970. Food habits of the western gray squirrel. *California Fish and Game* 56:36–48.

Stiles, E. W., and E. T. Dobi. 1987. Scatterhoarding of horsechestnuts by eastern gray squirrels. *Bulletin of the New Jersey Academy of Science* 32:1–3.

Stoddard, H. L. 1919. Nests of the western fox squirrel. *Journal of Mammalogy* 1:122–123.

Stone, K. D., G. A. Heidt, W. H. Baltosser, and P. T. Caster. 1996. Factors affecting nest box use by southern flying squirrels *(Glaucomys volans)* and gray squirrels *(Sciurus carolinensis). American Midland Naturalist* 135:9–13.

Stone, W. B., J. C. Okoniewski, and J. R. Stedelin. 1999. Poisoning of wildlife with anticoagulant rodenticides in New York. *Journal of Wildlife Disease* 35:187–193.

Sullivan, T. P. 1990. Responses of red squirrel *(Tamiasciurus hudsonicus)* populations to supplemental food. *Journal of Mammalogy* 71:579–590.

Sullivan, T. P., and W. Klenner. 1992. Response to Koford: Red squirrels and supplemental feeding. *Journal of Mammalogy* 73:933–936.

———. 1993. Influence of diversionary food on red squirrel populations and damage to crop trees in young lodgepole pine forest. *Ecological Application* 3:708–718.

Sullivan, T. P., and A. Vyse. 1987. Impact of red squirrel feeding damage on spaced stands of lodgepole pine in the Caribou Region of British Columbia. *Canadian Journal of Forest Research* 17:666–674.

Sur, M., R. J. Nelson, and J. H. Kaas. 1978. The representation of the body surface in somatosensory area I of the grey squirrel. *Journal of Comparative Neurology* 179:425–450.

Svihla, R. D. 1930. Development of young red squirrels. *Journal of Mammalogy* 11:79–80.

———. 1931. Captive fox squirrels. *Journal of Mammalogy* 12:152–157.

Swihart, R. K., and T. E. Nupp. 1998. Modeling population responses of North American tree squirrels to agriculturally induced forest fragmentation. In *Ecology and evolutionary biology of tree squirrels,* ed. M. A. Steele, J. F. Merritt, and D. A. Zegers, 1–20. Martinsville: Virginia Museum of Natural History, 311 p.

Swihart, R. K., and N. A. Slade. 1985a. Influence of sampling interval on estimates of home range size. *Journal of Wildlife Management* 49:1019–1025.

———. 1985b. Testing for independence of observations in animal movements. *Ecology* 66:1176–1184.

Tait, A. J., and E. Johnson. 1982. Spermatogenesis in the grey squirrel *(Sciurus carolinensis)* and changes during sexual regression. *Journal of Reproduction and Fertility* 65:53–58.

Tait, A. J., G. S. Pope, and E. Johnson. 1981. Progesterone concentrations in peripheral plasma of nonpregnant and pregnant grey squirrels *(Sciurus carolinensis). Journal of Endocrinology* 89:107–116.

Tappe, P. A., and D. C. Guynn, Jr. 1998. Southeastern fox squirrels: r- or K-selected? Implications for management. In *Ecology and evolutionary biology of tree squirrels,* ed. M. A. Steele, J. F. Merritt, and D. A. Zegers, 239–248. Martinsville: Virginia Museum of Natural History, 311 p.

Taylor, G. J. 1974. Present status and habitat survey of the Delmarva fox squirrel *(Sciurus niger cinereus)* with a discussion of reasons for its decline. *Proceedings of the Southeastern Association of Game and Fish Commissioners* 27:278–289.

———. 1976. Range determination and habitat description of the Delmarva fox squirrel in Maryland. Master's thesis, University of Maryland, College Park.

Taylor, J. C. 1966. Home range and agonistic behaviour in the grey squirrel. *Symposia of the Zoological Society of London* 18:229–235.

———. 1968. The use of marking points of grey squirrels. *Journal of Zoology* (London) 155:246–247.

———. 1969. Social structure and behaviour in a grey squirrel population. Ph.D. diss., University of London, London, 217 p.

———. 1977. The frequency of grey squirrel *(Sciurus carolinensis)* communication by use of scent marking points. *Journal of Zoology* (London) 183:543–545.

Teangana, D. O., S. Reilly, W. I. Montgomery, and J. Rochford. 2000. Distribution and status of the red squirrel *(Sciurus vulgaris)* and grey squirrel *(Sciurus carolinensis)* in Ireland. *Mammal Review* 30:45–55.

Terres, J. K. 1939. Gray squirrel utilization of elm. *Journal of Wildlife Management* 3:358–359.

Theobald, D. P. 1983. Studies on the biology and habitat of the Arizona gray squirrel. Master's thesis, Arizona State University, Tempe, 26 p.

Thompson, D. C. 1976. Accidental mortality and cannibalization of a nestling gray squirrel. *Canadian Field-Naturalist* 90:52–53.

———. 1977a. Diurnal and seasonal activity of the grey squirrel *(Sciurus carolinensis)*. *Canadian Journal of Zoology* 55:1185–1189.

———. 1977b. Reproductive behavior of the grey squirrel. *Canadian Journal of Zoology* 55:1176–1184.

———. 1978a. Regulation of a northern grey squirrel *(Sciurus carolinensis)* population. *Ecology* 59:708–715.

———. 1978b. The social system of the grey squirrel. *Behaviour* 64:305–328.

———. 1982. Grey squirrel (North). In *CRC handbook of census methods for terrestrial vertebrates,* ed. D. E. David, 164–165. Boca Raton, Fla.: CRC Press, 397 p.

Thompson, D. C., and P. S. Thompson. 1980. Food habits and caching behavior of urban grey squirrels. *Canadian Journal of Zoology* 58:701–710.

Thoreau, H. D. 1993. *Faith in a Seed: The Dispersion of Seeds and Other Late Natural History Writings.* Washington, D.C.: Island Press, 283 p.

Thorington, R. W., Jr. 1966. *The biology of rodent tails: A study of form and function.* Fort Wainwright, Alaska: Arctic Aeromedical Laboratory, 137 p.

———. 1972. Proportions and allometry in the gray squirrel, *Sciurus carolinensis. Nemouria* 8:1–17.

Thorington, R. W., Jr., A. L. Musante, and C. G. Anderson. 1998. Arboreality in tree squirrels (Sciuridae). In *Ecology and evolutionary biology of tree squirrels,* ed. M. A. Steele, J. F. Merritt, and D. A. Zegers, 119–130. Martinsville: Virginia Museum of Natural History, 311 p.

Thorson, J. M., R. A. Morgan, J. S. Brown, J. E. Norman. 1998. Direct and indirect cues of predatory risk and patch use by fox squirrels and thirteen-lined ground squirrels. *Behavioral Ecology* 9:151–157.

Toyne, E. P. 1998. Breeding season diet of the goshawk *Accipiter gentilis* in Wales. *Ibis* 140 (4):569–579.

Tufts, R. W. 1973. Is the grey squirrel invading Nova Scotia? *Canadian Field-Naturalist* 87:175–176.

Uhlig, H. G. 1955a. The determination of age of nestling and sub-adult gray squirrels in West Virginia. *Journal of Wildlife Management* 19:479–483.

———. 1955b. Weights of adult gray squirrels. *Journal of Mammalogy* 36:293–296.

Van Dersal, W. R. 1940. Utilization of oaks by birds and mammals. *Journal of Wildlife Management* 4:404–428.

Vander Wall, S. B. 1990. *Food hoarding in animals.* Chicago: University of Chicago Press, 445 p.

Verts, B. J., and L. N. Carraway. 1998. *Land mammals of Oregon.* Berkeley: University of California Press, 668 p.

Vinogradova, M. C., V. D. Schmidt, T. V. Sukhova, L. V. Shestopalova, and S. V. Aidagulova. 1996. Paneth cells of the eastern gray squirrel *(Sciurus carolinensis)* and red-cheeked suslik *(Citellus erythrogenys* Brandt). *Bulletin of Experimental Biology and Medicine* 121:195–198.

Wade, O., and P. T. Gilbert. 1942. The baculum of some Sciuridae and its significance in determining relationships. *Journal of Mammalogy* 23:52–63.

Walker, E. D., and J. D. Edman. 1985. Feeding-site selection and blood-feeding behavior of *Aedes triseriatus* (Diptera: Culicidae) on rodent (Sciuridae) hosts. *Journal of Medical Entomology* 22:287–294.

———. 1986. Influence of defensive behavior of eastern chipmunks and gray squirrels (Rodentia: Sciuridae) on feeding success of *Aedes triseriatus* (Diptera: Culicidae). *Journal of Medical Entomology* 23:1–10.

Wallach, J. D., and G. L. Hoff. 1982. Nutritional diseases of mammals. In *Noninfectious diseases of wildlife,* ed. G. L. Hoff, and J. W. Davis, 127–154. Ames: Iowa State University Press, 174 p.

Walls, G. L. 1942. *The vertebrate eye and its adaptive radiation.* Bloomfield Hills, Mich.: Cranbrook Institute of Science, 785 p.

Waser, P. M., and W. T. Jones. 1983. Natal philopatry among solitary mammals. *Quarterly Review of Biology* 58:355–390.

Webley, G. E., and E. Johnson. 1982. Effect of ovariectomy on the course of gestation in the grey squirrel *(Sciurus carolinensis). Journal of Endocrinology* 89:107–116.

———. 1983. Reproductive physiology of the grey squirrel *(Sciurus carolinensis). Mammal Review* 13:149–154.

Webley, G. E., G. S. Pope, and E. Johnson. 1984. Testosterone, 17-hydroxy–5 -androstan–3-one and 4-androstene–3,17-dione in the plasma of male and female grey squirrels. *Journal of Steroid Biochemistry* 20:1207–1209.

———. 1985. Seasonal changes in the testes and accessory reproductive organs and seasonal and circadian changes in plasma testosterone concentrations of the male grey squirrel (*Sciurus carolinensis). General Comparative Endocrinology* 59:15–23.

Weeks, H. P., and C. M. Kirkpatrick. 1978. Salt preferences and sodium drive phenology in fox squirrels and woodchucks. *Journal of Mammalogy* 59:531–542.

Weigl, P. D., and E. V. Hanson. 1980. Observations on learning and the feeding behavior of the red squirrel *Tamiasciurus hudsonicus:* The ontogeny of optimization. *Ecology* 61:213–218.

Weigl, P. D., L. J. Sherman, A. I. Williams, M. A. Steele, and D. S. Weaver. 1998. Geographic variation in the fox squirrel *(Sciurus niger):* Consideration of size clines, habitat vegetation, food habits, and historical biogeography. In *Ecology and evolutionary biology of tree squirrels,* ed. M. A. Steele, J. F. Merritt, and D. A. Zegers, 171–184. Martinsville: Virginia Museum of Natural History, 311 p.

Weigl, P. D., M. A. Steele, L. J. Sherman, J. C. Ha, and T. L. Sharpe. 1989. The ecology of the fox squirrel *(Sciurus niger)* in North Carolina: Implications for survival in the Southeast. *Bulletin of Tall Timbers Research Station* 24:1–93.

West, R. W., and J. E. Dowling. 1975. Anatomical evidence for cone and rodlike receptors in the grey squirrel, ground squirrel, and prairie dog. *Journal of Comparative Neurology* 159:439–460.

Wettstein, P. J., M. Strausbauch, T. Lamb, J. States, R. Chakraborty, L. Jin, and R. Riblet. 1995. Phylogeny of 6 *Sciurus aberti* subspecies based on nucleotide-sequences of cytochrome-b. *Molecular Phylogenetics and Evolution* 4:150–162.

Whishaw, I. Q., J. R. Sarna, and S. M. Pellis. 1998. Evidence for rodent-common and species-typical limb and digit use in eating, derived from a comparative analysis of ten rodent species. *Behavioural Brain Research* 96:79–91.

Whitaker, J. O., Jr., E. J. Spicka, and L. L. Schmeltz. 1976. Ectoparasites of squirrels of the genus *Sciurus carolinensis* from Indiana. *Proceedings of the Indiana Academy of Science* 85:431–436.

White, F. H., G. L. Hoff, W. J. Bigler, and E. Buff. 1975. A microbiologic study of the urban gray squirrel. *Journal of the American Veterinary Medical Association* 167:603–604.

Wild, A. E. 1965. Serum proteins of the grey squirrel *(Sciurus carolinensis)*. *Immunology* 9:457–466.

———. 1971. Transmission of proteins from mother to conceptus in the grey squirrel *(Sciurus carolinensis)*. *Immunology* 20:789–797.

Williams, G. C. 1966. *Adaptation and natural selection*. Princeton, N.J.: Princeton University Press, 305 p.

Williams, K. S., and S. R. Humphrey. 1979. Distribution and status of the endangered Big Cypress fox squirrel *(Sciurus niger avicennia)* in Florida. *Florida Scientist* 42:201–205.

Williamson, R. D. 1983. Identification of urban habitat components which affect eastern gray squirrel abundance. *Urban Ecology* 7:345–356.

Wilson, D. E., and D. M. Reeder, eds. 1993. *Mammal species of the world: A taxonomic and geographic reference*. 2d ed. Washington, D.C.: Smithsonian Institution Press, 1206 p.

Wilson, J. H. 1967. A test for homing in the gray squirrel. Master's thesis, Virginia Polytechnic Institute and State University, Blacksburg, 45 p.

Wobeser, G. 1969. Tetanus in a grey squirrel. *Journal of Wildlife Diseases* 5:18–19.

Wolf, T. F., and A. I. Roest. 1971. The fox squirrel *(Sciurus niger)* in Ventura County. *California Fish and Game* 57:219–220.

Wolff, J. O. 1996. Population fluctuations of mast-eating rodents are correlated with production of acorns. *Journal of Mammalogy* 77:850–856.

Wood, D. A. 1976. Squirrel collars. *Journal of Zoology* (London) 180:513–518.

Woods, G. T. 1941. Mid-summer food of gray squirrels. *Journal of Mammalogy* 22:321–322.

Wunder, B. A., and P. R. Morrison. 1974. Red squirrel metabolism during incline running. *Comparative Biochemistry and Physiology* 48A:153–161.

Yahner, R. H. 1980. Burrow system use by red squirrels. *American Midland Naturalist* 103:409–411.

———. 1986. Microhabitat use by small mammals in even-aged forest stands. *American Midland Naturalist* 115:174–180.

———. 1987. Feeding site use by red squirrels, *Tamiasciurus hudsonicus,* in a marginal habitat in Pennsylvania. *Canadian Field-Naturalist* 101:586–589.

Zegers, D. A., S. May, and L. J. Goodrich. 2000. Identification of nest predators at farm/forest edge and forest interior sites. *Journal of Field Ornithology* 71:207–216.

Zelley, R. A. 1971. The sounds of the fox squirrel, *Sciurus niger rufiventer. Journal of Mammalogy* 52:597–604.

Zigman, S., T. Paxhia, and W. Waldron. 1985. Biochemical features of the grey squirrel lens. *Investigative Ophthalmology and Visual Science* 8:1075–1082.

# Index

Boldface page numbers indicate
illustrations

## A

Abert's squirrel. See *Sciurus aberti*
acanthocephalans, 140
*Accipiter gentilis,* 140
*Acer rubrum,* 26
*Acer saccharinum,* 65
acorns, 69–78, 88, 99–102; carbohydrates, 86; consumption of, 72–78;
cotyledon of, 91; dispersal of, 72–78,
99–102; embryo of, 91; embryo excision of, **70**, 71, 78, 88, 100; germination schedules, **70**, 71, 72–75; and insect infestations, 73–74; lipid content,
69, **70**, 71, 98–100; perishability of,
69–78; protein, 86. *See also* partial
acorn consumption
Africa, 8
albinism, 13
anatomy, 3–8
Arizona, 103
Arizona gray squirrel. See *Sciurus: S. arizonensis*
Audubon, John J., 138

## B

black gum. See *Nyssa sylvatica*
blackjack oak. See *Quercus: Q. mari-
landica*

black oak. See *Quercus: Q. velutina*
black rat snake. See *Elaphe obsoleta*
black walnut. See *Juglans nigra*
blue jay. See *Cyanocitta cristata*
bobcat. See *Felis rufus*
body mass, 12, 20; and diet choice,
45–50; of newborns, 109; and reproduction, 113
botflies. See *Cuterebra emasculator*
brain size, 19
Brevard, South Carolina, 13
British Columbia, 87
bur oak. See *Quercus: Q. macrocarpa*
*Buteo lagopus,* 30, 83

## C

caching. *See* food hoarding
Canada, 13, 67, 87
*Carya,* 26, 85, 88; *C. laciniosa,* 41;
*C. ovata,* 41; *C. tomentosa,* 41
Cascade Range, 87
catkins, 11, 37
*Celtis,* 139
*Centurus carolinus,* 26
chestnut oak. See *Quercus: Q. prinus*
chipmunks. See *Tamias*
claws, 16
coevolution, 84, 87, 102–104
Colorado, 103
common grackle. See *Quiscalus
quiscula*

and energy content, 39–42, 45–50, 57; and energy maximization, 79; and handling costs, 40–41, 45–50, 58, 74–75; and metabolism, 41; patch use, 39, 51–63; and predation risks, 40–41, 45–50, 58; search costs, 42; and time minimization, 79. *See also* patch use; diet items
forelimbs, 16
foxes, 140
fox squirrel. See *Sciurus niger*
frosts, late spring, 138–139

### G

game theory, 124–125
*Glaucomys,* 29
goshawk. See *Accipiter gentilis*
great crested flycatcher. See *Myiarchus crinitus*
ground-dwelling squirrels, 1, 3, 18, 21

### H

habitat corridors, 10
habitat loss and fragmentation, 9–10
habitat use, 23–36; definition of, 24; and diet, 50; by fox squirrels, 34–36; by gray squirrels, 34–36; and habitat partitioning, 25, 36; and nest site selection, 28–30; by radio-tracked squirrels, 33–36. *See also* radiotelemetry
hackberry. See *Celtis*
Hamilton, William, 127, 130
Hamlet, North Carolina, 48
handling and marking, techniques for, 29–31, **31**, 134

hawks, 140
herbivory, 102–104; and nutrient consumption, 103–104; and tree genetics, 103–194
hickory. See *Carya*
holly. See *Ilex*
home range, 23–36, 113–114, 131, 51; and activity patterns, 51, 55, 113; and population density, 134; and space use, 55–57, 113–114
humans and tree squirrels: damage, 8; economic importance, 8; hunting, 139

### I

*Ilex,* 26
Illinois, 135, 136
inclusive fitness, 127–128, 130–132

### J

Janzen, Daniel, 101
jays. *See* Corvidae
*Juglans,* 85, 88, 139
*Juglans nigra,* 41

### K

keystone species, 104
kin selection, 127–128, 130–132

### L

largemouth bass. See *Micropterus salmoides*
Lawrence, Kansas, 117
*Liquidambar styraciflua,* 26